S0-AIG-674

15.75
XTIS

Prison Victimization

Prison Victimization

Lee H. Bowker, Ph.D.
University of Wisconsin—Milwaukee

Elsevier
New York · Amsterdam · Oxford

Elsevier Science Publishing Co., Inc.
52 Vanderbilt Avenue, New York, New York 10017

Distributors outside the United States and Canada:
Elsevier Science Publishers B.V.
P.O. Box 211
1000 AE Amsterdam, The Netherlands

© 1980 by Elsevier Science Publishing Co., Inc.
Third Printing, 1983.

Library of Congress Cataloging in Publication Data

Bowker, Lee Harrington.
    Prison victimization.

    Bibliography: p.
    Includes index.
    1. Prison violence—United States. I. Title.
HV9025.B68   365'.641   80-15727
ISBN 0-444-99077-1   hbd
ISBN 0-444-00551-X   pbd

Manufactured in the United States of America

Contents

Preface

I would like to begin by explaining how I came to write a book on prison victimization, which requires me to explain how I came to be involved in prison affairs. My initial introduction to prison occurred as a part-time instructor of college-level classes in a Washington State Penitentiary in 1968, and until 1976 I taught approximately 30 prison college classes at the community college and university levels. Thanks to a modest grant from the Wilken Fund at Whitman College, I began to do participant observation in the same institution, with my initial project being a study of Impact, a prison self-help group that was eventually destroyed when it became infiltrated by prisoner politicians. Between 1971 and 1973, I was the Director of the Social Therapy Program, which was a semi-isolated therapeutic community for violent drug abusers within the Washington State Penitentiary. About this same time, I became involved in other prison-related activities, including the Citizen Advisory Board to the Resident Government Council, the Research Review Board and the Governor's Task Force on Decision-Making in Corrections. These administrative and participant observation experiences allowed me to develop extensive personal relationships with prisoners as well as prison staff members, leading to an interest in understanding the dynamics of the subcultures that arise among incarcerated men and women. Several faculty research grants and additional funding provided under Ford Foundation Venture

Grant #710-0490 allowed me to visit research libraries and to make site visits to prisons in most of the western states plus additional institutions ranging from Canada to Florida in order to broaden my understanding of the changes that occurred in prisoner subcultures during the 1970s.

These activities gave me the background that was necessary to complement my scholarly research in connection with teaching a seminar on total institutions and gathering materials for a monograph, *Prisoner Subcultures,* which was published in 1977. Throughout these various experiences, I was constantly exposed to prison victimization. I observed hundreds of incidents in which prisoners psychologically victimized each other, and also a great many events in which they victimized staff members or were victimized by staff members. Although I did not directly observe many cases of physical victimization, I saw its effects on its victims and on uninvolved prisoners and staff members. *Prisoner Subcultures* contained a great deal of material about prison victimization, but that subject was not its primary focus. I continued to collect emperical reports on all sorts of prison victimization and also to think about its structure and meaning. This developmental process allowed me to present papers on prison victimization in 1977 and 1978 that embodied the theoretical typology that is used as the main organizing principle of this book. It was at this time that I expanded my conception of prison victimization from merely physical and economic to include psychological and social victimization. I also began to test out this classification by using specific incidents in order to understand how the different analytic classifications were intertwined as they occurred in day-to-day victimizing events.

The final series of events that led up to the writing of *Prison Victimization* began when I wrote sections on methodology and theory for a grant proposal on prison victimization to be submitted to the Law Enforcement Assistance Administration by the Socio-Environmental Research Center, Ltd. This proposal was later funded as part of a larger grant award, and I was subsequently employed by the Socio-Environmental Research Center, Ltd. to write first a literature summary on prisoner victimization entitled "Victimization in State Prisons: An Examination of the Literature" and later a set of interview guides, observation guides and other methodological material that was organized into the "Training Manual, Victimization in State Prisons Case Studies." This consulting activity allowed me to examine victimization records in several additional correctional institutions and to add to my collection of reports on prison victimization through a grapevine survey of research administrators, a visit to the Criminal Justice Reference and Information Center at the University of Wisconsin Law School, and the purchase of a number of unpublished doctoral dissertations related to prison victimization. The grant also funded discussions of prison victimization with colleagues such as Edith Flynn, James Jacobs, Jan Schreiber and Mary Knudten. Professor Flynn made a number of cogent criticisms of the first draft of the literature summary which I found extremely helpful as I wrote *Prison Victimization*. Three research assistants funded under the grant, Yvonne Johnson, Kathy Stamps and Marcia Wright, were most efficient in sifting through the prison literature in an attempt to fill in existing gaps in my knowledge of the field.

All of the activities described above have been oriented toward the scholarly community or the correctional profession. *Prison Victimization* is intended to be of use to these professionals, but it is also intended to serve the dual function of providing information to legislators and other creators of social policy about the nature and extent of prison victimization, its causes, and possible solutions to the problem. The solutions hinted at throughout the book are then organized in the final chapter under three headings with increasing degrees of social cost and occupational dislocation. In that way, all policy makers will be able to find something that is within their capability for implementation regardless of whether they take a status quo or radical approach to the problem.

This book begins with various reasons why we should find out about prison victimization and then goes on to examine the subject of prison victimization—in the eight chapters that follow. These present material on four types of prison victimization: (physical, economic, psychological and social) as it occurs in four different kinds of victim – offender caste relationships: prisoner – prisoner, staff – prisoner, prisoner – staff and staff – staff. The intersection of these dimensions produces a 16-cell property space into which all existing information on prison victimization can be sorted. In addition, most of the information is differentiated by age and sex of institutional population, with special attention being given to women's prisons and to institutions for juvenile delinquents. Following the final chapter on causes and possible solutions, the book concludes with the Appendix in which I briefly explain the various social science techniques for obtaining information on prison life, giving examples from the literature for each technique.

I thank William L. Gum at Elsevier and James Sprowls, my colleague, for their encouragement and suggestions; without them I would never have decided to proceed with this project. I would also like to thank Penny Thornton who typed several of the early chapters in the manuscript and Ann Schlesinger who typed all of the other chapters. Ann Schlesinger's ability to translate taped chapters into presentable manuscripts on the first draft was nothing short of amazing and allowed us to completely eliminate the second-draft stage of manuscript production. I would also like to apologize to Dee and Jessica, my wife and daughter, who gave up many weekends so that this book could be completed on schedule.

Prison Victimization

Prison Rapes and Their Origins

Feminists have presented convincing arguments that heterosexual rape symbolizes the condition of women in American society more than any other act. Similarly, homosexual rape symbolizes the condition of men in America's prisons. Like heterosexual rape on the streets, prison homosexual rape has effects that go beyond its immediate victims. Even in institutions where the rape rate is relatively low—perhaps averaging no more than a few incidents per year—there is widespread fear of being raped, and this fear motivates prisoners to defend themselves carefully against the possibility. Other prisoners are thrown into a panic by their fear of becoming a victim of sexual aggression, and some of them go so far as to mutilate themselves in order to be locked up in a psychiatric ward. There are numerous reports of men who have committed suicide because of their fear of sexual assaults. Just as women on the streets have come to see rape as a crime that affects all of them rather than just the victims of the crime, so must we realize that homosexual rape impacts all prisoners and fundamentally alters the social climate of correctional institutions. These general effects are perhaps even more destructive than the effects that rape incidents have on the victims themselves. This chapter explores the causes and varieties of forced homosexual behavior in American correctional institutions.

ESTIMATES OF THE PREVALENCE OF PRISON RAPE

The first attempt to estimate a sexual assault rate in correctional institutions was made by Davis in his study of sexual assaults in the Philadelphia prison system and sheriff's vans.[1] Davis and his staff worked with Police Commissioner Frank Rizzo in an investigation (1966–1968) of sexual assault in the Philadelphia correctional system. A total of 3,304 prisoners were interviewed during the investigation, and 156 sexual assaults were documented and substantiated through these interviews. Single reports of the sexual assaults were not accepted as true. Instead, all testimony had to be corroborated through institutional records, polygraph examinations or the testimony of witnesses. Since 4.7% of the men who were interviewed unquestionably were the victims of sexual assaults during their incarceration in Philadelphia, Davis felt justified in generalizing this rate to the entire population of prisoners who had paased through the system between June 1966 and July 1968—the period covered in his study. Doing so, Davis concluded that the true number of assaults in the 26-month period was in the neighborhood of 2,000.

Of the estimated 2,000 sexual assaults that occurred in the correctional system of a single city during the 26-month period, 156 were documented and fully described in the study. A number of these assaults had not been reported to institutional authorities when the incidents occurred. Of the 96 that were reported to institutional authorities, 32 were not mentioned in the prison records. Prison authorities, in essence, squashed these cases without further action. Only 40 of the 64 cases mentioned in prison records resulted in disciplinary action carried out against the sexual aggressors within the prison, and only 26 incidents were reported to the Philadelphia police department so that external prosecution of the aggressors could be considered. Because of the conservative methodology used by Davis and his associates, it is likely that his estimate of a 4.7% assault rate is low. There were probably additional assaulted prisoners who decided not to disclose their degrading experiences to the interviewers.

A second estimate of the sexual victimization rate in prisons is found in a technical report by Fuller et al.[2] They asked superintendents of ten North Carolina prisons how many incidents of homosexual rape or other sexual assaults they knew had been committed at their institution within the past three months. Sexual assault rates based on these reports were 0.17% for youth institutions and 0.26% for adult institutions. When the superintendents were asked how many incidents they recalled having occurred during the past year, the rates were 0.86% for youth institutions and 0.66% for adult institutions. These rates are quite a bit lower than the rate estimated by Davis, but there are several reasons for this. In the first place, Fuller et al. depended on reports of administrators, and Davis showed that these grievously understated the true incidence of prison rape. The second reason is that Davis included sexual attacks in which penetration was not achieved in his study while Fuller et al. excluded nonconsummated acts in the definition that they gave to the institutional superintendents. In addition to these factors, the Davis estimate was for 26 months rather than 12 months, and if we adjust for the time at risk, then the Philadelphia rate is reduced to 2.2% per year.

Other investigators have offered less precise estimates of the prevalence of homosexual rape in correctional institutions. For example, a technical report by Megargee cited in Nacci's article[3] states that approximately three out of every ten prisoners released from the Federal Correctional Institution at Tallahassee in the early 1970s had been propositioned for sexual activity. Not all of these propositions led to a forced sexual encounter, but Megargee's data give some idea of the widespread nature of sexual "pressure" in this institution. Toch agrees that pressure to engage in sexual behavior is fairly common in American prisons. However, he differs from investigators such as Davis in that he believes the actual occurrence of homosexual rape to be relatively low.[4]

A study conducted in the Tennessee State Penitentiary by Jones included questions about how many homosexual rapes prisoners had recently known about in the institution.[5] Approximately three-quarters of the prisoners recalled at least one rape per month; more than one-third recalled at least one rape a week; and 30% reported that such acts occurred more often than once a week in the institution. Because the prisoners were not asked how often they personally underwent sexual assaults, Jones was unable to construct a rape victimization rate for the entire institution. His data established that there was "the continuous commission of homosexual rapes at the Tennessee State Penitentiary."[6]

THE PHENOMENOLOGY OF PRISON RAPE

No analytic description can ever hope to portray prison rapes with such vividness that readers can understand the true impact of being a victim in a prison sexual assault. The only way to really get a feeling for this subject is to approach it phenomenologically. In this section, we present descriptions of rape events in the victims' own words. These descriptions have been taken from various case reports in the literature on prison sexual assaults.

All of a sudden a coat was thrown over my face and when I tried to pull it off I was viciously punched in the face for around ten minutes. I fell to the floor and they kicked me all over my body, including my head and my privates. They ripped my pants from me and five or six of them held me down and took turns fucking me.

My insides feel sore and my body hurts, my head hurts, and I feel sick in the stomach. Each time they stopped I tried to call for help, but they put their hands over my mouth so that I couldn't make a sound. While they held me, they burned my leg with a cigarette.[7]

■ ■ ■

The next day, on the 19th, he came to me again. I was in my cell, this was about the same time. He stated, "Today isn't your birthday, your going to do something." I told him I wasn't going to do anything. He started punching me again. I told him I was going to call the guard. He stated, "Go ahead and call, you'll only call him one time and I'll knock you out." He got the grease from off the table and handed it to me, told me to put some on, which I did. I laid down on the bed, he took out his penis and got on top. A friend he walks with, Kincaid, was standing out by the door, he was laughing. Joe got up after he got through, got toilet paper and wiped himself off. He then walked out of the cell.[8]

■ ■ ■

He couldn't take care of himself, you know. He wasn't a con, he wasn't a tough guy. He was just that kind of human being and, like, terrified, and the fucking guys just took advantage of him, you know. . . . I don't know how many fucked him, but like, there were others that were involved that were just harrassing him. . . . The kid went to Mattawan, because I remember the day that he wrapped shit in rags and toilet paper and stuffed it under his bed, and, like, before they sent him to Bellevue they had him clean it up—the hacks had him clean it out, and he wound up in the bughouse. He wound up in the bughouse.[9]

■ ■ ■

In the summer of 1973 a 28-year-old Quaker pacifist named Robert A. Martin, a former seaman with a background in journalism, held a stunning press conference in Washington, D.C. Arrested during a peace demonstration in front of the White House, Martin had chosen to go to prison rather than post a $10 bond. His first week in the District of Columbia jail, Martin told reporters, passed uneventfully enough in a quiet cell block populated by older prisoners, including Watergate burglar G. Gordon Liddy, but then he was transferred to Cellblock 2, a tier of "predominately young black prisoners, many of them in jail for serious crimes of violence." During his first evening recreation period on the new tier, the boyish-looking pacifist was invited into a cell on the pretext that some of the men wanted to talk with him. Once inside, he said, "My exit was blocked and my pants were forcibly taken off me, and I was raped. Then I was dragged from cell to cell all evening." Martin was promised protection from further assaults by two of his violators. The next night his "protectors" initiated a second general orgy of oral and rectal rape. The pair stood outside his cell and collected packs of cigarettes from other prisoners wanting a turn. When his attackers gave him a free rest period to overcome his gagging and nausea, Martin made his escape and alerted a guard. He was taken to D.C. General Hospital where he underwent VD tests and a rectal examination. The following morning a Quaker friend posted his bond.[10]

■ ■ ■

The guys were fooling around and grabbing me by the ass. He said I was a pussy and he was going to break me. So I picked him up and threw him against the wall. When he came off the wall I just beat the pulp out of him. I kind of just lost my head and I know that if I get in that state I'm really going to break because, you know, after awhile it builds up. You can't take it any longer.[11]

■ ■ ■

We were standing in the line and they yelled it down, "Three niggers and one homo," like that. . . . And then I heard the guys talking about me, and then the accidental ass-grabbing started.[12]

■ ■ ■

Soon after his return to the population he was approached by Willie, a large and powerful black inmate. Willie told him that he didn't approve of what the others had done, felt sorry for Alan, and would take care of him. He gave Alan a carton of cigarettes and signed over a five-dollar store order to him. Over the next several weeks the relationship developed into what Alan considered a real friendship. He was no longer harassed and his fears abated. One evening

5

Willie told Alan to "get off" with him. Alan accepted, but when he arrived at the back side of the third tier in the lower South State block, he found himself confronted with five or six other blacks. Willie demanded that he "take care of us. . . . I been taking care of you, now you gotta take care of me and my friends." Alan refused and tried to struggle free but was overpowered. Willie held him down by the head and shoulders while the others took turns committing buggery upon him.[13]

■ ■ ■

I was working and then got hit in the back of the head. And then five or six guys were holding me down and it didn't take but, say, 60 seconds from the time that I was hit on the head until the time that I was on the floor. There was three of them that did it, but the rest were their friends. You can say that it was rough. Scared, sure you were scared, but it's the realization that there is nothing that you can do about it. You can stand there and fight and fight, but within five minutes they're going to have it. And there is just so much that you can do. There is nothing that you can do about it. And you can throw a few punches and if you're caught totally by surprise then you're through before you start. The numbers alone were enough to defeat me, the surprise, though, didn't help much either.[14]

■ ■ ■

He then said that he heard something about me concerning homosexual acts. I told him what he had heard was not true. He then started to threaten me and if I didn't submit to him. Then I hit him with my fist in his face before he could hit me. Then about three more men came into the cell and they started to beat me up too. I fought back the best I could and then I fell on the floor and I got kicked in the ribs. Three guys were holding me while the other one tore my pants off; I continued to fight until one of the guys knocked me out. One of the guys was holding me on the floor and had my arm pinned to the floor. And about seven or eight guys came into the cell and they took turns sticking their penis up my ass. When they finished they left my cell, and I was still laying on the floor.[15]

■ ■ ■

I asked Sergeant Brown. And he told me to go ahead, "Pick up the nearest thing around you and hit him in the head with it. He won't bother you no more."

I went over to another sergeant and I asked him and he said, "Pick up the nearest damn thing to you and just hit him with it; that is all."

I looked at him and I said, "All right. If I do this I ain't going to get locked up for it am I?"

He looks at me and he says, "No." Because I am using self-defense.[16]

■ ■ ■

After this he came back to his bed and he was crying and he stated that "they all took turns on me." He laid there for about 20 minutes and Cheyenne came over to the kid's bed and pulled his pants down and got on top of him and raped him again. When he got done Horse did it again and then about four or five others got on him. While one of the guys was on him, raping him, Horse came over and said, "Open your mouth and suck on this and don't bite it." He then put his penis in his mouth and made him suck on it. The kid was hollering that he was gagging and Horse stated, "You better not bite it or I will kick your teeth out."

While they had this kid they also had a kid named William in another section in E Dorm. He had his pants off and he was bent over and they were taking turns on him. This was Horse, Cheyenne, and about seven other colored fellows. Two of the seven were brothers.[17]

I should apologize to the reader for presenting such upsetting material, but there is no other way to make the point that prison rapes are not very sexual—just as heterosexual rapes on the street have only a very limited sexual component. Instead of an emphasis on sexuality, prison rapes emphasize brutality, dominance, and the affirmation of the masculinity of the aggressors. There is an obvious coupling of sexuality with sadism in many of the vignettes presented above.

It is important to realize that not all homosexual behavior in prison is coerced. There are also many couples who engage in consensual homosexual relations, and these men are much more loving in their expression of sexuality. It is not homosexuality per se that is violent and brutal, but rather rape as a generic entity that subsumes brutality and sadism by the very nature of the act.

RAPE AND RACE

Rapes are not randomly distributed within the prison population, especially with respect to race. When Jones asked prisoners at the Tennessee State Penitentiary about the races of the aggressors and victims in rape incidents, nearly all whites agreed that the aggressors were black and the victims were white. Black prisoners differed, with most of them holding that the race of both aggressor and victim varied according to the circumstances of the incident. At the same time, not one of the black prisoners was able to recall a single occurrence in which a white prisoner had raped a black prisoner, so their responses to the general question about the relationship between race and rape must be questioned. Most black respondents claimed that both blacks and whites raped whites frequently, and that there were occasions when blacks raped blacks. However, white respondents indicated that they did not follow the habit of blacks who raped members of the other race when they wanted to get back at them. They would instead stab blacks or burn them out of their cells in retaliation for having molested white prisoners.[18]

Davis also provides us with information about the relationship between race and rape. He found that 56% of the rape incidents involved black aggressors and white victims. In comparison, 29% of the cases involved black aggressors and black victims; 15% of the cases involved white victims and white aggressors; and there were no cases involving white aggressors and black victims. These percentages are consistent with the general opinions expressed by prisoners at the Tennessee State Penitentiary. They also reflect the fact that approximately four out of every five prisoners in the Philadelphia system at the time of the Davis study were black. We might argue that the relationship between race and rape would be very different if the situation were reversed and only 20% of the prisoners were black.

Davis explains the relationship between race and rape in two ways. First, many of the black groups are organized into gangs, and the participation of individual blacks in gang rapes is a way of keeping their standing in the gangs. Should they refuse to participate in the gang rapes, it is possible that they might become victims in the next incident. The second factor contributing to the relationship between race and rape in Philadelphia is a general factor that also applies to heterosexual rape on the streets. That is that the lower-class black males who are typically incarcerated in correctional institutions have generally been unable to use the means of affirming their own masculinity that are commonly used by middle-class blacks and whites. Some of them deal with this deprivation and assert their masculinity by demonstrating dominance over other men and women, and rape is the crime of choice in demonstrating that dominance. The shock

8

to their masculinity that occurs when they are incarcerated further exacerbates this deprivation and enhances their motivation to engage in sexual assaults. According to Davis, they have become "almost totally dependent for self-esteem upon an assertion of their sexual and physical potency."[19]

Would the relationship between race and rape reverse if most prisoners were white? Carroll's study of an eastern penitentiary answers that question in the negative. Only 22% of the men in the institution he studied were black, yet the rape distribution was quite similar to the situation in the Philadelphia prison system. Blacks were far better organized than whites, and they had a much higher degree of group solidarity. As a result, they were the most powerful clique in the prison, and they had much greater power than one would expect from their numbers alone. This facilitated their victimization of white men who were not effective in defending themselves. Another element in the black rapes of white victims was that white leaders who wanted to have those victims as permanent sexual partners cooperated with the black rapists in seducing and degrading the victims. When they had been repeatedly used and abused by gangs of blacks, they would be more than happy to agree to a consensual relationship with one of the white prisoner leaders. Thus, we see that one facet of interracial rape is that it may be facilitated by members of the victim's own race.[20]

Carroll also deals at length with the influence of black rage on interracial sexual assault. He points out the extent to which blacks have been generally oppressed, and links that to their motivation to humiliate and degrade white victims in the prison setting. A quote from one of his interviews is worthwhile.

> To the general way of thinking it's 'cause we're confined and we've got hard rocks. But that ain't it at all. It's a way for the black man to get back at the white man. It's one way he can assert his manhood. Anything white, even a defenseless punk, is part of what the black man hates. It's part of what he's had to fight all his life just to survive, just to have a hole to sleep in and some garbage to eat. . . . It's a new ego thing. He can show he's a man by making a white guy into a girl.[21]

Carroll found that although very few black prisoners were known as "rippers" or "wolves," nearly all of the blacks had participated in sexual assaults upon whites at some time in their prison stints. This relationship between black rage and interracial rape has been forcefully expressed with respect to heterosexual rapes on the street by Eldridge Cleaver in *Soul on Ice*.[22]

It is unwise to discuss statistics on the relationship between race and rape, for there are many who would see these statistics as proof that blacks are more criminal or more violent than whites. By "more violent," is meant inherently more violent—that there is something that is part of the makeup of black people that makes them more violent than whites rather than that there are compelling external environmental conditions that cause a temporary racial imbalance in the statistics on rape and other violent crimes. Such an argument could be further buttressed by showing that blacks on the streets have higher violent crime rates than whites, and that because most black rapes are intraracial rather than interracial, black women suffer a particularly high risk of being raped. I explicitly reject any attempt to link the current racial imbalance in violent crime and rape rates with inherent racial differences. Arguing that blacks are inherently more violent than whites is like arguing that Italians are inherently more likely than Germans to become members of Mafia-type organized crime. It confuses the historical context of events with biology and visible physical differences between ethnic and racial groups. How can we believe that blacks have a racial affinity for rape and violence when we know that just a hundred years ago, almost all interracial rapes committed in the United States were committed by white men on black women? Although there is no solid empirical evidence on the matter, it is likely that this was the situation with respect to sexual exploitation in America's prisons up until the middle of the 20th century. Interracial rape is like all other social phenomena in that its epidemiology changes over time in response to changes in the social environment. Therefore, the language of timeless invariant relationships that is appropriate when dealing with biology, physics, and the other physical sciences cannot be meaningfully applied to the distribution of criminal acts such as rape.

OTHER CAUSES OF PRISON RAPES

Racial tensions and the discrimination against black males in American society are not the only factors that contribute to the incidence of prison rape. There are also other causes such as the American propensity for violence and the influence of rigid sexist conceptions of male and female roles. The United States has one of the highest heterosexual rape rates in the world,[23] so it should be no surprise that its prisons are similarly afflicted. Indeed, it is probably true that many of the "wolves" who rape "punks" within the prison are merely continuing behavior in which they raped women on the streets before they were incarcerated. Both white and black men, particularly those who come from poverty backgrounds, define masculinity in terms of domination and commonly force their sexual attentions on their wives and women friends as a way of affirming their masculinity. Even at the college level, where most of the men are from middle class backgrounds, approximately half of the coeds report being the victims of sexual aggression during the current academic year.[24] It appears that some of the impetus for sexual aggression comes directly from the way sex roles are defined in America.

Prisoners who are raped differ from their rapists in more than their racial heritage. They are also more likely to be middle class, young, inexperienced, convicted of minor property offenses, and slight of build. In the prison environment, men with these characteristics are perceived as being rather feminine. From the viewpoint of the rapist, nothing could be more natural than "making a woman" out of someone who already has characteristics of a woman. If prison rapes are demonstrations of domination rather than consummations of sexual desire, then why should the rapists choose victims whom they view as being particularly feminine? One reason is that weaker victims are more easily subdued. More important than this, it is necessary for prison rapists to participate in homosexual activity without thinking of themselves as homosexuals in order to preserve their masculine identity. When they redefine their victims as females, and even refer to them as "girls," then they are free to refer to themselves as "studs" or "real men." Their homosexual activity is thus redefined as heterosexual activity. They are not less masculine for having raped other men; they have shown themselves to be masters of men and have proved that they can play the masculine role even where sex role reciprocity is impossible because there are no women.

It would be a mistake to search for all the causes of prison rape in the character and situation of the rapist. Sexual deprivation within the prison may contribute to the frequency of rape, although it is perhaps the least important causal factor in prison rape. Masturbation and consensual homosexual activity are available to all who desire them. In addition, there are homosexual prostitutes in prisons who will sell themselves for a few packs of cigarettes. It is not the restriction of sexual outlets that is a problem within the prison. It is the restriction of social outlets for playing masculine roles. This deprivation cannot be alleviated through masturbation, and participation in a consensual sexual relationship adds to the masculinity threat that already exists in the prison setting. If it is true that conjugal visits reduce the incidence of prison rape, as Hopper alleges,[25] this is because the conjugal visits are used as a social control technique by the prison administration to make prisoners think twice before they commit rapes, nonsexual assaults, or other major rule infractions. The policy followed by administrators who have conjugal visits at their disposal is generally to exclude all prisoners who have recent major rule infractions from the possibility of a conjugal visit.

If prisoners with certain characteristics have a notably high risk of suffering sexual assaults, then there is no reason why these prisoners cannot be identified at the point of entry into a correctional system. These men could then be placed in institutions that do not include potential rapists and that are more intensively supervised than other correctional institutions. When we realize this, we see that the policies followed by state correctional administrators must also be considered to be causal factors in producing prison rapes. These systemwide administrators are generally unwilling to spend the time and effort as well as the money necessary to protect easily victimized prisoners. At the local level, prison wardens add to this when they sometimes reject requests for protective segregation from prisoners who are experiencing sexual pressure. They are more limited in what they can do for potential rape victims than state correctional administrators because they have less resources at their disposal. The number of segregation cells in prisons is strictly limited, and many of them are used for prisoners who have committed serious rule infractions rather than for those who wish to seek shelter from the general population. Nevertheless, there are other strategies that individual wardens could follow if they wished, such as creating special therapeutic communities for potential victims in sealed-off parts of the prison environment.

Correctional officers must also bear some blame for the existence of prison rapes. Many of them carry out their jobs responsibly, but there are those who prefer to let the prisoners do whatever they want as long as they do not make a commotion. These latter officers are the ones who knowingly or unknowingly permit prison rapes to be consummated at the far end of the tier while they sit comfortably in their offices. When potential victims come to them for protection, they may do nothing for them, or just tell them to fight it out, as is illustrated in the following case vignette.

> I went and said, "Look this guy is bothering me, man. He kept coming out with these sexual remarks and I want somebody to do something about this guy—tell him something."
> He said, "Well, there is nothing that we can do about it, and there is nothing that the brass can do about it, so hit him." He came right out and told me just like that.[26]

This vignette illustrates poor judgment on the part of the prison officer. A more serious indictment of the behavior of correctional officers is contained in the following passage from the Philadelphia study.

> Then too, some guards put pressure on victims not to complain—such complaints, after all, would indicate that the guards were failing in their duty. We found many cases where victims, after filing complaints, had "voluntarily" refused to prosecute, and a number of them told us that guards urged them to rely on prison discipline rather than to bring the facts out into the open. Very often, these guards asked the victim if he wanted his parents and friends to find out about his humiliation.[27]

We might also discuss the legislators and citizens who are generally responsible for underfunding correctional institutions—a situation that decreases the number of staff members who can be hired at the same time that it sets salaries too low to attract highly capable applicants. However, this topic will be treated later.

EFFECTS OF PRISON RAPE

Homosexual rapes are carried out within the boundaries of prisoner roles. The "wolf" is the aggressor and the "punk" is the victim. These terms are nearly universal, although there are additional terms that are found from institution to institution. Descriptions of sexual roles in prison settings have been consistent from the 1930s up to the present—and cross-culturally. Fishman[28] described active and passive homosexual roles in 1934 similarly to those described by Scacco in 1975.[29] Srivastava's study of life in an Indian prison differs from both these American accounts in only the terminology. He found that "punks" were men who had accepted their inferior sexual status either for economic reasons or to be protected from the "prison bullies" and the "barrack hawks." Prisoners known as "boyhunters" were preoccupied with bullying and sexually exploiting younger prisoners. Another term for the sexual aggressors was "toughs": these were men who wielded immense coercive power over many of the less violent prisoners around them.[30]

In all of the settings discussed in this chapter, the inexperienced "fish" who does not know his way around the prison is easily manipulated by the more experienced "wolf," who is willing to use "shivs" and other weapons to force his attentions on the "fish" if more subtle manipulations fail. A "pressure punk" is forced into sexual behavior by violence or threats of violence. The slightly different social role of the "canteen punk" is occupied by young men who have been initially raped and then continue to participate in homosexual behavior in return for material items obtained from the prison canteen. In a sense, the "canteen punk" plays a role very similar to the role of the prostitute on the street. Men who give in to aggressors and are "punked" may all of a sudden find themselves owned by predatory groups of "jockers" who not only use them themselves whenever they wish, but who also may force the "punks" to prostitute themselves for profit or to rob the cells of other prisoners.

One of the vignettes presented earlier in this chapter is a story of Alan and his suffering in a group rape by Willie and his friends. Following his story a little further will tell us something about the effects of prison rape. After his initial group rape, during which he was degraded verbally as well as raped repeatedly, he was subjected to numerous assaults of a similar nature by a large number of blacks. He suffered these assaults over a period of months and then accepted the offer of a well-known and powerful white prisoner and became his "kid." This meant that Alan had agreed to provide his new mate and several of his friends with unlimited sexual services in return for cigarettes, store orders, and some degree of protection. Alan's experience is an example of a "train job" in which a number of offenders attack a single victim. Willie played the role of the "ripper" and set up Alan for the attack following which he organized additional sexual assaults. Only when the victim has become completely submissive and there are new fields to be sown do the victimizing inmates lose interest in him and cease the attacks. This is the point at which rape victims generally are converted to "canteen punks."[31]

The story of Alan illustrates the way in which "fish" are processed into prostitutes who are willing to do practically anything to avoid further brutal mental and physical assaults. In confronting this transformation, we see that one of the effects of prison rapes is to force people to become consensual homosexuals against their will. This calls into question the entire idea of the consensual homosexual in a prison setting. One must wonder how many so-called consensual homosexuals would never have engaged in this behavior were it not for having been raped or threatened with rape and exposed to the example of other rape victims.

A second effect of rape is to create a climate of fear that makes the prison a hostile and threatening environment in which to live. Prisoners who are stable and tough can deal with this fairly effectively by being very careful about their behavior. Thinking about the possibility of being victimized and modifying your behavior to minimize that possibility at all times probably means a considerable deflection from the possibilities of participation in more positive pursuits, and this is one of the ways in which prison rape affects all prisoners rather than a relatively small group of victims. For those prisoners who are less stable and unable to successfully modify their behavior so as to minimize the risk of rape, there is a possibility that they may engage in self-destructive behavior as a way out of the situation. Hans Toch and his students at the State University of New York at Albany have specialized in the study of the varieties of self-destructive behavior in correctional institutions.[32] In some of the self-destructive situations, the self-mutilators had never been raped or even severely assaulted. It was the fear that these things might occur to them, heightened by psychological games played on them by their fellow prisoners, that drove them to inflict self-damage.

Another negative effect of prison rape comes from an unexpected direction. The work of Lockwood[33] is convincing proof that many men who are threatened with being raped, or who have perhaps already been raped but are not yet completely cowed, strike back at their attackers, and harm them severely. There is a certain rough justice in this kind of behavior, particularly from the viewpoint of the victim. At the same time, any student of prison affairs who is concerned about the welfare of victims must, to be consistent, also be concerned about the welfare of aggressors. The analysis of human affairs in terms of "good guys" and "bad guys" is never humanistically appropriate. Prison "wolves" sometimes make mistakes and attack victims who have not yet been completely manipulated into submission, and victims sometimes find reserves of strength and courage that they never knew they had. One of the victims interviewed by Lockwood stated:

> I wanted to protect myself and the only way that you can protect yourself is with violence. And it was getting to the point where after a while I was starting to do pushups every night. And then as I would get tired, I said that I would kick that guy's ass as I got stronger. I noticed that there was a bunch of them around, I thought when he hit me, "This is it, that will show the other guys when I get into a fight with this one that I am not going to quit." So I fight and get punched a few times and I punch him a few times and they see that I'm a man.[34]

Another victim killed his aggressor when the man began to pressure him for sex.

> At that certain time, I had a whole lot on my mind. He caught me at the wrong time to talk to me about that stuff. If it was another time, I don't believe that I would have tried to kill him or would have tried to do anything to him. I had a whole lot of little things on my mind. It was the time. When I was finished, I felt sorry for him. I really shouldn't have done that, but I did it.[35]

Capping all of the effects that we have mentioned above, there are the physical and psychological effects of the victimization upon the victim. Social status and a positive self-image in prison settings are acquired as part of a zero-sum game. If "wolves" are to gain in status, then "punks" must lose status. If some men improve their self-images, then other images must deteriorate. Prisons, more than any other places in which human behavior occurs, are battles of all against all in a brutal struggle for dominance and privilege. Prison rapes usually include lacerations in the anal area and the excess brutality of the rapes usually means that there will be contusions on other parts of the body. In addition, victims commonly suffer such severe emotional reactions that they have physical consequences such as nausea, cramps, insomnia, and headaches.

The devaluation of the self is swift and severe in prison rapes. Victims often feel that they cannot face their fellow prisoners afterward, and they fear that news of their degradation will get back to their wives and parents on the streets. The brutality and disregard of the victim's wishes in a rape guarantee that there will be some degree of devaluation of the self as a result of rape incidents. In a prison setting, this is magnified because of the social definition that is forced upon rape victims. This definition proclaims that they have become "women" and can never again be men. Furthermore, their only value in the prison setting is in their "womanhood." Disparaging remarks will constantly be made about the newly minted "punk" for the rest of his prison life, and may even be carried over to the streets when he is released.

What is the effect of homosexual rape on a prisoner's ability to make a satisfactory adjustment after he is released from the prison? We have no competent research studies with which to answer this question. It is fair to guess, however, that the heterosexual life of prison rape victims may be damaged by their experiences. They may suffer from impotence and lack confidence in their dealings with women. If they have been "punks" over a long period of time and had never established a heterosexual pattern on the streets previous to their incarceration, they may find it easier to continue homosexual behavior after their release from prison than to attempt to switch to heterosexuality. Even more important than these effects is the possibility that playing a consistently passive and demeaning role in the prison may interfere with the newly released person's ability to cope actively with the myriad challenges of the outside world. If the released rape victim finds it more difficult to meet life's challenges and to make decisions for himself than the average parolee, then he is going to suffer severe adjustment problems, for there is much evidence that prisoners in general experience a great deal of difficulty in this area of their readjustment to freedom.

NOTES

1. Alan J. Davis, Sexual assaults in the Philadelphia prison system and sheriff's vans, *Trans-Action* 6 (December 1968): 8–16.
2. Dan A. Fuller, Thomas Orsagh and David Raber, "Violence and Victimization Within the North Carolina Prison System," paper presented at the annual meeting of the Academy of Criminal Justice Sciences, 1978.
3. Peter L. Nacci, Sexual assault in prisons, *American Journal of Correction* 40 (January–February 1978): 30–31.
4. Hans Toch, A psychological view of prison violence, in A. Cohen (Ed.), *Prison Violence* (Lexington, MA: D.C. Heath, 1976), pp. 43–52.
5. David A. Jones, *The Health Risks of Imprisonment* (Lexington, MA: D.C. Heath, 1976).
6. Ibid., p. 156.

7. Davis (1968), p. 12.
8. Ibid., p. 10.
9. Hans Toch, *Living in Prison: The Ecology of Survival* (New York: Free Press, 1977), pp. 151–152.
10. S. Brownmiller, *Against Our Will* (New York: Simon and Schuster, 1975), pp. 258–259.
11. Daniel Lockwood, "Maintaining Manhood: Prison Violence Precipitated by Aggressive Sexual Approaches," paper presented at the annual meeting of the Academy of Criminal Justice Sciences, 1978, p. 17; and *Prison Sexual Violence* (New York: Elsevier, 1980), p. 45.
12. Toch (1977), p. 147.
13. Leo Carroll, *Hacks, Blacks, and Cons* (Lexington, MA: D.C. Heath, 1974), pp. 182–183.
14. Daniel Lockwood, "Sexual Aggression Among Male Prisoners," Ph.D. dissertation, State University of New York at Albany, 1977, p. 260; and Lockwood (1980), p. 92.
15. Davis (1968), p. 10.
16. Lockwood (1978), p. 35; and Lockwood (1980), pp. 55–56.
17. Davis (1968), p. 9.
18. Jones (1976).
19. Davis (1968), p. 16.
20. Leo Carroll, "Race and Sexual Assault in a Prison," paper presented at the annual meeting of the Society for the Study of Social Problems, 1974.
21. Leo Carroll, Humanitarian reform and biracial sexual assault in a maximum security prison, *Urban Life* 5 (January 1977):422.
22. Eldridge Cleaver, *Soul on Ice* (New York: McGraw-Hill, 1968).
23. Lee H. Bowker, *Women, Crime, and the Criminal Justice System* (Lexington, MA: D.C. Heath, 1978).
24. Eugene J. Kanin and Stanley R. Parcell, Sexual aggression: A second look at the offended female, *Archives of Sexual Behavior* 6 (1977):67–76.
25. Columbus B. Hopper, *Sex in Prison* (Baton Rouge: Louisiana State University Press, 1969).
26. Lockwood (1978) p. 33; and Lockwood (1980), p. 54.
27. Davis (1968), p. 11.
28. Joseph F. Fishman, *Sex in Prison* (New York: National Library Press, 1934).
29. Anthony M. Scacco, Jr., *Rape in Prison* (Springfield, IL: Charles C. Thomas, 1975).
30. See for example S. Srivastava, Social profile of homosexuals in an Indian male prison, *The Eastern Anthropologist* (October–December 1973):313–322; Sex life in an Indian male prison, *Indian Journal of Social Work* 35 (April 1974):21–23; *The Indian Prison Community* (Lucknow: Pustak Kendra, 1977).
31. Carroll (1974).
32. See for example Hans Toch (1977); and *Men in Crisis, Human Breakdowns in Prison* (Chicago: Aldine, 1975); and Robert Johnson, *Cultural and Crisis in Confinement* (Lexington, MA: D.C. Heath, 1976).
33. Lockwood, (1977;1978;1980).
34. Lockwood (1978), p. 23; and Lockwood (1980), p. 49.
35. Lockwood (1978), p. 18; and Lockwood (1980), p. 46.

Other Forms
of Violence Among Prisoners

 Prison is a barely controlled jungle where the aggressive and the strong will exploit the weak and the weak are dreadfully aware of it.[1]

Prison rape is the most spectacular of all the criminal acts committed behind the walls, but it is not the most common. In most prisons, there are a dozen nonsexual physical assaults for every sexual assault that occurs. The degree of control over prisoner behavior exercised by correctional officers and the physical environment are sufficient to prevent escapes and riots, and to dampen the amount of violence that occurs among prisoners. Unfortunately, there are very few institutions in which architecture and supervision are of such a high quality that assaults among prisoners are uncommon. Keve's metaphor of the jungle is an apt one for our correctional institutions. Prisoners are surrounded with possibilities for personal victimization, and many of them are visible to only the most experienced jungle traveler. To the neophyte, danger can strike at any moment and without warning.

I had my introduction to prison violence during my years as the administrator of a therapeutic community for violent drug abusers in a maximum security prison during the early 1970s. This program was created because the warden of the institution wished to terminate the drug dependence of a number of the prisoners and to reduce the number of violent acts that were occurring within the institution. Threats of violence against hospital personnel were used in often successful attempts to gain access to psychoactive drugs through the sick line. These threats became so bad that all of the physicians resigned from the prison out of fear for their lives. Before they did so, conditions had deteriorated to the point at which the examining physician was forced to have a stalwart hospital attendant at his side at all times in order to ensure his safety. At the same time, there was also a high level of violence between prisoners, and this violence was carried over into the security and detention area when the offenders were given time "in the hole." The warden's request for help resulted in the establishment of a semi-isolated therapeutic community for the worst offenders. The incidence of violence within the program was much lower than it had been for these men outside of the program. Despite this, there were still a number of violent incidents that occurred during the first year of the program's operation.

Shortly after the program was implemented, two prisoners who were competing for a leadership role in the program settled their differences temporarily when one pursued the other around the tier with an ax. Even though most of the men had forsworn violence on the tier, they felt it necessary to carry weapons during their brief forays outside of the isolation area to bring in supplies or to meet visitors and escort them to the tier. Some carried knives, one had a sawed off baseball bat, and still another had a machete so carefully concealed on the tier that nobody knew about it until it was discovered a year later. Had any "enemy" prisoners tried to force their way onto the tier, he would have run for his machete to defend his turf. As the program developed, it became defined as the most desirable of the available prison "goodies," and prisoners began to pressure me for admission to the program. After one direct threat to my life had been made, a system was adopted whereby armed members of the program met me at the front gate of the prison and walked with me to the tier on my daily visits to the program.

The nature of prison violence is exemplified by a series of incidents that occurred after the program had been in existence for six months. It began when a white prisoner hurled a number of racial slurs at a militant black prisoner. Other prisoners on the tier avoided an immediate confrontation because the program administrator was on the tier. As soon as he had left for the evening, the white prisoner went into the black prisoner's cell with a hammer in each hand and beat him on the top of his head.

The black prisoner fought back with a baseball bat, and then stabbed the white prisoner three times in the chest. This confrontation took less than a minute, so that by the time the administrator had reached the front gate of the prison, he was notified to go directly to the prison hospital where the white prisoner was in danger of dying from stab wounds. There was no physician available in the hospital, but several highly skilled prisoners were able to reduce the pressure on the heart caused by internal bleeding and to bring the prisoner back to life on three occasions when his heart had stopped. Amazingly enough, he made a complete recovery and was eventually released from the prison after having threatened the life of the program administrator and numerous other people. He moved on to another state after his release, committed a crime there, and was incarcerated, following which he was killed in a fight with another prisoner. Meanwhile, the black prisoner who had stabbed him was placed in segregation for the offense, and he was apparently m..rdered there by several white prisoners who poisoned him under the guise of giving him a recreational drug. This could never be proved, and so his death was officially defined as an accidental overdose. This account seems a bit outlandish, and yet anyone who has worked in a maximum security, custody-oriented correctional institution for an extended period of time can relate similar stories.

PRISON ASSAULT RATES

Recent interviews with 36 ex-prisoners from the Cook County Department of Corrections revealed that 22% of them had been the victims of beatings—some severe enough to cause concussions and fractures—during their stay in the Cook County jail. They witnessed approximately 75 beatings and a similar number of sexual attacks. Eleven percent of the men admitted that they had themselves been sexually attacked, and they also reported that four of their fellow prisoners had been deliberately set on fire as a result of prisoner altercations.[2] Are these incidence statistics typical of American prisons in general?

There are a few surveys of prisoner assaults and homicides in the literature. One of the earliest of these is a study of assaults in Canadian penitentiaries during 1964 and 1965. In this study, Akman identified 35 serious prisoner–prisoner assaults during each year, most of which occurred in Canada's maximum security institutions. The assaults occurred among those serving sentences of short or medium length more than would be expected by chance, and young offenders (age 20–24) were more likely to use cutting and stabbing instruments than older offenders, who were proportionately more likely to use their fists in inflicting injuries.[3] Because Akman counted only serious prisoner assaults, his statistics cannot be used to establish an accurate assault rate for Canadian penitentiaries.

Sellin matched Akman's survey of Canadian penitentiaries with a similar survey of American prisons. He found that 26 homicides occurred between prisoners in 1964. In addition, there were 88 aggravated assaults reported in the questionnaires that he received from prison administrators. Sellin also reported historical assault information for several prisons. For example, Joliet prison in Illinois recorded 25 aggravated assaults between 1956 and 1964, of which 19 were committed on fellow prisoners. These assaults were carried out with weapons such as hammers, knives, blackjacks, pipes, cell stools, iron rods or shovels. Again, only the most severe offences were reported by Joliet officials. When a more careful count of prisoner assaults was made in the Kentucky State Penitentiary, 110 assaults were documented during 1964, with a total of 138 victims because some of the assaults were carried out against multiple victims.[4] These data show that a single institution that takes the trouble to count assaults carefully and fully can record more assaults among prisoners than were reported nationwide by prison administrators in the questionnaires distributed by Sellin.

A followup study conducted by Sellin produced comparable data for 1965. Being more complete enumeration, this survey identified 603 victims of prison aggravated assaults, of which 61 died of their injuries.[5] The difficulties experienced by Sellin in amassing reliable data on assaults among prisoners suggest that questionnaires directed to prison administrators are not adequate as a method for developing reliable estimates of prison victimization. There is no way that Sellin's material can be translated into a meaningful national assault rate. The on-site examination of official records by objective investigators yields more meaningful results, although official records will always seriously underestimate the true prevalence of assaults among inmates. Using this approach, Buffum found an inmate homicide rate of 0.8 per 10,000 per year in Pennsylvania prisons between 1964 and

1973.[6] Guenther's studies in two federal institutions yielded prison assault rates of 1.8 and 0.9 per 100 prisoners per year.[7]

These early surveys of prisoner violence have recently been supplemented with reports on prisoner violence from four states and several national surveys of prison homicide. Official records at the Tennessee State Penitentiary show that 19 prisoners were stabbed by other prisoners between early 1972 and the middle of 1973, an average of slightly over one stabbing per month. More than two-thirds of the prisoners surveyed by Jones indicated that they thought the stabbing problem at the Tennessee State Penitentiary was very serious. Reasons for stabbings that the prisoners gave included (1) punishment for having "snitched off" another prisoner, either before or after entering the penitentiary, (2) punishment for failure to pay a debt, (3) the result of a homosexual entanglement or (4) the result of a trivial argument that got out of hand. A great many of the stabbings occurred in the prison yard, which is located next to the hospital, and that is one of the reasons why only four of the 19 victims died as a result of the attacks. It is evident that there is a considerable component of unpredictability in the stabbings, for 48% of the black prisoners and 72% of the white prisoners thought it likely that they might be the next victim of a stabbing. Most prisoners apparently felt that there was no way that they could be sure to avoid becoming the victim of a stabbing attack.

Prisoners at the Tennessee State Penitentiary were murdered by being beaten to death as well as by being stabbed, and ten prisoner homicides were recorded in the official prison records during 1972. This amounts to a homicide rate of 617 per 100,000 prisoners, as compared with a homicide rate for the state of Tennessee of 11 per 100,000 in 1972. Black prisoners at the Tennessee State Penitentiary were more likely to be victimized than white prisoners, and if we look only at them, the homicide rate is inflated to 1,290 per 100,000 prisoners. For black prisoners between the ages of 17 and 24, the risk of homicide is raised still higher to 5,172 per 100,000, or approximately one out of every 19 young black prisoners per year.[8] Jones does not give us a comparable rate for nonfatal assaults, but we can imagine how high they must be when we see the size of the prisoner homicide rate.

In an investigation of officially recorded inmate stabbings at Angola Prison in Louisiana between 1969 and 1972, Astrachan found records of 211 incidents. Eleven of these 211 stabbings were fatal. Astrachan did not calculate the stabbing rate per prisoner, instead counting the number of stabbings per month. This yielded a rate of 5.9 stabbings per month between 1969 and 1972. When he continued his study into subsequent years he found that the rate rose sharply to 12.5 stabbings per month the first 11 months of 1973 and then mellowed slightly to 11.8 per month through mid-1975. The total number of fatalities due to stabbings between 1973 and 1975 was 39.[9] Can anyone dispute the conclusion that the stabbing problem at Angola was of epidemic proportions during these years?

Violence in the California system has been more carefully documented and publicized than violence in other American prison systems. This documentation allows us to gain an impression of the extent to which prisoner violence has increased in the California prison system in the past decade. There were relatively few stabbing incidents in the California prison system in the early 1960s, so few that when Conrad wrote on the subject in 1966, he felt constrained to offer reasons why the incidence of California prison violence was so low.[10] The California prison system, which is one of the largest in the world, recorded 27 male stabbing incidents in 1960 and 44 in 1965. By 1970 the number of stabbings had increased to 73, which became 117 in 1972, 203 in 1973 and 197 in 1974.[11]

The decline in the California prison stabbings that occurred between 1973 and 1974 is presumably the effect of increased security procedures that were instituted in the California system at the end of 1973. These included collective lockdowns, additional gun coverage by correctional officers, the reclassification and reduction of certain prisoner assignments, the cancellation of evening activities, the elimination of most vehicle traffic in security areas, tighter controls on visiting, the standardization of furniture in prisoner cells, rearranging the location of certain dangerous offices and shops, and other schedule and facility modifications. Seen in terms of the mean rate of stabbings per 100 prisoners, the effect of these increased security procedures was to lower the stabbing rate from .098 to .069. Interestingly, the rate for stabbings in the general population declined even more steeply, from .089 to .037, and the rate for stabbings in security housing increased from .253 to .557. It appears that security housing in the California system is not terribly secure, and that one effect of increasing security procedures in the general population was probably to remove a number of violent prisoners into security housing where they continued to prey upon their fellow convicts.[12]

The extent to which data on prisoner stabbings underreport total violence among prisoners can be estimated by comparing the California stabbing rates developed by Bidna with reports on all known violent incidents in the California prison system that have been published by Carter et al. and Park. There were 303 officially recorded violent incidents in the California system in 1969, a rate of 1.08 per 100 prisoners per year.[13] This level of officially recorded violence rose from 465 incidents in 1971 to 777 incidents in 1973 and 1,022 incidents in 1974. The comparable rates for these years are 2.00, 3.67 and 4.30 per 100 prisoners, respectively.[14] This means that the increased security procedures that dampened prisoner stabbings did not have the same effect on total prisoner violence, and that by 1974, one in every 23 California prisoners suffered a violent assault. In view of the likelihood that the majority of assaults between prisoners did not come to the attention of California officials, the true prisoner assault rate for 1974 may have been as high as one in ten. Looking only at official figures, it appears that the California prison assault rate was approximately four times the stabbing rate in 1973 and six times the stabbing rate in 1974. If these ratios hold equally well for Angola, then that institution has regularly experienced between 50 and 75 officially recorded assaults per month, to say nothing of those that escaped official attention or were suppressed by correctional officers.

Another state study of the incidence of prison violence is contained in an in-house technical report written by Grasewicz for the Virginia Department of Corrections. She counted 586 officially recorded assaults among prisoners in four Virginia institutions between 1974 and mid-1976. The prisoner assault rate for these institutions was 9.96 attacks per 100 prisoners per year. The State Penitentiary, which housed the most serious offenders, had a prisoner assault rate that was slightly below the average for the four institutions studied, while the juvenile institution had an assault rate that was more than twice the average—21.7 per 100 prisoners per year. Grasewicz comments that the classification system used in the state predetermines the violence rate in institutions to the extent that it sends young violence-prone offenders to one institution and older prisoners who are likely to adjust well to institutional life to a different institution.[15]

The final state prison study of prisoner assaults gives us a direct estimate of the extent to which official assault rates under-estimate assault rates as perceived by the victims in American prisons. In North Carolina, Fuller et al. generated four different estimates of prisoner victimization rates, ranging from 6.8 to 77.6 per 100 prisoners per year. The 6.8 rate was based upon official offense reports while the 77.6 rate was based upon gross victim-ization reports made by prisoners in interviews. This suggests that the assault problem as viewed by prisoners is 11 times as great as the assault problem that is officially recognized by prison administrators. Fuller et al. take a different tack in their analysis of the data, for they consider the true victimization rate to be limited to those incidents in which the victim did not contribute in any way to the violence. This, of course, eliminates the vast majority of prison assaults from consideration, so it is no surprise that their restrictive definition reduced the assault rate to only 2.4 per 100 prisoners per year. The reported reasons for the incidents included verbal abuse, debts, revenge, sex, horseplay and mental illness. Victimization varied systematically by age and race with the victimization rate declining steadily with older inmates and with white prisoners being more likely to be victimized than black prisoners. In interracial assaults, white prisoners were much more likely to be attacked by blacks than the reverse.[16]

National prisoner assault rates have never been calculated, but we do have estimates of prison homicides for the nation as a whole. Sylvester et al. identified 128 homicides in American correctional institutions during 1973, of which 113 were among prisoners. Three-quarters of the victims died as the result of stabbing injuries, a few were strangled, and the others were beaten to death, killed by firearms or burned to death in their cells. Official records relating to these incidents indicate that homosexuality was the most important precipitating factor, fol-lowed by "snitching," arguments, money and property disputes, collective violence, drug use, gang activity and racial tension. In contrast to the high estimate of victim precipitation by Fuller et al., Sylvester et al. estimate that only one-fifth of the homicides were victim-precipitated.[17] Translating this into more meaningful terms, a prisoner serving a sentence of 20 years mandatory time would have a probability of being murdered of one in 67. The level of prisoner homicides reported for 1973 was unchanged in the following two years, according to a report published in *Corrections Compendium*, which cited 114 prisoner homicides in

1974 and 111 prisoner homicides in 1975 with 45 of 50 states reporting.[18]

An unpublished doctoral dissertation by Wolfson continued the analysis of prison homicides that was begun by Sylvester et al. Wolfson found that there was considerable variation in the homicide rates from state to state in 1973, ranging from zero to 100 per 10,000 prisoners. In general, homicides were more likely to occur in cells and cell blocks than in prison yards and in recreation areas. Twenty-six percent of the homicide incidents were alcohol- or drug-related. Both the victims and the offenders in homicide incidents generally had violently aggressive behavior in their prison records, and yet four out of every five of them were not classified as management problems prior to the homicide. The national homicide rate in 1973 was 18.9 per 10,000 in state prison, and 7.4 per 10,000 in the Federal Prison System.[19]

PRISON ASSAULTS FROM THE PRISONER'S PERSPECTIVE

When prisoners rioted and gained control of a Canadian institution in 1971, a group of sex offenders and alleged informers selected from among the inmate population were dragged from their cells, tied to chairs in a circle, and viciously assaulted by another group of inmates.[20] The entire prisoner population witnessed the beatings and tortures that led to the deaths of two of the prisoners. This incident illustrates three important facts about assaults among prisoners in correctional institutions. First, the rate of violence rises drastically during a prison riot because correctional officers cannot protect the weak from the strong and the socially undesirable from the prisoner elites. The second principle is that certain types of sex offenders, especially those who have violently assaulted very young people, are commonly beaten up by other prisoners as a demonstration of the contempt in which they are held. Finally, it is traditional that informants, called "rats" or "snitches," are to be punished with severe beatings or death. An example of this sort of incident is given by Toch in his book, *Police, Prisons, and the Problem of Violence.*

Inmate B is released from his daily exercise period, requisitions a "long-handled, heavy duty brush," and assaults inmate attendant O with his utensil. He testifies that he "felt that O had been 'snitching' on him," that O was the cause of his cell having been searched by custodial personnel.[21]

Several of the other examples given by Toch are instructive of the variety of violence between prisoners.

Inmate A sits in C's cell listening to C play his guitar; four other inmates enter. Situation looks sufficiently unpromising for A to attempt an exit, but he is stopped as he tries to leave. He gets a beating from C (which fractures his jaw). Following this beating, A is forced to lie down on the floor, where C performs sodomy on him. After lunch, A is "escorted" back to A's cell, where another inmate (M) rapes him.[22]

■ ■ ■

H is stabbed to death in a shower room, with L doing the stabbing, and D holding H until he collapses. H had owed L five cartons of cigarettes and also had incurred a debt (of 15 packs) with D. L indicates that he had decided that if H "did not pay me the cigarettes he owed me, I was going to kill him." He stabbed H some 16 times and explains that "I wanted to kill the guy. The – – – – deserved it."[23]

Stang tells a brutal tale of prisoner–prisoner victimization that was apparently condoned by the authorities in an Arkansas prison.

LL-33 stated that he and three other prisoners were planning to escape because of the treatment and not enough food. He stated that they were all "slapped" around by three inmate yardmen, because they would not give them money. He stated that a line rider[24] found out about the escape and brought them to the superintendent who whipped them with the "hide" on the buttocks with their pants down, and on the back and head. He further hit them with his fists and kicked them. The superintendent then left the building and told the riders to work them over real good. One rider got four others to help him beat them up. He stated that they came into the building with "blackjacks," wire pliers, nut crackers, and knives. He stated that they stripped all the clothes off of LL-33 and the rider stuck needles under his fingernails and toenails. They pulled his penis and testicles with wire pliers and kicked him in the groin. Two riders ground out cigarettes on his stomach and legs. One rider squeezed his knuckles with a pair of nutcrackers. He stated that they worked on him all afternoon, and the next day, he was put out in the field and made to go to work. He stated that he was unable to work, and they put him in the hospital and would not let anyone see him until he healed up.[25]

The Arkansas prison system has provided endless tales of brutality among prisoners, with the worst abuses occurring because some prisoners were given power over others due to inadequate funding for the hiring of correctional officers. Bruce Jackson tells what it was like in the Arkansas prison system during the 1960s.

So he put me in a two-spot. In two-spot you have to pick eighty pound or more or get your head whupped with a hoe that's tapered off kind of like a blackjack. So I picked about 40 pounds.

He whupped my head. He first comes out there, he kicks you about four times until he gets you down, kicks you in the head, kicks you in the stomach and finally gets you down there on the ground. And you can't do nothing 'cause the highpower got a rifle down on you (the inmate guard points his rifle at the man being beaten) ready to kill you just in case you strike back at the rider. The rider was an inmate too.[26]

■ ■ ■

This old convict doctor had a pet coon down in the hospital and if you said anything insubordinate, he'd set the coon on you. That sonofabitch could tear your ass up. Coon's name was Oscar. I never will forget that mean sonofabitch. You could hit him, knock him all the way across the hospital over there, and he'd come right back at you.

They had a field superintendent here that time they called "White Gas" because he drove a little ole white Chevrolet. And he'd call you over to the car on the turn row and say, "You stick your head in here a minute, I can't hear you." You stick your head in his goddamned window and he'd roll the glass up on you and whip you head with a blackjack.[27]

Francis Marziani, who was an inmate at Lewisburg Federal Prison, was set free by a United States District Judge after filing a petition based on the prevalence of violence at that institution. He said that the going price for a contract murder at Lewisburg was two cartons of cigarettes, and that he would be killed if he was returned to Lewisburg because he had broken the convict code by talking to prison officials. While at Lewisburg, Marziani had been gang-raped and repeatedly beaten. In his statement, Marziani said:

I'm going to be executed soon . . . but it won't be by the gas chamber or electric chair. . . . No, I'll be executed with a shank after I'm returned to Lewisburg. In case you're not familiar with a shank, it's a two-foot long piece of sheet metal, sheared off in one of the machines in the metal shop . . . It'll probably take 5 or 13 minutes with that thing shoved through me. If there's anyone around when I get it, they'll stare for a few seconds and then turn away and go about their business. . . . When I'm finally executed it will be for a reason. I broke the rules. No, not the rules laid out by your court. That's the bitter irony of it. Exactly because I obeyed your rules, I broke an even more important set of laws. The laws imposed on everyone who walks into Lewisburg. They're more important than yours, because if you break them, you're killed as soon as there is a chance. And there's no way to appeal.[28]

ASSAULTS IN AN ASSAULTIVE ENVIRONMENT

It is more than a play on words to say that prison assaults occur in an environment that is itself an assault upon the senses. The noise is deafening, the architecture obnoxious, and most of all, the prisoners have little control over their fate. They must live in the area to which they are assigned, or at least in the institution to which they are classified, and have very little choice as to the people they will see and be exposed to every day in the yard. It is no accident that prisoners living in dormitory settings have higher blood pressure than prisoners living in single cells.[29] There is greater exposure to continuous danger of assault and other forms of victimization in dormitories than in single cells, and the stress of being constantly alert and wary, as well as of actual victimizations suffered, results in higher blood pressure levels. This can also be conceptualized in terms of overcrowding, although to do so misses the point that it is not overcrowding per se that is necessarily important here; it is with whom one is overcrowded.

Even those prisoners who take care to develop their bodies and to seek out some sort of training in self-defense are not safe from the possibility of victimization. Homemade weapons, which are endemic in America's prisons, are a great unequalizer in prison battles. Extensive collections of confiscated weapons are exhibited at most American penitentiaries, and these are but a small portion of the total number of weapons that are available in the prisoner populations of these institutions. In addition to cutting instruments and clubs of various kinds, prisoners may make bombs, particularly fire bombs, and even guns from scrap materials that are available within the prison walls. As one author says, "A spray of buckshot from a pipe-barreled 'zip' is as lethal as that of a riot gun."[30] In his study of prison-made weapons, Rees describes items such as a hand-cannon shooting two-ounce cubes of brass out of a square pipe, and ballpoint pens that have been turned into disposable launchers for their own brass tips. Ballpoint pen guns, if correctly constructed, are capable of firing projectiles that will penetrate a sheet of plywood one-inch thick. Improved security in industrial areas can cut down on the amount of metal entering the prison to be transformed into knives or guns. However, no security system could intercept materials such as rolls of paper that were glued and overlapped in such a way as to form the barrel of a gun designed to guide a payload of ground glass to its target in Folsom Prison. The barrel was taped to a handle and a compote of crushed match heads set off the gun when it was fired with a match or heated wire. Such a weapon could be constructed practically anywhere if prisoners were aware of the proper construction techniques.[31]

I am suggesting that the prison environment combines the ready availability of homicidal weapons, prisoners who are often violence-prone, inadequate architecture and supervision, and a constant round of explosive situations and pressures to create what is no less than a controlled war. The general causes and consequences of prison violence are the same as the causes and effects of prison rape that were discussed in the previous chapter. All of the forms of prison victimization are related so that each becomes a causal factor in the other, forming an insane feedback system through which prison victimization rates are under constant pressure to increase. A similar feedback phenomenon occurs when prisoners feel constrained to take revenge for past victimizations and to defend themselves in current victimizations. The interaction takes on the form of a macabre version of the game of musical chairs in which today's aggressor may become tomorrow's victim. Things become even more confusing when, as Lockwood has shown, the aggressor turns into the victim during a single incident in which the aggressor intended the violence level of the encounter to be minimal and was surprised by a victim who topped his bid with an all-out physical attack.[32]

It is appropriate to inquire as to the benefits gained from violently attacking others. There are presumably a great many—

or violence would not be so common in prison settings. The most important of these advantages is increased social status in the prisoner subculture. Violent inmates tend to have higher status than nonviolent prisoners—everything else being equal. Foolish violence does not necessarily produce higher status, but it is rather the judicious use of violence in the right places and against the right people that is maximally status-enhancing. Along with the increase in status, there are self-image benefits that accrue from assaulting one's fellow prisoners. Perhaps the most important of the self-image benefits is reassurance in playing the stereotypic masculine role that is so highly respected in prisons. The appropriate use of violence demonstrates that its perpetrator is "tough"—a "real man" who is someone to be reckoned with.

The old adage that the best defense is a good offense suggests a third benefit of prison violence, which is that those violent prisoners who have reached a comfortably high place on the prisoner status ladder are less likely to be habitually victimized in a variety of ways than men who are, in essence, defenseless. For example, an acquaintance of mine had a rather small build and was not particularly strong. Nevertheless, no one ever bothered him because he was known to be "crazy with a knife" and always armed. It was rumored that he had killed a number of his fellow prisoners over the years and that since he did not fear loosing his own life, he would fight against any odds, flailing wildly with his knife to do as much damage as possible before he was subdued. Even if his reputation was somewhat overblown, it was believable enough to restrain any sane prisoner from getting into a fight with him. The student of prison violence must be careful not to be sidetracked into meaningless arguments about the difference between reality and reputation. In the prison as on the streets, reputation is far more important than empirical reality. This is just another application of the principle developed by W.I. Thomas that "If men define situations as real, they are real in their consequences."[33]

Prison violence can also provide the offender with sexual release without responsibility. Engaging in a consensual relationship would not only prove a greater threat to the aggressor's masculinity, it would also cost a great deal more in time and effort. All of the elements of courting and mutuality are bypassed when sex can be demanded as a tribute by virtue of the threat of violence. Sexual release is a form of tension release, which reminds us that all varieties of prison violence are self-reinforcing to the extent that they provide the aggressor with a measure of tension release. The continual buildup of pressure in prison settings demands some form of tension release, which makes violence potentially more intrinsically rewarding in this setting than in less tense environments.

A direct benefit of assaulting another inmate is economic gain. Simple "rip-offs" can produce canteen items, minor appliances, and either prison scrip, illegal "white money" (street money) or cigarettes. The range of material items available through violence does not end here. It includes desirable cell furniture and perhaps even "celling" in the most favorable location. This relates to another benefit of violence: to establish oneself in a more pleasant or otherwise desirable social setting. For example, becoming a member of a desired group or gang or gaining access to recreational facilities that are particularly desired are eased if one has a reputation for violence. Violence or the threat of violence can compel fellow prisoners to give up their place in line or leadership in a group in deference to the desires of a "real man" and staff members in most institutions will go along with these arrangements rather than interfere in the prisoner subculture.

There is just one more advantage that prisoners might achieve by using their violence judiciously: they may be able to manipulate themselves right out of the door. That is to say, they may be able to shorten their sentence by being enough of an aggravation to administrators so that they will get a positive recommendation when they see the parole board, which in turn increases their chances of being released from prison at an early date. If a prisoner goes too far in the use of violence to this end, he runs the risk of accumulating so many disciplinary actions that the parole board may extend his term or perhaps even the possibility that he could be prosecuted in a court of law. The myth that this is an easy way to work your way out of prison is certainly exaggerated. A more sophisticated version of this benefit probably holds true. In this scenario, the newly admitted prisoner commits a number of minor violent acts shortly after entering the institution and then "straightens up" and has a clean record for the remainder of his career. With the cooperation of his counselor, he can then argue to the parole board that he has "seen the light" and, having reformed, is ready to return to the free community.

What kind of a place is prison when we are able to list so many important benefits that can be gained by the violent victimization of one's fellow prisoners? Isn't prison a place where people are supposed to learn how not to be violent? The better we understand behavior in the prisoner subculture and the interaction among prisoners, correctional officers and administrators, the more surrealistic prison life seems to become. And so we return to the jungle metaphor with which I opened the chapter, having little hope that a better understanding of prison life will suggest easy solutions to the problem of prison assaults.

NOTES

1. Paul W. Keve, *Prison Life and Human Worth* (Minneapolis: University of Minnesota Press, 1974).
2. Charles A. Felton, "Violence in Prison," paper presented at the annual meeting of the Academy of Criminal Justice Sciences, 1979.
3. B. Akman, Homicides and assaults in Canadian penitentiaries, *Canadian Journal of Corrections* 8 (1966): 284–299.
4. Thorsten Sellin, Homicides and assaults in American prisons, 1964, *Acta Criminologica Medicalis Legalis Japonica* 31 (1965): 139–143.
5. Thorsten Sellin, Prison homicides, in T. Sellin (Ed.), *Capital Punishment* (New York: Harper and Row, 1967), pp. 154–160.
6. Peter Buffum, Homicides in Pennsylvania prisons, 1964–1973: A preliminary research note, in *Report of the Governor's Study Commission on Capital Punishment* (Harrisburg: Commonwealth of Pennsylvania, 1973), pp. 111–114.
7. Anthony Guenther, "Violence in Correctional Institutions: a Study of Assaults," unpublished paper, College of William and Mary, 1974.
8. David A Jones, *The Health Risks of Imprisonment* (Lexington, MA: D.C. Heath, 1976).
9. A. Astrachan, Profile/Louisiana, *Corrections Magazine* 2 (September–October 1975): 9–14.
10. John P. Conrad, Violence in prisons, *The Annals of the American Academy of Political and Social Science* 364 (March 1966): 113–119.
11. L. Bennett, Study of violence in California prisons: A review with policy implications, in A. Cohen (Ed.), *Prison Violence* (Lexington, MA, D.C. Heath, 1976), pp. 149–168.
12. Howard Bidna, Effects of increased security on prison violence, *Journal of Criminal Justice* 3 (1975): 33–46.
13. R. Carter, D. Glaser and L. Wilkins, *Correctional Institutions* (Philadelphia: Lippincott, 1977).
14. J. Park, The organization of prison violence, in A. Cohen (Ed.), (1976), pp. 89–96.
15. Linda Grasewicz, "A Study of Inmate Assaults in Major Institutions," unpublished paper, The Virginia Department of Corrections, 1977.
16. D. Fuller, T. Orsagh and D. Raber, "Violence and Victimization Within the North Carolina Prison System," paper presented at the annual meeting of the Academy of Criminal Justice Sciences, 1977.
17. Sawyer S. Sylvester, John H. Reed and David O. Nelson, *Prison Homicide* (New York: Wiley, 1977).
18. *Corrections Compendium* (February and March 1977).

19. Wendy P. Wolfson, *"The Patterns of Prison Homicide,"* Ph.D. dissertation, University of Pennsylvania, 1978.
20. Fred Desroches, Patterns in prison riots, *Canadian Journal of Criminology and Corrections* 16 (1974): 332–351.
21. Hans Toch, *Police, Prisons, and the Problem of Violence* (Washington, DC: U.S. Government Printing Office, 1977), p. 59.
22. Ibid., p. 57.
23. Ibid., p. 58.
24. A line rider is an armed prison guard on horseback. This use of prisoners as correctional officers was once common in many southern prisons.
25. David P. Stang, The inability of corrections to correct, in Burton M. Atkins and Henry R. Glick (Eds.), *Prisons, Protest, and Politics* (Englewood Cliffs, NJ: Prentice-Hall, 1972), p. 37.
26. Bruce Jackson, *Killing Time, Life in the Arkansas Penitentiary* (Ithaca, NY: Cornell University Press, 1977), p. 183.
27. Ibid., p. 189.
28. Lewisburg inmate testifies on widespread prison violence, *Corrections Digest* 7 (June 16, 1976): 7–8.
29. David A. D'Atri, Psychophysiological responses to crowding in prisons, in Laura Otten (Ed.), *Colloquium on the Causes of Crime and the Determinants of Criminal Behavior* (McLean, VA: The MITRE Corporation, 1978).
30. C. Rees, Arsenals behind prison walls, *Guns and Ammo* (January 1970), p. 30.
31. Ibid., pp. 29–33.
32. Daniel Lockwood, *Prison Sexual Violence* (New York: Elsevier, 1980).
33. Quoted in G. Duncan Mitchell, *A Hundred Years of Sociology* (Chicago: Aldine, 1968), p. 167.

Variations on a Theme:
Prisoner Violence Among Females and Juveniles

 Most of the individuals behind bars at any given point in time are adult males. Similarly, most studies of prison life and prison violence have been conducted in institutions for adult males. The image of the maximum security prison is derived exclusively from institutions for adult males, and so I have taken care to present data about men's prisons in the two previous chapters without confusing the issue by simultaneously discussing differences between these institutions and institutions for delinquents and females. In this chapter, I turn to these two other categories of correctional institutions. Having laid out a model of prison violence among men, I will now contrast that model with violence in correctional institutions for women and children.

VIOLENCE IN JUVENILE INSTITUTIONS

I mentioned in the last chapter that Grasewitz found that the assault rate in an institution for male juvenile delinquents was more than twice the rate for a maximum security prison in Virginia.[1] Is this an unusual finding? Or are juvenile institutions generally more violent than adult institutions? Although we do not have other comparisons based on precise assault rates, we know that within maximum security prisons for adult males, it is the younger men (many are not yet 21) who are most heavily involved in prison violence, both as victims and as aggressors. If we extrapolate this relationship down to boys in their midteens, then we can assume that juvenile institutions are indeed very dangerous places in which to live. This conclusion is also supported by a study of violence in North Carolina prisons by Ellis et al.[2] Further evidence in support of this conclusion can be drawn from a number of descriptive studies of institutions for male juvenile delinquents that have been carried out over the past 20 years.

In an early report of victimization in juvenile institutions, Ward analyzed homosexual behavior among institutionalized delinquents. He found that bullying and aggressive homosexual behavior became confused with masculinity and that dependence and submission became confused with femininity in boys' training schools. This confusion was reflected in the terminology used by the prisoners. For example, the word "punk" was used as much for a passive participant in homosexual behavior as for a boy who behaved in a generally unmasculine fashion. In the process of collecting his data, Ward found that many boys who were forced to become "punks" in a sexual sense when they were first imprisoned later became con-wise and attained the status of "wolves." They then preyed on the newer prisoners just as they themselves had been the prey of "wolves" when they were "fish."[3]

A similar situation was found by Fisher at Lomo, a small state institution for delinquent boys in California. He found that victimization and patronage were the two central social processes at Lomo. There were three basic types of victimization among the boys: physical attack, agitation and exploitation. Agitation was verbal abuse and manipulation whereas exploitation was the use of threats to coerce inmates to give up material items or engage in sexual activity against their will. Those boys who were physically weak or relatively incompetent at self-defense were the prime targets of all three types of victimization. Instead of protecting the weaker prisoners from those who were abusing them, staff members sided with the aggressors. The aggressors were the elites in the prison subculture, so that staff members catered to them in order to obtain their cooperation in keeping the institution quiet. A quiet institution produces good staff job performance ratings and also makes their day-to-day duties easier. At Lomo, the patronage system flowed from staff members to prisoner elites, who in turn used their special privileges continually to victimize and abuse their fellow prisoners.[4]

Polsky did not begin his study of prisoner behavior in *Cottage Six* with the idea of studying prisoner victimization. The institution that he studied was one of the better-staffed institutions in the northeast and had an excellent reputation in the field of juvenile delinquency. Despite this, there was heavy victimization in the cottage, and Polsky's participant observation study led him deeper and deeper into this matrix of victimization. Polsky was directly introduced to some of the techniques of victimization in use in the cottage because they were used against him. He suffered minor physical attacks and psychological manipulation by various boys during his stay there, and only his six-foot-six size saved him from further indignities.

There was a clear status structure in the cottage, with scapegoat roles such as the "queer" and "rat" being at the bottom of this status pyramid. Polsky lists five deviant interactive modes as occurring in the cottage: aggression, deviant skills and activities, threat-gestures, ranking and scapegoating. The one behavioral form of victimization missing from his study is rape. There are hints about it in his book, but nothing is spelled out. Perhaps he found the subject too offensive to deal with in the early 1960s. Of the five interactive models that he identified, only deviant skills and activities were nonvictimizing. The other four social processes all entailed diminishing the status of the victim so that the aggressor could rise still higher in the eyes of his peers. Victimization in the cottage was so bad that upper-status boys turned some of the scapegoats into virtual human punching bags. Newcomers and social isolates were heavily victimized, and unless they fought their way up the social status ladder, this abuse would continue throughout their entire stay in the institution. In one incident,

> Foster swung out at Werner and hit him hard in the stomach. Werner of course couldn't do anything about it. George Little came up and slammed him. He was followed by Drake and Parker. Werner swore at Little but didn't want to get into a fight with him. In all of their eyes Werner was a punk.[5]

The beauty of the use of physical violence as a control technique is that once physical superiority has been established, it is not necessary to continue to attack the others physically to gain their submission. Threats of physical violence are very effective where the victim is all too aware that they can be carried out any time that the aggressor wishes to do so. It is entirely possible for marital dominance to be established by one incident of assault on a woman by her husband and to have that dominance maintained over a period of years with verbal threats that remind her that her husband is capable of assaulting her whenever she does not give way to his wishes.[6] Polsky found that threats of physical violence were very effective in upsetting the weaker boys. Ranking, which is a form of verbal abuse, constantly reminded the victims of their inferior status. For example, a "queer" would be told that "Your mother is a subway and you can get in for fifteen cents," and "Your mother is like a subway—you can get in for nothing by getting under the turnstile."[7] Whenever the elites were displeased with how things were going in the cottage, they took it out on the weaker members of the group through the scapegoating process. Although some victims succeeded in fighting their way up the status ladder, a more common end for the boys at the very bottom of the status system was to be incarcerated in a mental institution, presumably at least partially as a response to the severe and continual victimization they suffered during their time in the cottage.

The problem in *Cottage Six* was that the houseparents were the only staff members in regular contact with the boys. The professional staff in the institution stayed away from the cottage and only worked with the boys in their offices. Whatever therapeutic benefits they tried to accomplish in these isolated sessions were lost on the boys when they returned to a cottage in which violence and the threat of violence were the only principles of any consequence. Houseparents tended to be rated according to how well they kept the cottages in order, and that meant no trouble from the boys. Therefore, the prisoner leaders were in a position to blackmail the houseparents by threatening to cause a great deal of trouble if they did not cooperate to the extent of allowing the leaders to dominate the weaker prisoners completely. So long as the victimization proceeded unhindered, the leaders kept their bargain with the houseparents and things ran smoothly. Houseparents who were consistently rewarded for turning their backs on boys crying out for help were not exactly contributors to good citizenship.

The basic pattern of victimization uncovered by Polsky in a small, therapeutically oriented cottage was also discovered in a larger, more custodial institution by Rubenfeld and Stafford.

Group interaction in the institution they studied was characterized by a vicious struggle for power, material goods and privilege. Boys at the bottom of the status ladder were called "girls." Just above them, there were the "sweet boys," and then the "punks." All three of these roles were in the category of scapegoats and were considered to be untouchables. Like the scapegoats in Polsky's study, the untouchables were relegated to the position of nonpersons. For example, if a "punk" was smoking a cigarette, no self-respecting prisoner would take a drag on that cigarette since it implied fellating by proxy.[8]

Although blacks constituted only one-third of the boys in the institution, they dominated the prison social structure because they were so much better than whites at defending themselves, both verbally and physically. Their dominance was so complete that whites always deferred to blacks in the use of preferred recreational facilities. Black "fish" were recruited directly into one of the two higher status groups without any hazing experiences. This contrasts sharply with the extensive testing that white "fish" experienced when they entered the institution. The predatory core of the inmate leaders harassed them continually.[9] The same sort of testing behavior was found by Allen in his study of a Federal Youth Center. At this institution,

> A boy who submits is then tested to see to what degree he will submit, and their particular concern is the sexual area. If he submits in this area he is ostracized from the fellowship of the rest of the youths and taunted as well. Had the other youths wanted merely to use this boy for sexual purposes, then ostracism and taunting would not only be unnecessary, but would work against their interests and would not make any sense. Rather, it appears that they are trying to determine the degree of homosexual temptation that the new member represents, and if this is too great, they react by behavior such as exclusion designed to encourage him to cross over to nonhomosexual behavior.[10]

Now this is a strange interpretation. Are we to believe that inmate elites try to convince "punks" to give up their homosexual behavior by demanding that they engage in sexual behavior? Allen has identified a legitimate problem for the aggressors who have problems about masculinity, and these problems are heightened by the homosexual temptations that exist in an all-male institution. There is also some truth in the idea that engaging in sexual assaults is one way of dealing with homosexual temptations in that the extreme aggressiveness of the homosexual attack really covers up sexual excitement with pure aggression. There is certainly no tender loving care involved in these sexual encounters. These activities permit the aggressor to achieve sexual release and support his masculinity at the same time that they rule out any chance of a consensual love affair that would be more threatening to his self-image. Consensual homosexuality practiced in stable dyads is apparently much less common in juvenile institutions than in correctional institutions for men. The problem in Allen's formulation is in his implication that the aggressors are consciously dealing with their homosexual temptations through aggression, whereas it appears more likely that this is one of the unconscious supports for what they consciously perceive as simply "getting their rocks off" and letting everyone know who's who in the institution.

Prisoner exploitation was not completely out of hand in the Federal Youth Center, for there was a counterbalancing mechanism institutionalized as part of the prisoner subculture there. This was the mythic process of "creeping." In "creeping," a weaker inmate who was regularly victimized and exploited by one of the prison elites would creep up on him at night when the lights were out and cut his throat. "Creeping" was a strong part of the beliefs held by the boys in the prisoner subculture even though it had rarely occurred in the history of the institution.[11] Because definitions of the situation are more important in determining human behavior than an objective portrayal of the situation, this myth had a much greater retarding effect on prisoner victimization than one would expect given the rareness of its empirical occurrence.

VIOLENCE AMONG BOY PRISONERS IN THE 1970s

A number of studies of prisoner victimization in juvenile institutions have been carried out in the past few years. The work of Johnson,[12] Feld,[13] the John Howard Association,[14] Bartollas and his associates[15] and Cottle[16] suggests that the patterns of juvenile prison violence have not changed even slightly since 1960. For example, a respresentative of the John Howard Association took testimony from a number of youths who described fighting and other mistreatment as being rampant in their institution *even* in the presence of staff members. Some of these staff members would move away from victimization incidents and allow the boys to fight it out until one them was hurt. They would then step into the fight and call a halt to the activity. The boys also reported widespread homosexual activity that sometimes involved coercion through physical intimidation. Homosexual assaults had become so common in the institution that the lights had to be kept on in the dormitory every night. This apparently did little good, since the night watchman was also victimized by some of the delinquents while he was supposed to be enforcing order. In one specific instance, a staff member allowed one of the prisoner leaders to act as a supervisor because the cottage was understaffed that day, and the prisoner permitted one of the weaker boys to be gang raped by three other prisoners as a result.[17]

A recent article by Johnson gives us a number of instructive examples of violence between prisoners in correctional institutions for delinquent boys.

> I was just sitting in my cell and this guy comes in and grabs me by the arm, by my bicep and pulls me out and tells me to get down on my knees. I mean, you wouldn't know what that guy wants you to get down on your knees for. You can't tell what the guy wants, you know? But I mean I'm small, you know, and you see all these big guys, you hear all this stuff and getting taken off and all this dumb stuff in jail. And you've never been in jail and you don't know what they're about, and it gets to you.[18]

■ ■ ■

> They slapped me in the face and another one kicked me in the spine. And they said if I didn't give in to them by tomorrow then that's what would happen. They would bring me into the shower room and beat the shit out of me and force me. And they said if I wasn't forced, that if I gave it to them, then it wouldn't be so bad. So I couldn't tell the guard what was going on and I figured that the guard wouldn't listen to me . . . they thought I was going crazy. They wouldn't listen to me. So I thought I would just go along and do something about it myself. So I was praying to myself, saying "dear God please be with me all night." And then when the gates closed I just stuck my fingers in there.[19]

■ ■ ■

> I was just hoping things wouldn't happen to me more than they were. I was just more or less imagining what could happen. I was just frightened. I wasn't thinking about how I could handle it. Like

I said before the only way they would get it is if they sliced my throat or knocked me out or I just couldn't get up off my feet. And I said that automatically, but I knew there were other ways. Guys in here they come up behind you and put a blanket over your head and knock you out. And you don't know what happened to you, because I see this happen. I was scared of things like this.[20]

■ ■ ■

Prior to my release time these guys had me buying them cigarettes in the commissary and other items. And I was doing this to avoid getting beat up or in any kind of scuffle. So this went on for quite a few months. And each week it got larger and larger. And they were calling me names, punk and easy to bulldoze. I knew that practically everyone was taking advantage of me. . . . And this particular day I was in my cell and these three colored guys who I had been paying off from the commissary came in and started laughing and they wanted to indulge in some sexual behavior. I was frightened and punched around a few times and I was sexually assaulted. I was deathly afraid of going to the officer or any of the brass, that I would be held back from being cut loose. So I just held it to myself.[21]

These boys are trying to act in what they take to be a masculine fashion. And yet their fear shows. The terror of prison life for those who are not powerful and who do not have influential friends is barely controllable. All other aspects of their lives become distorted by their fear and by the manipulations of those who would take advantage of them. However, not all prisoners are equally terrified by the prospect of an assault. For example, consider the ritual encounter between two prisoner leaders that is described by Feld.

Finally, they squared off in the middle of the room, kicking over some chairs in the process. They were only a few steps apart, yet neither moved forward. Instead, they kept saying to each other, "Come on sucker," until one of the staff members stepped between them and forced them to sit down at their respective tables. The staff intervention saved face for each of them and they retired to their tables and continued their verbal abuse, saying "Come on sucker," "Why didn't you fight when you had the chance?" "You can't fight," and the like. After this had continued for some time, one said to the other, "I don't say I can beat your ass. But you can't make me a punk."[22]

Because Feld studied a number of institutions simultaneously, he was able to go beyond the descriptive analysis provided by Polsky in *Cottage Six* to show how variations in the orientation of the institution and its staff members directly impact the behavior of the prisoners. In the Massachusetts juvenile institution that he analyzed, the inmate social structure paralleled the institutional orientation in that those institutions that were more treatment-oriented experienced considerably less prisoner victimization than those institutions that were more custody-oriented. As a matter of fact, there were no instances of sexual exploitation in the treatment-oriented cottages. In the custody-oriented cottages, the lower-status boys used various techniques to try to minimize their exposure to victimization by their fellow prisoners.

> They sat near the staff for physical protection to avoid being beaten by the other boys. When residents moved from place to place, the punks walked at the back of the lines to stay close to staff and to prevent inmates from getting behind them. One consequence was that in lines for food or desserts they received what was left, but that was a small price to pay for security. In Cottage 9 they asked to be locked in the isolation rooms to sleep, in order to avoid being beaten or raped in the dormitory. Because of the alienation between inmates and staff, however, cottage personnel provided them with little comfort or reassurance beyond the scant protection afforded by their physical presence.[23]

Feld analyzes victimizations in these institutions with compassion and insight. He concludes that the inmate code, which is a set of norms prescribing appropriate behavior among prisoners, benefits only the interests of the prisoner elites. The primary tenet of the code is *never* to "snitch" and this prohibits victims from complaining to staff members. If they do not complain, victimization will continue, but if they do snitch and it becomes known to other prisoners, they will be marked for the remainder of their stay in the institution and will almost certainly suffer greatly increased victimization as punishment for having broken the code.

> . . . for those inmates who become targets of assaults and rapes, the loss of physical integrity is the ultimate victimization. These victims, apart from the physical pain, are without recourse or remedy, and the ensuing feelings of helplessness and futility can only have damaging consequences. Victims can either resist and become

involved in an escalating cycle of violence, or they can acquiesce and thereby further assure their exploitation and the internalizing of their "loser" status.[24]

The most extensive study of victimization in juvenile correctional institutions was carried out in an Ohio institution for boys by Bartollas et al. Their work has been reported in a great many journal articles and papers[25] and also in their book, *Juvenile Victimization: The Institutional Paradox*.[26] The following summary of their findings is derived from this book. New boys arriving at the institution were terribly fearful, as they had already heard about the institution's reputation. They were so totally paralyzed by fear that they were unable to pay attention to the institutional orientation given by staff members. It was clear to them that they would shortly be given a very different kind of orientation to institutional life. As soon as a new boy is released into the institution, he is subjected to a testing process by the inmate leaders who want to know whether he will defend himself when he's attacked and whether he has a history of sexual exploitation. The worst of the exploiters are probably the "booty bandits,"[27] who make a career of harassing passive youths and exploiting them in every possible way, especially sexual.

No help is offered to the new boys from staff members or from other prisoners. They are completely left to their own devices. The less able they are to defend themselves, the further down the exploitation matrix they are pushed. The most innocuous form of victimization in the exploitation matrix is to take the victim's dessert at meals. If he permits this, then the aggressors next will take his favorite foods. The other victimizing acts in the matrix, arranged in the order of increasing severity of victimization, are confiscation of the victim's canteen pop and candy, pop and candy given to him by his parents, institutional clothing, toilet articles, cigarettes, personal clothing and his radio, followed by physically beating him, forcing him to play the passive role in anal sodomy, to masturbate others and to be the receptor in oral sodomy. Being the "girl" in oral sodomy is the ultimate in degrading victimization experiences as seen in the eyes of the prisoners. Any boy who can be forced to participate in this activity is, by definition, fair game to be exploited in all of the lesser forms of victimization.

Like most urban institutions, the one studied by Bartollas et al. was dominated by black prisoners. It follows from this that the victims were usually white prisoners. Other characteristics associated with victimization included tone of voice, facial expression, posture and confidence projected in interpersonal relations. These characteristics were crucial in establishing an image of someone who was not appropriate material for victimization. Prospective victims had poor impression management. They were likely to back off slightly when talking to other prisoners, and they had less than average direct eye contact with the other boys. They had generally been sent to the institution for relatively minor crimes, and they were usually without experience in street fighting. With inadequate fighting skills and impression management, there was no way that they could defend themselves against the depredations to which they were subjected. The boys at the bottom of the status structure were so fearful that they broadcasted this fear with every word and motion. They were often willing to allow themselves to be exploited for sex in the hope that they would not be beaten up, but this hope was rarely fulfilled.

One would expect that the aggressors would be physically larger than the victims in addition to being tougher and more skilled in street fighting. Surprisingly, this was not true. Victims and aggressors were approximately the same age, weight and height, and they also had approximately the same intelligence level. The number of offenses recorded in their records was also equivalent. Even the number of previous commitments to institutions did not differentiate between the sexual victims and their exploiters, although this dimension did differentiate between aggressors and victims in general. Boys with a greater number of previous institutional experiences were more likely to be aggressors than to be victims.

The experiences of the scapegoat who inhabits the lower regions of the status structure in the prisoner subculture can be conceptualized in terms of stages. The initial stage is the testing to which a boy is subjected when he is admitted to the institution. If any fearfulness is shown, the prisoner elites victimize and harass him unmercifully. If they are successful in forcing him into sexual acts such as oral sodomy, this "dramatic event" is publicized throughout the institution and it is defined as his "status degradation ceremony." He is then considered to be a social outcast and is avoided by self-respecting prisoners, except when they decide to victimize him. The next stage in the process can be labeled "role engulfment." In this stage, the scapegoat comes to accept his low social standing and to internalize the hatred of himself that is part of the scapegoat's social role. He displays little outward emotion and keeps his guilt, shame and indignation to himself. His personal habits deteriorate, and he may no longer brush his teeth or take regular showers. Many boys in this situation end up mutilating themselves in their despair.

Not all of the scapegoats continue to occupy this role for their entire institutional stay. Perhaps as many as one out of every three is successful, eventually fighting his way up from the bottom. Those who do not manage their way off the bottom of the heap are considered to be untouchables by the other prisoners. They are not allowed to serve food, smoke the same cigarettes, or even sit beside the other prisoners. The staff members are little better than the other prisoners. They generally reject and ignore the scapegoats, and give them fewer institutional privileges than the other boys. The scapegoats internalize their lower status to such an extent that they may injure themselves. Here are two of the many examples of the discouragement and hopelessness that these boys feel.

> The first day I got up in the cottage I got in a fight. I was pushed by homosexuality and I got in a fight. The "Man" blamed me for it and made me do some work and all that. So as it went on, I was down in the school area, and I was approached about four or five times. I had to fight myself out of it. It really messed me up mentally, you know. I was really bothered by it. . . . So then they started bothering me more. And everything kept building up, so I drank some metal polish. I thought that maybe if I drank some metal polish, they would take me to the hospital and I could run. Because this place was pretty well laid out; I couldn't run from it.[28]
>
> ∎∎∎
>
> I'm weak, I'm kindhearted. Take, for instance, my cigarettes. People keep coming up and asking for one and I would say, "Yeah, take one." But they would take the whole pack. And then I began to give up sex. I'm always tense and anxious. I've always been degraded. I'd rather be dead than continue to suffer in this hell hole.[29]

Nineteen percent of the boys were pure exploiters, 34% exploited others but were also exploited themselves on occasion; 21% were occasionally exploited; 17% were commonly exploited; and 10% were able to keep themselves completely aloof from the exploitation matrix. They were neither exploiters nor exploited. Boys who suffered victimization in the institution tended to be better adjusted than the aggressors in their lives outside of the institution, but they were the most poorly adjusted of the prisoners within the institution. The final irony of their victimization is that they scored the highest of all the prisoner groups on heterosexuality in the Gough Adjective Check List.

Victimization within the prisoner subculture is aided by architecture and by the unwillingness or fearfulness that keeps staff members from interfering in many victimizing occurrences. It is unlikely that the topic of victimization never occurred to the architects who originally designed the institution studied by Bartollas and his associates. As a result, the institution possessed numerous areas in which victimization was comparatively easy if staff members were not constantly vigilant. Sexual exploitation was particularly likely to occur in single rooms and showers. Recreational and educational areas were also burdened with a heavy incidence of victimization events. Any area in which supervision was not adequate was sought out by victimizers and incorporated in their plots to make use of the bodies and possessions of others. In some cases, it didn't even matter if staff members were present because they were so cowed that they felt unable to do anything about it.

> One youth, for instance, was ordered by several others to masturbate them while the teacher was still present in the room. Unable to do anything about it, the teacher stood by, permitting the group masturbation. In another situation, the teacher was ordered to leave the room while one youth was compelled to commit oral sodomy for other boys. In still another incident, a college female was visiting a class and when she went outside the classroom for a cigarette, she was attacked by several inmates. It took a valiant effort by school personnel to avert a rape.[30]

The ecology of victimization incidents varied with the type of the incident. For example, economic victimization did not have the same ecological distribution within the institution as physical victimization. It was more common in the cottages where the boys kept most of their material items and in which staff members showed little concern when boys lost their possessions. The educational area, vocational area and recreational area were also sites for a considerable number of economically victimizing incidents.

The institution studied by Bartollas, Miller and Dinitz was rated to hold seriously delinquent youths, so one might expect that victimization there would be more severe than in institutions for less serious delinquents. Unfortunately, the other publications that we have examined in this chapter do not support this conclusion. It appears that juvenile victimization is rampant in a wide variety of institutions across the country. Bartollas and his colleagues have given us a detailed portrayal of prisoner victimization and they have analyzed victimization phenomena much more fully than any previous investigator. However, there is no reason to think that the institution they studied has had an unusually high incidence of prisoner victimization.

VIOLENCE IN INSTITUTIONS FOR WOMEN AND GIRLS

There are three reports in the literature containing victimization rates for female institutions and comparing them with male institutions. The earliest of these reports is a study of serious assaults in Canadian penitentiaries that was carried out by Akman in the mid-1960s. The serious assault rate in the Kingston Prison for Women in 1976 was .019, or approximately one in every 50 prisoners.[31] Although this is a higher serious assault rate than the rate in any other Canadian penitentiary in 1965, it is hard to know what this means. There were 14 serious assaults in the Kingston Prison for Women during 1965, which translates into a high assault rate only because of the small number of women incarcerated there. Rates based on small numbers are subject to severe fluctuations from year to year, so it may be that 1965 was atypical for assaults in this institution. The other two studies of female correctional assault rates were carried out in the 1970s, and both of them report much lower assault rates among women than among men. In one of these, the rate was equal to the rate experienced in a drug rehabilitation halfway house that was included in the study, although it was much lower than the maximum security men's prison.[32] In the other study, the assault victimization rate was one-fifth of the average rate for all the male institutions in that state.[33] If we combine these data with qualitative studies of female prisons, it seems safe to say that violence in prisons for women and girls is considerably lower than it is in prisons for men and boys.

Being less common than male violence does not mean that female violence is less severe on those occasions when it occurs. Here are some examples of violence in women's institutions.

Another night, this other women comes up to me in the hall with a goddamm tonic bottle. You believe this? I goes, "What the hell you think you're going to do with *that?*" She goes, "Come on baby lady, let's see what you got under there." So she starts to lift up my shirt and I push her away, only she laughs. Then she's coming at me again, only this time she's starting to take off her dress. No kidding. She ain't got anything on underneath. So here I am, standing in this goddamm corridor of this goddamm jail with a sex maniac coming at me with a root beer bottle in her hand. And she ain't kidding either. . . .

So I start pulling off my own dress real slowly and she starts to calm down. Like before, she looked like she could either shove that bottle up inside me or split my face open with it. But when she sees maybe I'm going to get it on with her, she kind of relaxes. So then I say, "Take it easy, okay, cause I'm on the rag." I thought that would stop her, which it did, sort of. Only she says, "Okay, I'll leave you alone, only let me suck your tits." I figured, why not, the poor woman'd probably been in here a hundred years without seeing nobody half my age.[34]

■ ■ ■

A quiet girl was severely kicked in the stomach and the breast by five other inmates, evidently because, after first encouraging them, she would not submit to homosexual threats. None of the officers (guards) saw what happened, as it occurred in a bedroom, but when she told the officer in the next shift, they attempted to beat her again—right in the presence of the officer.[35]

■ ■ ■

This giant weighing in at two hundred fifty pounds, grabbed hold of me—all 110 pounds—and swung me around so I was facing Jacky. I thought she was going to hold me so Jacky could beat on me and I was worried about my glasses. Jacky pulled off her bandana, so that it wouldn't pull over her eyes, I suppose, and then struck me on the cheek.

I felt the impact, but it didn't hurt too much. I was worried that she would break my glasses with another blow. But there wasn't one. Jacky turned and ran, throwing a shiv to one of her women as she fled. She had it in her hair. The women ducked into an A & O with the shiv and probably flushed it down a john. End of the evidence. . . . My face! That bitch Jacky had slashed my face![36]

■ ■ ■

When a mommy and a daddy had a fight at Westfield, the bull-dyker would stick scissors in the girl's back, twist it and pull it out, then dare her to go to the clinic to have it treated. There were always deaths from blood poisoning or loss of blood because the kids who got stabbed with scissors or knives were afraid to tell the guards or go to the clinic. They knew they'd be killed when they got back.[37]

■ ■ ■

"The bitch is repulsive. I'd as soon do it with a dog as that stud broad," said Jane. "But I keep getting these kites. She has treatened me, she hangs around my room, and she's got her hands all over my ass all day long. How do I get that bitch off my case? I can't hold out much longer. Last night she gave me gum for my lock. Hey, I ain't got nothing against a good screw or even making it with the right broad but I'll barf if that bitch touches me. Problem is I'll get the shit kicked out of me or worse if I don't spread 'em in the next couple of days."[38]

These examples illustrate the viciousness of violence in women's prisons. Fear may not permeate these institutions to the extent that it does male institutions, but there are evidently many individuals who suffer horribly victimizing experiences. The use of cutting weapons to permanently disfigure the victim's face is a unique characteristic of violence in female institutions, and this adds a touch of threat and horror that goes beyond most of the fights that occur in men's prisons.

Homosexuality is much more likely to occur consensually in female subcultures than among incarcerated males. There is quite a bit of violence that is related to homosexuality, but the nature of the relationship is different. Homosexual rapes are relatively rare, and most of the fights develop out of lover's triangles. The masculine role player in a female prison relationship does not use physical violence to subdue her victim. Instead, homosexual relationships develop consensually or perhaps with a moderate degree of psychological manipulation. So long as only two people are involved in the relationship, the likelihood of violence is relatively small. The danger of a fight skyrockets when one number of the dyad finds a new lover and jealousies get out of hand.[39] Giallombardo tells us that there were a great many fights between women at Alderson, particularly for homosexual reasons, and the women there feared not for their lives so much as that they would be disfigured by a razor or scissors.[40]

Homosexual attacks on female prisoners may occur as punishment or as initiation rites, as in a western facility where new females were allegedly initiated by being raped with a broom handle. The only mention of this sort of behavior in the formal sociological literature on women's prisons is Giallombardo's comment that homosexual attacks sometimes occurred in all three of the girl's institutions that she studied, usually victimizing prisoners who had made a great deal of fun of those who engaged in homosexual behavior.[41] The legal literature contains a number of discussions of the famous case of People vs. Lovercamp in which testimony was given about sexual pressuring and assaults in the California Rehabilitation Center. In this institution, assaults and threats of assaults were used to coerce women into homosexual behavior against their will.[42] The events described in this court case do not differ in any way from homosexual coercion as practiced in male prisons.

At Frontera in California, four times as many homosexuals had three or more disciplinary reports as nonhomosexuals.[43] This illustrates the tendency toward violence that is inherent in homosexual jealousies, and it may also be indicative of other differences between homosexual and heterosexual roles as played in female institutions. The concentration of infractions among a small subgroup of the total female population was also found in the Florida Correctional Institution for Women by Lindquist. At this institution, one-twentieth of the women committed more than half of the disciplinary offenses, but there is no indication of the sexual orientation of these women in Lindquist's report.[44]

An unpublished doctoral dissertation by Simmons sheds some light on how activities by staff members may lead to violence between prisoners. She found that staff members in the women's prison that she studied were excessively concerned about homosexual behavior and were quick to separate lovers in order to prohibit any possible sexual contact between them. This enforced segregation invariably led to one of the members of the dyad finding a new lover, which set up a homosexual triangle. The jealousies engendered in this process and the damage to the status of the deserted lover were so great that a fight was a foregone conclusion.[45] It should also be mentioned that even if neither of the separated lovers find a new mate, their separation will create suspicions that will often have the same result.

Violence at Occoquan, an institution studied by Heffernan, was concentrated in the "life" subculture, one of the three dominant subcultures within the institution. One of the roles found in the life subculture was the "guerilla." Members of the life subculture in general, and guerillas in particular, were much more likely to be involved in fighting than the members of the other two subcultures. Sixty-one percent of the women in the life subculture had officially recorded disciplinary infractions for fighting, as compared with 22% of the women in the "cool" subculture and 9% of the women in the "square" subculture. As in the other prison settings, aggressive prisoners at Occoquan caused violence both through their own victimization of others and by threatening others in such a way that they suffered retaliatory attacks motivated by self-protection. One of the Heffernan's interviewees said:

> Then some people are looking for fights. Violence is the way they take care of things. With some of us, we know that it doesn't solve things, but sometimes if a person has a certain attitude, you just finally have to show her physically that she can't get away with it. They respect you and don't tangle with you.[46]

Except for the behavior of a few "guerillas," it appears that violence is only used in women's prisons to settle questions of dominance and subordination when other manipulative strategies fail to achieve the desired effect.

The studies which have been discussed thus far in this section have all been carried out in correctional institutions for women. It is legitimate to wonder whether female juvenile delinquents are more violent than women when incarcerated in view of our finding that institutions for male juvenile delinquents appear to experience more violence than institutions for adult males. The two studies that are available to us on this subject unfortunately offer contrasting answers to this question. The first, by Giallombardo, replicated her earlier study of a women's prison in three institutions for adolescent girls. She did not deal with violence to any great degree, and leaves us with the impression that other techniques of social control and exploitation were sufficient to maintain the prisoner social structure most of the time in these institutions. At Western, one of the three institutions in her study, the girls attempted to draw a newcomer into some of their deviant activities in order to control her behavior. This seemed to work in most cases, and it diminished the amount of overt violence that was necessary to support the social order.[47] In contrast, the situation at Lancaster, a girls' institution studied by Feld, was as vicious and degrading as conditions in correctional institutions for boys. There was even a "punk" role at the bottom of the status structure at Lancaster, a role filled by young women who were continuously victimized by their peers.[48]

Feld found that the inmate elite constantly directed verbal abuse toward lower-status girls for trivial reasons and assaulted them violently to reinforce their own status positions. In doing so, they were able to avoid unpleasant tasks such as fixing meals, clearing tables and washing dishes at the same time that they increased their social status. The lower-status girls were only too glad to perform any task they were asked, hoping that it would put off an imminent beating. The use of threats when actual violence did not occur reminds one of Polsky's *Cottage Six*. Common comments by inmate leaders at Lancaster were, "One more time, and I'll punch you in the mouth," or openly warning those around them, "I'm going to do a number on that girl."[48]

When new girls were admitted to Lancaster, they were subjected to the same kind of testing procedures that are described for boys by Bartollas, Miller and Dinitz. Anyone who capitulated to the aggressor invited further aggression rather than an end to the battle. One of the girls expressed this process as, "The girls would stop picking on them if they fought back. Fighting depends on if you're scared of them or not. You should still fight with them even if you can't fight."[49] The only way to get off the bottom of the status pyramid was to fight and continue fighting until one achieved a high enough status level to be left alone. This is very important because, "The girls will fight with someone they know won't fight back, and then threaten them so they won't say anything. They'll rarely fight with ones that will fight back."[50] Feld's conclusion from his study was that "Aggressiveness and boldness appeared to be an even more effective unequalizer among the females than among the males."[51]

CONCLUSION

The evidence that has been presented in this chapter suggests rather strongly that the violence and degradation that occurs in prisons for men is paralleled in institutions for women and adolescents. The differences that exist are differences in degree rather than differences in kind. Institutions for delinquent boys may be a little worse and institutions for women and girls, perhaps a little better than the average men's institution, but all three categories of correctional institutions have high enough rates of assault and associated victimization phenomena so that we must consider exposure to the probability of victimization to be the most severe of all the punishments that we inflict on correctional clients. Furthermore, there is convincing evidence that the burden of the punishment of victimization falls more heavily on those who have committed relatively minor crimes and those who are first offenders than it does on multiple and hardened offenders. To the extent that there is any deterrent effect associated with the threat of imprisonment, we might expect that this effect would be stronger for relatively law-abiding people than for the habitual and serious criminals through our society. This is, of course, just the opposite of the effect needed if we want to maximize the positive contributions of imprisonment to the social defense against serious crime.

The similarity of victimization phenomena in different types of institutions also calls to our attention the possibility that there might be something in the very nature of prison life that leads to these incidents. If this is true, then we can understand prison victimization as more the product of structural conditions than the accomplishment of a relatively limited number of "evil" persons who merely need to be reformed in order to solve the problem. Zimbardo's unique prison simulation experiment supports this conclusion. When he and his associates created an artificial prison in a Stanford University basement, they found that psychologically normal college students rapidly took on not only the official duties and responsibilities of the roles of prisoner and correctional officer, but also the negative aspects of these roles which are conducive to prison victimization.[52] When psychologically normal college students can spontaneously develop victimization-related aspects of their social roles in a few days while participating in an experiment that they know to be a simulation, then it appears justified to conclude that there is something in the structure of prisons that predisposes people to engage in dehumanizing forms of human behavior. This is a question that I will examine in greater detail in a later chapter.

NOTES

1. Linda Grasewicz, "A Study of Inmate Assaults in Major Institutions," unpublished paper, The Virginia Department of Corrections, 1977.
2. Desmond Ellis, Harold G. Grasmick and Bernard Gilman, Violence in prisons: A sociological analysis, *American Journal of Sociology* 80 (1974): 16–43.
3. Jack L. Ward, Homosexual behavior of the institutionalized delinquent, *Psychiatric Quarterly Supplement* 3 (1958): 301–314.

4. Sethard Fisher, Social organization in a correctional residence, *Pacific Sociological Review* 4 (1961): 87–93; Informal organization in a correctional setting, *Social Problems* 13 (1965): 214–222.
5. Howard Polsky, *Cottage Six* (New York: Wiley, 1962), p. 58.
6. Lee H. Bowker, *Women and Crime in America* (Encino, CA: Glencoe, 1980).
7. Polsky (1962), p. 62.
8. Seymour Rubenfeld and John W. Stafford, An adolescent inmate social system—A psychological account, *Psychiatry* 26 (1963): 241–256.
9. Ibid., p. 252.
10. Thomas E. Allen, Psychiatric observations on an adolescent inmate social system and culture, *Psychiatry* 32 (1969): 296.
11. Ibid., pp. 292–302.
12. Robert Johnson, *Culture and Crisis in Confinement* (Lexington, MA: D.C. Heath, 1976); Youth in crisis: Dimensions of self-destructive conduct among adolescent prisoners, *Adolescence* 13 (1978): 461–482.
13. Barry C. Feld, *Neutralizing Inmate Violence* (Cambridge, MA: Ballinger, 1977).
14. John Howard Association, *Illinois Youth Centers at St. Charles and Geneva* (Chicago: John Howard Association, 1974).
15. Clemens Bartollas, Stuart J. Miller and Simon Dinitz, *Juvenile Victimization: The Institutional Paradox* (New York: Wiley, 1976).
16. Thomas J. Cottle, Children in jail, *Crime and Delinquency* 25 (1979): 318–334.
17. John Howard Association (1974).
18. Robert Johnson (1978) p. 475.
19. Ibid., p. 476.
20. Ibid., p. 477.
21. Ibid., p. 478.
22. Feld (1977), pp. 154–155.
23. Ibid., p. 160.
24. Ibid., p. 199.
25. See, for example, Clemens Bartollas, Stuart J. Miller and Simon Dinitz, The exploitation matrix in a juvenile institution, *International Journal of Criminology and Penology* 4 (1976): 257–270; Becoming a scapegoat: Study of a deviant career, *Sociological Symposium* 11 (1974): 84–97; White victim in a black institution, in M. Riedel and P. Vales (Eds.), *The Offender—Problems and Issues* (New York: Praeger, 1977).
26. Clemens Bartollas et al. *Juvenile Victimization,* op. cit.
27. Clemens Bartollas, Stuart J. Miller and Simon Dinitz, The "booty bandit": A social role in a juvenile institution, *Journal of Homosexuality* 1 (1974): 203–212.
28. Clemens Bartollas et al. *Juvenile Victimization,* op. cit., p. 165.
29. Ibid., p. 173.
30. Ibid., p. 252.
31. D. Akman, Homicides and assaults in Canadian penitentiaries, *Canadian Journal of Corrections* 8 (1966): 284–299.
32. Donald J. Shoemaker and George A. Hillery, Jr., "Violence and Commitment in Custodial Settings," paper given at the annual meeting of the American Sociological Association, 1978.
33. Dan A. Fuller, Thomas Orsagh and David Raber, "Violence and Victimization Within the North Carolina Prison System," paper presented at the annual meeting of the Academy of Criminal Justice Sciences, 1978.
34. Thomas J. Cottle (1979) pp. 328–329.

35. Gene Kassebaum, Sex in prison, *Sexual Behavior* 2 (January 1972): 39.
36. G. Allen, On the women's side of the pen, *The Humanist* 38 (September–October 1978): 31.
37. Vergil L. Williams and Mary Fish (Eds.), *Convicts, Codes, and Contraband: The Prison Life of Men and Women* (Cambridge, MA: Ballinger, 1974). p. 113.
38. Kenneth Dimick, *Ladies in Waiting Behind Prison Walls* (Muncie, IN: Accelerated Development Inc., 1979), p. 90.
39. Charles A. Ford, Homosexual practices of institutionalized females, *Journal of Abnormal and Social Psychology* 23 (1929): 442–448; David A. Ward and Gene G. Kassebaum, *Women's Prison: Sex and Social Structure* (Chicago: Aldine, 1965); Rose Giallombardo, *Society of Women: A Study of Women's Prison* (New York: Wiley, 1966); *The Social World of Imprisoned Girls* (New York: Wiley, 1974).
40. Giallombardo (1966).
41. Giallombardo (1974).
42. Criminal law—California court holds the defense of necessity available to prison escapees—People v. Lovercamp, "43 Cal. App.3d 823, 118 Cal Rptr. 110" (1974), *University of Illinois Law Forum* 1975 (1975): 271–280; D. Deckert, Criminal law—Prisons—Necessity a defense to escape when avoiding homosexual attacks—People v. Lovercamp,"43 Cal App.3d 823, 119 Cal. Rptr.110" (1974), *Western State University Law Review* 3 (Fall 1975): 165–175.
43. Ward and Kassebaum (1965).
44. Charles A. Linquist, "Female Violators of Prison Discipline: Backgrounds and Sanctions," paper presented at the annual meeting of the American Society of Criminology, 1978.
45. Immogene L. Simmons, "Interaction and Leadership Among Female Prisoners," Ph.D. Dissertation, University of Missouri, 1975.
46. Esther Heffernan, *Making It in Prison: The Square, the Cool, and the Life* (New York: Wiley, 1972), pp. 108–109.
47. Giallombardo (1974).
48. Feld (1977), p. 162.
49. Ibid., p. 134.
50. Ibid., p. 134.
51. Ibid., p. 162.
52. Phillip Zimbardo, Mythology of imprisonment, *Society* 9(6) (1972): 4–8.

Psychological Victimization Among Prisoners

In the struggle for status, a positive self-image, and material goods, prisoners cannot afford to limit their aggression to the physical level. The risk of being injured by one's victim is too great. An effective strategy for minimizing this risk is to use verbal aggression wherever possible, resorting to physical aggression only when absolutely necessary to achieve desired goals. I have stated that prisoner status is substantially determined by the demonstrated domination of others. The higher the ratio of victimizing others to being the victim of others, the higher one's social status. Psychological victimization is probably not as status-enhancing as physical victimization, but the accumulation of results of hundreds of psychological victimizations has the same effect as a much smaller number of physical victimizations. In addition to being a safer strategy, psychological victimization also involves the expenditure of a smaller amount of energy by the aggressor than physical victimization, and so it is possible to use it more extensively in the daily routine of exploitation that characterizes most correctional institutions.

PSYCHOLOGICAL VICTIMIZATION AMONG
MALE PRISONERS

In psychological victimization, the aggressor manipulates other prisoners into giving up material goods, sex or some other desired commodity without actually having to fight for it. Some aggressors deviate from this general pattern in that they perpetrate psychological victimization purely for the pleasure they gain from seeing the suffering of the victim. In some cases, the victims are driven to such a state of self-destructive personality disorganization that they mutilate themselves or commit suicide.

The general term for psychological manipulations in prison is *con games*. One way of conceptualizing con games is to follow the form used by Berne in his classic book, *Games People Play*.[1] This has been done for correctional institutions in an insightful booklet by Heise, *Prison Games*.[2] Heise includes three major psychological manipulations that prisoners use against each other along with a few manipulations between staff and prisoners and a number of psychological games that are nonvictimizing. The names of the three Heise games that I will discuss are "Rats, Punks and Snitches," "Inmates and Convicts" and "Shot Picking."

"Rats, Punks and Snitches" is the most serious of all prison games. The victim's life is always at stake, and there is often danger to the life of the aggressor, too. At the very least, this game threatens the good standing of the victim in the prisoner subculture. The aggressor begins the game by accusing the victim of being an informer, which is intolerable under the convict code. If the accusation is made directly and in front of witnesses, it will probably provoke a fight on the spot. A safer way of beginning the game is to make the accusation behind the victim's back. Regardless of whether the accusation is made face-to-face or behind the back, the victim is automatically assumed to be guilty unless he immediately challenges the aggressor to a fight. Should he fail to do so, perhaps out of knowledge that the aggressor would easily win the battle, the minimum penalty will be ostracism and the limitation of friendships to other informers and prison untouchables. In addition to the ostracism, there is an obvious loss of status by the victim and increased risk of future physical victimizations. Under the traditional convict code, the victim would most likely have been assassinated. Today, one hears that the victim should be assassinated, but it is unlikely that the homicide will actually be carried out. Heise includes piping (being attacked with a lead pipe), stabbing and sexual assault among the punishments that may be meted out to an alleged prisoner informer.

The game of "Rats, Punks and Snitches" can be played more subtly. For example, the aggressor can mention informally to his friends that the victim has a "snitch jacket" and warn them that they probably would not want to get too involved with him. Alternatively, the aggressor may say something like, "You knew that guy there is a punk, didn't you?" Or, "When I was in Folsom, that guy was known as a rat, so watch yourself around him."[3] An even weaker form of the game occurs when these terms are teasingly or harassingly used without the imputation of truth. Heise identifies this variety of the game as "Let's Hang a Lightweight Jacket." The more indirect ways of playing the game are used by the older and more experienced prisoners, while the direct challenges are usually employed by young, immature prisoners who are hungry for fast status and who do not fully appreciate the danger in which they are putting themselves.

"Inmates and Convicts" is closely related to the game of "Rats, Punks and Snitches." The aggressor in the game says something like, "He's no convict! He's an inmate!"[4] He then goes on to explain that the victim is not a true convict, as defined under the convict code. This claim is not as serious as the claim that the victim is an informer, and does not necessarily result in any physical harm to the victim. Rather, it serves to lower the status of the victim by suggesting that he is not a "true" convict and, at the same time, to raise the status of the aggressor, who is posing as a defender of traditional values in the prisoner subculture.

Heise's final game is "Shot Picking." The aggressor in this interpersonal game identifies an inept and inexperienced prisoner, sometimes called "lame," and then deliberately insults him in a loud voice. Again, the purpose is to reduce the status of the victim while increasing the status of the aggressor in the incident. This is a unique exception to the zero-sum limitation in prisoner status games, for the aggressor in "Shot Picking" has the opportunity to gain more status than is lost by the victim. This occurs because the aggressor manipulates the situation so that he is doing the loud-mouthing in a setting where most prisoners within hearing distance of the incident cannot see his victim. They are thus likely to think that he is arguing with someone less inadequate than the "lame," which naturally enhances his status more than it would if the identity of his victim were known to all. "Band Wagon" is a variety of "Shot Picking" in which the victim is such an easy target that all the prisoners on the tier jump on the bandwagon and verbally abuse him. At this point, however, there is little status to be gained from the verbal mistreatment because the mark is known to be such a pushover.

A more graphic example of psychological victimization between prisoners has been reported by Carroll in his book, *Hacks, Blacks, and Cons*.

Soon after he arrived, this inmate was approached by two others carrying a jar containing some orange liquid. They told him the liquid was acid and threatened to throw it over him if he did not "come across" for them which he immediately did, only to find out the liquid was orange juice. Hereafter he was repeatedly coerced into performing sexual activities, and eventually placed himself into protective custody.[5]

The victim in this incident was not psychologically tough enough to resist the pressure that was brought to bear upon him because he was a "fish" (a neophyte prisoner) and so was confused and vulnerable. In addition, being new to prison life, he was not aware of the fact that there probably was not any acid available in the prison. Experienced "wolves" are always on the lookout for prisoners who have not yet learned how to defend themselves psychologically as well as physically, and turnover in prisoner populations is always high enough so that there is a ready supply of these potential victims.

A variation of this manipulation that has been traditionally used to victimize new prisoners is to provide free canteen items and other favors to the newcomer and to befriend him. Then, after an accomplice has threatened to rape him, the aggressor defends him and the victim becomes even more psychologically dependent on him. At some point in this process, the victim is no longer able to make independent judgments. He is then highly vulnerable, and the aggressor moves in to offer him the alternative of becoming a "kept man" or being turned loose on his own—to be victimized by others. The victim is shocked at this betrayal and yet has nowhere to turn. If he has been set up properly, he will almost always accede to the aggressor. This process of psychological manipulation is a delicate one, and it requires a great deal of skill and sensitivity on the part of the aggressor. It is analogous to the psychological manipulations used by pimps to keep their prostitutes working for them on the streets.

In the discussion of Polsky's study of *Cottage Six* in Chapter 3, I mentioned a number of deviant processes that were used to enforce social control in the prisoner subculture of the cottage. Three of these processes—threat-gestures, ranking and scape-goating—are essentially types of psychological victimization. The threat-gestures kept the lower-status boys in the cottage in a constant state of psychological turmoil. Threat-gestures are a series of quick motions that appear to the victim as if he is going to be beaten, such as lunging at him, pretending to kick him or throwing a mock punch at him. The victim's fearful reaction, such as jumping back or otherwise cowering, reinforces the aggressor in this form of behavior. In ranking, numerous insults are heaped upon the lower-status boys to make clear to everyone that they are truly "punks." Scapegoating combines these two techniques with physical aggression to keep the victims on the bottom of the prisoner status structure. These psychological manipulations can best be understood as serving several functions at the same time. They maintain the status quo in the cottage social structure; they heighten the status of the leaders; and they serve as social control mechanisms to keep everyone, including those not involved in the incident, in his place.[6] There is probably more of a deterrent effect associated with many of these forms of psychological victimization than with the formal responses of the criminal justice system in the free society.

The psychological pain that is suffered by prisoners who are being manipulated and humiliated is difficult for an outsider to appreciate. Knowing about these manipulations in the prisoners' own words will make it easier for the reader to identify with their predicament. The following three vignettes have been taken from Toch's book, *Living in Prison, The Ecology of Survival:*

> Any new person, they hollered obscenities at them and all sorts of names, and throwing things down from the gallery and everything. They told me to walk down the middle of this line like I was on exhibition, and everybody started do throw things and everything, and I was shaking in my boots . . . they were screaming things like, "That is for me" and "This one won't take long—he will be easy." And "Look at his eyes" and "her eyes" or whatever, and making all kinds of remarks.[7]

■ ■ ■

> Sometimes there's 20 or 30 people in the showers, and they're always making remarks to you, and you don't feel free. I'm used to, on the streets, where you don't have any paranoia. Taking a shower is a beautiful thing. Here it's a paranoia thing, where they have you back against the wall, and if you turn around and wash your legs and you're bent over, besides getting remarks you might really get hurt . . . and you take your shower in 30 seconds, and you feel really stupid, and you just pull your pants down and there's all these guys waiting for you to pull your pants down. It's a sick thing. Even though the physical pressure is there for a short time, the mental pressure is there permanently. And if you're on the toilet and everybody's just walking by, then it's a really intense thing.

I've been to the bathroom in front of people on the streets, and it's just nothing at all like it is in here. You just want to say, "Jesus, leave me alone." But you can't close the door, and it's a cell and people are looking at you . . . sometimes I have some heavy thoughts to myself, thinking about why all this happened. Is this pressure going to build up to a point where I say I'm actually going to be a fag? I really wonder where and why all of this is happening. What I was into. I never dreamed that I was going to be in this condition and in this kind of place and around these kind of people and around this kind of environment, where I would want to leave and couldn't.[8]

■ ■ ■

From one minute to the next you don't know what an inmate is going to say. You don't. You could be discussing a fishing trip for a few minutes, and then the next thing you know the guy next to him is yelling that he is going to get into your buns or he thinks you're cute or how about a blow job or something like this. But the few minutes you were talking about this fishing trip your mind was relaxed and you were settled down and then right away somebody has to start. It's always that way. Somebody has to start. No matter what the conversation is, it always comes into it . . . he'll say, "How's your buns today?" Just to keep his image up. And then you have to start, because if you don't start on the defensive, then they're going to say that so-and-so doesn't defend himself, so we'll ride him a little more.[9]

The point made by these vignettes is that even brief comments in a prison can carry emotional impact because of the degradation that they imply. Psychological games that cheat prisoners out of money may be angering, but they are threatening only to the extent that they imply something that goes beyond mere financial loss. In contrast, direct references to sexual victimization arouse a considerable amount of fear in all but the toughest prisoner. This fear clouds the victim's thinking and makes it easier to victimize him in ways other than sexual. For example, sexual inuendos could be used to weaken the resistance of a victim where illicit sex was the not the goal of the manipulation at all, but rather some sort of economic gain. The victim would then be manipulated into a position where he was so relieved to escape sexual victimization that he would make no resistance to the loss of material goods.

The victim of physical aggression always knows that he has been victimized, although he might resist applying the label of a victim to himself. This is not necessarily true with psychological victimization, for many of these victims are not even aware that they have been engaged in a contest, let alone that they lost it. For example, Mann identified a relationship called "lugging" in his study of the prisoner social system at Guelph Reformatory in Canada. When the older prisoner "lugs" a young, attractive "fish," he takes him under his wing, befriending him and giving him tobacco and other gifts in return for personal or sexual favors. The senior partner in seven consecutive "lugging" relationships describes this process:

> It all sounds very easy to him, and he's going to make something on it — new clothes and more tobacco, etc. So he never thinks of what it's going to cost him. The brighter the picture you paint him, the better he likes it. That's just the start. After he's in it for a while, it lowers his dignity to a certain level and then it doesn't really matter. [Here he is referring to homosexual acts.][10]

There is nothing brutal about the way that these "sweet kids" are treated by their older partners. They recognize that they are benefiting from the attentions of their mates, not considering themselves to be victims. They may be only dimly aware that their degrees of freedom have been attentuated by the psychological manipulations practiced on them. From our perspective, we can clearly identify the element of victimization as psychological in that these "punks" are coerced into relationships that are not in their best interests—relationships that lower their social status and harm their self-image—just after they have arrived at the penitentiary and before they have had a chance to really understand all of the social roles that are open to them.

PSYCHOLOGICAL VICTIMIZATION AMONG PRISONERS IN FEMALE INSTITUTIONS

Although there are no objective studies of the matter, administrators generally agree that psychological victimization is extremely high in women's prisons; there is speculation that it is even higher than in men's prisons. The theory is that incarcerated women and men carry out similar levels of aggression against their fellow prisoners, but a much higher proportion of the women's aggression is psychological and a much higher proportion of the men's aggression is physical. I cannot offer sufficient evidence to either confirm or discredit this theory, but I will offer a few examples of psychological victimization in women's prisons.

Like men, incarcerated women are deprived of structural supports for their gender identification. Their loved ones are separated from them and communication links are tenuous. This provides endless opportunities for psychological victimization. For example, it may be rumored that the husband or lover of the victim in a psychological manipulation has been seen with a new mate. The aggressor in this manipulation releases increasingly threatening rumors about the victim's mate as time goes on, driving her to distraction. The goal in this manipulation may simply be to see her suffer but it is more likely to be to upset her enough so that she gives up a leadership or friendship role that is desired by the aggressor—or perhaps so that she becomes embittered about heterosexual relations and is willing to undertake a homosexual relationship with the aggressor. The danger of this kind of manipulation is that if the victim finds out that she has been manipulated and that none of the rumors is true, she is likely to lose self-control and physically assault the aggressor.

Dimick discusses the ways in which prisoners take advantage of any of their sisters who show signs of paranoid thinking. Once the word is out, the aggressors "slip objects like magazines, pictures or maybe even extra furniture into their cells just so they will be bewildered when they find them. Comments such as 'I told you that three times yesterday' are made about subjects that were never discussed. Or they may allude to what somebody said 'about you.'"[11] The victim is probably a little disoriented to start with, and with so many fellow-prisoners willing to help her over the edge, a minor problem may soon develop into a major psychological breakdown.

Females are rarely forced into homosexual relationships against their will by physical aggression. A very high proportion of lesbian relationships in the prison are consensual. When coercion does exist, it is psychological in nature. Ward and Kassebaum show how women were sometimes seduced into homosexual affairs at Frontera in California by the use of material goods. A new and attractive prisoner would be given many presents of material items by an older, more experienced prisoner, and after a time, she would come to depend on these items to support her standard of living. At the same time, she would become somewhat emotionally dependent on the supplier of these items. When the aggressor felt that the victim was caught in the net, she would refuse to provide additional material items unless the victim would engage in overt sexual behavior. Despite the overt sexual elements of the relationships developed in this fashion, Ward and Kassebaum comment that most of these relationships were based on an exchange of commisary items for continued interest and loyalty rather than for overt sexual behavior. The sex simply accompanied the interest and loyalty.[12]

In her study, *Society of Women*, Giallombardo identifies two types of psychological victimization. These are "panning" and "signifying." "Panning" is derogatory gossip about a prisoner who is not present while "signifying" is negative gossip about a prisoner in her presence. Mimicking, biting sarcasm and scorn are all used as informal social control mechanisms. They tend to be used to maintain the social structure of the prisoner groups rather than to produce sexual or economic acquiescence. The status of the aggressor is enhanced indirectly through continued occupation of a leadership position rather than directly by an immediate status gain. On the social roles described by Giallombardo, the "jive bitch" provides the best example of the use of psychological victimization. She deliberately spreads misleading rumors with the intent of causing conflict between other prisoners for her own benefit.[13] Giallombardo's more recent study of three institutions for delinquent girls continues her tradition of minimizing the discussion of the unpleasantries associated with prisoner victimization. She comments that one of the functions of the pseudofamily systems in all three institutions was to protect the girls from their fellow-prisoners, but she says very little about from what there is need to be protected. There are apparently few serious assaults in the institutions she studied. Most fights do not result in substantial physical injury. Interpersonal difficulties are normally settled by verbal aggression and manipulation rather than in a physical test of strength. Pseudofamily members counteract verbal attacks made against their relatives, minimizing or denying any harmful statements that have been made about them. The only direct victimization that is discussed by Giallombardo is the use of verbal pressure or small gifts as part of the manipulation to attempt to seduce the desired partner to a lesbian relationship.[14] However, she does not describe the process in enough detail so that we can understand how it actually occurs.

There was a considerable amount of verbal aggression at Lancaster in Massachusetts, another institution for delinquent girls.

At this institution, "the female leaders directed a considerable amount of verbal abuse against lower status girls for trivial reasons, such as giving them the wrong brand of cigarette, accidentally splashing water while swimming and the like."[15] In addition to the direct verbal aggression at Lancaster, there was also the indirect use of threats by the lieutenants of the inmate leaders, who constantly warned lower-status girls that they would be beaten if they did not please the leaders or if the leaders got into trouble. There was also a great deal of ranking, in which "the girls used negative imputations of homosexuality in much the same fashion as the boys did, ranking on girls for being 'lessies' or lesbians, just as the boys derided others as 'faggots.' "[16]

The power of psychological aggression in serving an economic goal is illustrated in the following quote from a prisoner at Occoquan, the District of Columbia Women's Reformatory.

> First time down I got a terrific "bullying." There are a group of five or six "bullies" that take everything—cosmetics, soap, everything you lay down—and make life miserable for you, unless you "bully back" or go along and don't bother them.[17]

It is clear from this quote that the content of the aggression is verbal. Victims are threatened into giving up material items rather than having them stolen by unknown thieves. Once a bully has a tough reputation that matches her aggressive demeanor, new prisoners who are not well-versed in street fighting and prison manipulations will give up some canteen items rather than take the chance that the verbal aggression will turn into physical aggression if they resist.

SUICIDE AND SELF-MUTILATION AS CONSEQUENCES OF PSYCHOLOGICAL VICTIMIZATION

Suicides, attempted suicides and self-mutilations, some of which have a suicidal intent and others of which do not, are all part of life in penal institutions. Most studies of the subject say little about prisoner victimization and its possible relationship to the self-destructive acts.[18] The common assumption is that self-destructive behavior is due to the mental illness of certain prisoners, a manipulative attempt to gain "illegitimate" ends, an immediate reaction to the shock of the first days of imprisonment, or a response to problems with family members or the criminal justice system outside of the prison microcosm. Helgemoe began his study of self-injury among prisoners assuming that problems with family, the courts and parole were uppermost in the instigation of self-injuries. To his surprise, these factors were much less important than the stressfulness of the prison setting itself.[19] Because this was an unanticipated result, Helgemoe did not gather as much data on the subject as he might have, and it is not clear to what extent psychological or physical victimization by other prisoners might have contributed to the high degree of prison stress that led to the self-injuries. Gibbs, in an unpublished doctoral dissertation, states that the dominant theme emerging from a content analysis of interviews with prisoners who harmed themselves was fear, and his description of these self-injurers as inexperienced, nonviolent young prisoners is also the description of prisoners who are most likely to become victims. He recommends that staff members devote greater attention to diagnosing difficulties that have arisen out of fear of victimization or sexual pressure as a way of preventing self-damaging actions.[20]

Self-mutilation or suicide may occur because of self-hatred after a number of degrading victimizations have occurred, out of fear and despair of anticipated future victimizations, or perhaps as a way of forcing prison authorities to pay attention to the victim and to grant protective custody. Gibbs' findings notwithstanding, most self-mutilations and suicides probably have very little to do with victimization phenomena. I do not mean to say that victimization is the main cause of self-destructive acts—only that it is an important cause. Here are four vignettes in which prisoners who damaged themselves explain the situation, as they perceived it, when they decided to carry out the self-destructive act.

> Yeah, there were a lot of people riding me, because, like, guys were coming by, guys would say in a crowd, "I would get him myself, but I don't want to get the extra time for it." Because the word was already out that I was a rat; it was put out by the two guys that came up to prison with me.[21]
>
> ■ ■ ■
>
> This harassment just stops my normal procedure, my everyday life. Everything just seems to stop immediately. . . . You get scared and you don't eat or sleep or use a toilet regular. Everything tightens up on you. That fear . . . you lose interest in doing anything.[22]
>
> ■ ■ ■
>
> They put a note in my cell and say they're going to come and kill me, they're going to hang me. So I showed the note to the police

and told them I didn't know what was going on. Because I had heard that they will kill you in the Tombs, people have told me that on the outside . . . and the day before that they tried to kill another guy. They stabbed him with a piece of wire. . . . So nothing couldn't tell me that they wasn't going to do the same to me.[23]

■ ■ ■

Like guys, they kept tripping at me, you know? When you come upstairs and go back upstairs, they start playing with you and I just stuffed that stuff off, because I didn't want do get no ticket for getting in a fight or nothing. So I've been here about 13 months and haven't had no fights, just stuff it off. But I just keep thinking about it and guys keep bothering me. . . . And I went to program and the same guys right away started tripping on me. So I'd just think about it and then let it slide. Go out to rec, play cards, and forget about it. Then another guy would come up and do the same thing.[24]

Vignettes such as these suggest that many potentially self-destructive prisoners are not afforded enough protection from would-be victimizers in the prison population so that they can live tolerable lives until their sentences have been completed.

NOTES

1. Eric Berne, *Games People Play* (New York: Grove, 1964).
2. Robert E. Heise, *Prison Games* (Fort Worth: Privately published, 1976).
3. Ibid., p. 17.
4. Ibid., p. 23.
5. Leo Carroll, *Hacks, Blacks, and Cons* (Lexington, MA: D.C. Heath, 1974), p. 80.
6. Howard W. Polsky, *Cottage Six* (New York: Wiley, 1962).
7. Hans Toch, *Living in Prison: The Ecology of Survival* (New York: Free Press, 1977), p. 148.
8. Ibid., p. 149.
9. Ibid., pp. 148–149.
10. W. E. Mann, Socialization in a medium security reformatory, *Canadian Review of Sociology and Anthropology* 1 (1964):146.
11. Kenneth Dimick, *Ladies in Waiting Behind Prison Walls* (Muncie, IN: Accelerated Development Inc., 1979), p. 72.
12. David A. Ward and G. Kassebaum, *Women's Prison: Sex and Social Structure* (Chicago: Aldine, 1965).
13. Rose Giallombardo, *Society of Women: A Study of a Women's Prison* (New York: Wiley, 1966).
14. Rose Giallombardo, *The Social Work of Imprisoned Girls* (New York: Wiley, 1974).
15. Barry C. Feld, *Neutralizing Inmate Violence* (Cambridge, MA: Ballinger, 1977), p. 162.
16. Ibid., p. 163.

17. Esther Heffernan, *Making It in Prison: The Square, the Cool, and the Life* (New York: Wiley, 1972), p. 148.
18. See, for example, Elmer Johnson, *Correlates of Felon Self-Mutilations* (Carbondale, IL: Center for the Study of Crime, Delinquency and Corrections, Southern Illinois University: 1969).
19. Raymond A. Helgemoe, "A preliminary Inquiry into the Prediction of Self-Injury Among Prison Inmates Based on Stressful Incidents," paper presented at the annual meeting of the Academy of Criminal Justice Sciences, 1979.
20. J. J. Gibbs, "Stress and Self-Injury in Jail," Ph.D. dissertation, State University of New York at Albany, 1978.
21. Hans Toch, *Men in Crisis* (Chicago: Aldine, 1975), p. 67.
22. Ibid., p. 69.
23. Robert Johnson, *Culture and Crisis in Confinement* (Lexington, MA: D.C. Heath, 1976), p. 107.
24. Ibid., p. 128.

Economic Victimization Among Prisoners

 Unlike psychological victimization, economic victimization among prisoners has been recognized since the earliest days of the existence of penal institutions. As a result, the literature is saturated with information on the subject. Even the early sociological classics on prison life, such as those by Clemmer and Sykes, include a modest discussion of economic victimization. As with other aspects of the study of prison life, these comments are invariably descriptive rather than theoretical in nature. Perhaps the closest approach to the general theoretical statement about prison economic victimization is the comment by Srivastava that economic victimization can be expected to be higher in an impoverished prison community than in a less-deprived population,[1] which suggests the more general statement that the level of economic victimization in a prison is inversely proportional to the level of availability of material goods in that institution. If this is true, then we should expect to find higher levels of economic victimization in austere prison environments than in some of the relatively "plush" minimum security institutions that have been constructed recently. It also implies that as the material level of prisoners has increased over the last several decades, economic victimization should have decreased. Although we lack adequately standardized statistics on economic victimization, the many descriptive

accounts that are available lead us to believe that Srivastava's idea will hold for American prisons only if we measure economic victimization as a proportion of economic goods available rather than in an absolute sense. That is to say, because modern prisons have so much more available to steal than traditional prisons, the total amount of goods stolen and otherwise extorted from prisoners is almost certainly higher than it was under traditional conditions. What has probably decreased is the proportion of the economic items owned by prisoners that is illegitimately taken from them even though the absolute value of the stolen material is greater than it was in the days when prisoners were permitted to have very few economic items in their possession. This is analogous to the comparison of victimization rates between blacks and whites in American society. Whites are more likely to suffer economic victimization than blacks in an absolute sense, but if we control for the greater wealth of whites, we will see that a different pattern emerges. Blacks, with less wealth than whites, on the average appear to actually lose a greater proportion of their material posessions than whites do.

EARLY CLASSICS ON ECONOMIC VICTIMIZATION

Clemmer's classic description of prison life, *The Prison Community,* contains several examples of economic victimization during the mid-1930s. One of these illustrates robbery and the other burglary.

> In the quarry one day while the inmates were at work one man approached another with a drawn knife. The "chiv" had been fashioned from some scrap steel, sharpened to a fine point by rubbing it on the stone floor of the cells, and inserted in a piece of wood. He approached a man who carried money and, at the point of the knife, forced him behind a large rock and robbed him. The man who was robbed could not tell officials because he was not supposed to have the several dollars which were taken from his person. He did tell other inmates, but no effort was made to retrieve the money as the thief was dangerous and armed with "chiv."[2]
>
> • • •
>
> There is much thievery and a thief in prison respects nobody. I have seen them take the last sack of tobacco a man had, take pens and valuables from guards, and even as little as a box of matches. It just

seemed they wish to acquire articles, sometimes having no use for the same.

Where there was a "task" (prescribed amount of work) to be done, I have seen some slow, mischief-making prisoners idle away the hours and then steal articles from others to make up the sum allotted to them.[3]

In his study of Trenton State Prison in New Jersey in the 1950s, Sykes provides a description of victimizing prisoner roles. Along with the physical victimizers, such as the "gorilla" and "wolf," he identified the "hipster" and the "merchant." The hipster used psychological manipulations to gain his ends, while the merchant or "peddler," as he was sometimes called, used a combination of psychological and economic strategies to increase his material wealth at the expense of other prisoners. Hipsters talked like "real men," but were not actually very good at fighting—always careful to choose relatively weak victims. Sykes comments that it is men such as these "who convert the prison into what one inmate has described as a gigantic playground—a place where blustering and brawling push life in the direction of a state of anomie."[4]

Sykes found that there was a great deal of fraud and chicanery in the economic relations among prisoners. This included failure to carry out a bargain in the exchange of goods or services, cheating on gambling debts, and more elaborate frauds such as those that are perpetrated by prisoners who are able to convince the men around them that they have special information about prison affairs that they have gained through associations with staff members. If a prisoner can establish this kind of definition of the situation, then he is in a position to demand various special favors in return for passing along this information. If the aggressor is nimble of wit, the victims may never realize that they have been subjected to a very sophisticated manipulation.

The merchant or peddler role contradicts the convict code as practiced in the Trenton State Prison in that goods that should be freely exchanged between prisoners on the basis of need were instead being sold at a profit by the incumbents of these roles. Although this was defined as illegitimate in the prisoner subculture, it was not necessarily victimizing in universal terms. Selling goods for even a rather outrageous profit is considered appropriate activity in a capitalist society. Victimization entered into the dealings of the merchants and peddlers only when they charged exorbitant prices, in situations where competitors had been eliminated, or where there was unfair price-fixing.

The analysis by Sykes represents an important advance over the earlier work of Clemmer in that economic victimization is no longer seen as an isolated individual act. Instead, it is reconceptualized in terms of social roles. This means that economic victimization in prison is socially patterned. One implication of this is that the prisoner social system is willing to tolerate a certain amount of economic victimization without applying informal sanctions against the offenders. Otherwise, it would be difficult for offenders to operate over a long enough period of time for patterned social roles and their attendant norms, beliefs, and values to develop and become part of the informal social structure of prison life.

The degree of role definition appears to vary from prison to prison. Economic victimization in an Indian prison studied by Srivastava was extensive, and the prisoner leaders were the heaviest victimizers of all.[5] However, no social roles were elaborated around economically victimizing activities as they were in the Trenton State Prison. In contrast, information gathered at Pentonville in England by Morris and Morris included the specific role of the "baron." Individuals playing this role normally involved themselves in economic activities of a speculative, risk-taking nature—such as marketing tobacco and bookmaking. Prisoners were manipulated into situations where they owed debts to the barons. They were then kept perpetually in debt by excessive interest rates. If payments on debts were not made on time, the barons arranged to have beatings administered to the debtors. These beatings were generally administered by henchmen rather than by the barons. In most cases, the mere threat of beatings produced the desired results. Once a debt became as large as three or four ounces of tobacco, the victim was almost never able to pay it off completely.[6]

A TYPOLOGY OF PRISON ECONOMIC VICTIMIZATION

The combination of a decade of observation behind prison walls and a careful scrutiny of the literature suggests that there are eight different kinds of prison economic victimization. Some prisoners specialize in one or two of these types while others participate in most of them from time to time. Although the types are analytically distinct, they are often combined into complex systems of economic manipulation when they are implemented by sophisticated prisoners.

Loansharking

The prison is always a tight money market whether the money is scrip, United States currency or tobacco. Those who wish to borrow money so that they can buy drugs, gamble or achieve some other kind of goal are willing to pay very high interest rates to secure a loan. In loansharking, the aggressor takes advantage of the eagerness of the victim and charges interest rates that are usurious by any reasonable standard and which would be, in any case, illegal anywhere in the free society. The high interest rates are made doubly devious if a "fish" is the borrower and the loan shark does not even tell him what the interest rate is at the time that the loan is made. A variation on this is that the victim is told the initial rate of interest when he accepts the loan, but he is not informed of the fact that the interest escalates when debt payments are not made on time. Consider the following example.

"You got my stuff?" Chilly asked, automatically falling into the tone and vocabulary he used for these exchanges.

"Well, no, as a matter of fact I haven't. That's what I wanted to see you about."

"All right, when do I get my stuff?"

Juleson shrugged, meeting Chilly's level gaze with difficulty. "To be honest with you, I don't know."

"You be honest. That's a keen virtue. But I can't smoke it, and I can't pay the people I owe with it. How much you figure you'll owe me next month?"

"Why fifteen packs, a box at three-for-two. That's right, isn't it?"

"No, that isn't right," Chilly repeated with satirical patience. "You had one month to get up fifteen packs. Now it's twenty-two packs. Another month and it's three cartons. Are you following me?"[7]

Gambling Frauds

Gambling frauds occur when the gambling activity is manipulated so that the aggressor has an unfair advantage. The is particularly common where the victim is a "fish," not very bright or otherwise disadvantaged. Card games, dice, betting pools of all kinds and many other forms of gambling are used in this type of economic victimization. Rudoff describes how this was done in a California institution.

> Some enterprising inmates basked in luxury through the profits earned in the management of football or baseball pools. Others did not do too well as they bet on the outcome of a variety of sporting events. It was a group of losers who became the source for staff problems. Many inmates were exploited and manipulated by the more experienced gamblers and contracted debts far beyond their means to pay. Subsequent pressures and demands for payment led to assaults, requests for protection, and in general, a number of painful experiences. The best the staff was able to do about gambling was to control it and keep it at a minimum so that it did not get out of hand.[8]

The excerpt implies that the gambling frauds were linked to loansharking. This is very common, since loansharking can more than double the profits from a gambling swindle. A passage from a study of a Canadian institution paints a graphic picture of how this is done.

> They (new inmates) gamble among themselves before they gamble with anyone else in the joint. Then they think, "Well, I am good," so they go in and lose their shirts to someone else who is a little better, and that's it, you have to keep gambling to repay your debts . . . if they can't pay off, the debt goes up. Interest. You owe $5.00 and every day it goes up, say $1.00 and pretty soon they owe their life and they're hooked.[9]

Many prisoners gamble because they did so on the streets. Others do so to reduce the boredom and sensory deprivation of prison life. Whatever the reason, they are always in danger of being victimized by gambling fraud. It is only among close friends that gambling operations can be assumed to be honestly conducted.

Pricing Violations and Related Phenomena

When demand exceeds supply by a wide margin in an illegal market, sellers are free to charge all the trade will bear. It is difficult to say at what point this systematic overcharging becomes victimizing in nature, just as it is difficult to say when industrial overpricing in the free society has become excessive. Two related activities are clearly victimizing, and these are price fixing and market manipulation. Price fixing occurs when there is enough competition in the market to drive prices down to a reasonable level but this is counteracted by an agreement among competitors to standardize prices at an unnaturally high level. Market manipulation refers to victimization among sellers to reduce the degree of competition in the market. This can be accomplished in a direct but dangerous manner by threatening the life of a competitor. A more sophisticated way of accomplishing the same goal is to send a "snitch kite," exposing the illegal activities of a competitor to the administration. Here is an example of such a note that was sent in the United States Penitentiary at Atlanta, Georgia, on December 18, 1969.

> To alleviate the drug traffic over the holiday it would be wise to pay particular attention to Mc Pherson 27014, who is currently trafficking "Pills" and "Pool" tickets, which are being typed on his typewriter at the Industries Payroll office. He turns over those tickets to Freeman and Caplowe, likewise with the pills.[10]

Guenther points out that it is difficult for correctional officers and administrators to know when a snitch kite is accurate. Some economic victimizers attempt to remove their competition by revealing the truth about them while others prefer to make up stories that are untrue. A third ploy is to arrange to have a snitch kite submitted about oneself to achieve a goal that is unlikely to be obvious to the administration of the penitentiary. In one case, a prisoner arranged to have a "head-knocker" concealed under his bed and revealed to the administration through a snitch kite. His goal was to be locked up in segregation with his business partner, without whom he was not sure he could defend himself from prisoners who were angered because of their victimization in the racket that the two of them ran together. The prisoner was successful in being locked up with his partner, and then apparently returned to the general population when the full story was pieced together in the Adjustment Committee.[11]

Theft

Theft refers to the stealing of goods while the victim is not present. Items may be taken from a person's pants while he is in the shower, or from his locker in the industrial area. A great deal of stealing occurs in the cells due to the fact that officers are not careful to keep them locked whenever their occupant is not present. This kind of stealing runs contrary to the convict code and was once fairly rare in correctional institutions. It has been on the rise in the past several decades partially because of the decrease in the normative power of the convict code. Bartollas et al. comment that even in an institution for delinquents that experienced extremely high levels of exploitation, the convict code prohibited stealing personal goods from the rooms of the prisoners. Known thieves suffered decreased social status and even physical abuse as their punishment for breaking this tenet of the code.[12]

Robbery

Relatively weak prisoners may be content to steal behind the backs of their victims, but any aggressor who wishes to see himself as a "true man" will prefer to confront his victims face-to-face. Instead of theft, the macho convict prefers robbery. Most robberies are petty in nature because there is nothing of any great value to take from anyone in the prisoner subculture. The low absolute value of these goods is misleading, however, because of the great subjective value that these goods develop in prison settings. A man who has waited for a week to be able to buy a few candy bars at the prison canteen may feel just as victimized when he is strong-armed into giving them up on the way back to his cell as someone on the streets who has just lost two hundred dollars in a mugging.

Aggressors can have the best of both worlds if they gang up on victims. The direct confrontation preserves the illusion of masculinity at the same time that odds of two, three or four to one make it impossible for the victim to successfully resist the attack. Mann describes what happens to young "fish" in the following excerpt.

> Immediately the typical 17-year-old arrives he is bait for the upper strata of the inmate group. Upon his first appearance in the exercise yard, a competition almost develops among them as to who will own and influence him. This is usually not too overt, although sometimes it is. He can, within a matter of hours, have taken from him his lighter, his ration of tobacco, or if it's in the wintertime, and he happens to have a fairly good smock, this may be changed for a more beaten-up sort of thing. . . . He then realizes he can't by

himself exist in a prison, because these "exchanges" are always made by two or three people at a time. He may be physically fairly powerfully built, but he has no chance against odds of three of four to one.[13]

Protection Rackets

Activities such as theft and robbery, carried out on a rather disorganized basis, do not provide a very steady source of material goods. They also have the disadvantage of being rather risky operations. The sensible alternative for a group of prisoners who have rational control of their behavior is to organize their economic victimization on a regular schedule and to minimize the possibilities for violence to themselves by achieving a degree of consensus with their victims. This is done through a form of extortion known as protection rackets. Protection rackets exchange a promise of freedom from harassment for regular payments of money, goods or services. It works the same way in prison that it does on the streets. The victim is approached by someone claiming to be the agent of a group that can protect him from vitimizations that are predicted to becoming his way. If the victim resists, a brutal incident is arranged to convince him that he is truly in danger. This is how one prisoner explains the process.

> The victim is warned that he is in danger of being hi-jacked by some unnamed mob; but that for so many sacks of weed a month his friend the gangster will save him from harm. Since the gangsters choose their victims with care, selecting only the more spineless and helpless of the cons, this threat usually suffices. If a man should refuse to pay, or if he squeals, he will likely be knifed or slugged quietly, which not only settles his case but has an excellent moral affect on the other suckers.[14]

Blackmail differs from a protection racket only in that the victim is buying protection from having his reputation damaged instead of protection from having his body damaged. The disadvantage in blackmail is that it is harder to find subjects to blackmail weak prisoners about than it is to extort money from them using threats of violence because they have so few things to hide from anyone. People who are already at the bottom of the status structure have little reputation to lose. However, those who could be most easily blackmailed are near the top of the status structure and have considerable ability to defend themselves. Attempting to blackmail such individuals might result in the unfortunate maiming of the blackmailer.

Deliberate Misrepresentation of Products

The deliberate misrepresentation of products is a direct outgrowth of the accepted marketing practices. We are all accustomed to discounting many of the exorbitant claims that are made about products in television commercials. The pressures and instabilities of prison life make it difficult for many prisoners to exercise a similar judgment about the products that they are offered. When a new drug comes on the prison market, sophisticated prisoners will wait until they have seen the results of the drug before they buy some to use themselves. The younger, more impulsive men are more likely to make immediate purchases and then take their chances with the quality of the product. Sometimes they get rat poison instead of LSD. On other occasions they buy marijuana that has been mixed with tobacco or they rent a highly touted pornographic pamphlet that turns out to be not terribly exciting. The sales pitch on these items is called a "hype," and one might argue that the excitement of the hype is part of what prisoners are paying for, so that even though they are victimized in a strict sense, they sometimes get their money's worth anyhow in a rather backhanded fashion.

Nondelivery of Products

It is only a short step from the misrepresentation of delivered products to failing to deliver them at all. In this form of economic victimization, a prisoner is "burned" by paying money for products that he never receives. It would be bad form for the aggressor in a "burning" to just laugh at the victim and tell him that he had been a fool to give his money for nothing. A much better technique is to sympathize with the victim and claim that some third party force beyond anyone's control has resulted in the nondelivery of the purchased products. The aggressor may claim to have been hijacked by "gorillas" or that the "horse" (a correctional officer who smuggles contraband into a prison for a fee) was unable to make the proper connection on the streets so the money was lost. Since gorillas and horses also victimize prisoners with whom they are economically involved from time to time, it is very difficult for the ultimate victim—the consumer —to ascertain exactly who is ultimately responsible for the burning. The prisoner who is con-wise estimates the odds of being burned at the time that he makes the purchase and refuses to pay for products offered by those whose reputation suggests a high probability of nondelivery or product misrepretentation.

Drug dealers in the eastern penitentiary studied by Carroll protected themselves from inmate predators by forming alliances with small groups of other prisoners. These groups consisted of one "stash" and two or three "runners." Drugs brought in from outside the prison would be given to the stash, who hid them from the general population. Being a nonuser, the stash would not generally be suspected of hiding drugs. The runners would give the "hype" to the perspective customers and then collect their money and give it to the dealer. Once the money was carefully salted away, the dealer would obtain the drugs from the stash and then distribute them to the runners, who would then deliver the drugs to the customers. The runners never know who the stash is in this kind of an operation and therefore cannot join up with him to eliminate the dealer from the racket. Unfortunately, there is no way for the dealer to cover all bases, and he too may be burned if the stash takes the drugs and goes into business for himself or if the runners steal all or part of the drugs and claim that they themselves were victims of theft.[15]

When dealers, consumers or other actors in the economic marketplace are cheated, violence is often the result. Three recent killings in the Atlanta Federal Penitentiary (revealed in testimony before the Senate Permanent Subcommittee on Investigations) are examples of this form of retaliation. In the first incident, a prisoner who bought narcotics that turned out to be basically sugar paid $500 to a third prisoner to have the offender who had misrepresented his product disemboweled. Another prisoner who had stolen narcotics was immolated in his cell as retribution by his victim. The third aggressor turned victim sold "bad" narcotics and was chopped to death by his hatchet-wielding victim.[16] The violence in these incidents was particularly gruesome as a deterrent to future economic crime.

THE TAKEOVER OF ECONOMIC DISTRIBUTION SYSTEMS BY PRISONER GANGS

Williams and Fish claim that the most powerful economic figures in prisons are really "right guys" rather than "merchants." Although the convict code specifies that right guys should share goods rather than sell them, a right guy can successfully profiteer if he puts together a gang to carry out what amounts to an organized crime operation. The lieutenants in the gang buffer him from the ultimate victims of the economic manipulations. Because he is so well insulated, the prisoners, paying weekly for protection services or making their loan payments to avoid being assaulted, will know the name of only the lowest-level gang member who collects their payments. These social organizations are far more elaborate than the simple drug distribution rings that I have described above. The only difference between them and Mafia organizations in the free society is that they lack the position of counselor, an elderly legal advisor who is probably omitted from these prison gangs because such people are almost never incarcerated.[17] The ultimate development of prisoner organizations, specializing in economic victimization, occurs when large prisonwide gangs force all independent economic victimizers out of business and either divide up the spoils among themselves or fight to the death to determine who will establish a monopoly over the entire correctional institution. These gangs may have their bases on the streets rather than behind the walls, and they may also have branches in more than one correctional institution. Jacobs describes what happened to the old style "merchants" when gangs began to take over economic activity at Stateville in Illinois.

> For the first time in history, the old cons who "knew how to do time" found their lives disrupted and in danger. Gang members moved in to take over the "rackets." One informant described an instance where half a dozen "gang bangers" simultaneously put knives to his throat. Rather than cut the gangs in, many of the dealers went out of business.[18]

Stateville has gone through two distinct stages of economic victimization. Until 1968, the traditional convict code was held in high regard and prisoners rarely stole material items from each other. When the gangs began to take over economic operations in 1969, they first wiped out any competition from isolated individuals and then greatly increased the level of economic victimization that was occurring in a prison. Propinquity was no longer one of the bases of social organization. Gang members thought it quite appropriate to steal from nongang members living in adjoining cells. Anyone who was not affiliated with a gang was fair game. The only exception to this was the Spanish origin group, which was left alone out of fear that they would engage in mass action against anyone who victimized a member of their ethnic group.[19]

Like organized crime groups in free society, prisonwide gangs prefer to suppress disorganizing violence in order to maximize their profits and to minimize any disruption in social affairs that might temporarily decrease their control over economic matters. The violence that remains tends to be instrumental in nature, that is to say, it is used in the service of gang goals and ordered by gang leaders. The high level of violence that occurrs when gangs are solidifying their control of a prison or when they are in conflict with each other contrasts sharply with the relatively modest level of ongoing violence when these jurisdictional matters have been settled to the satisfaction of gang leaders. Davidson did a participant observation study of Chicano prisoners at San Quentin in California during such a lull in prisoner violence and interpreted this as a positive contribution made by organized prison crime to the well-being of prisoners in general.[20] He managed to describe economic victimization in positive terms, and was apparently conned so well by the gang leaders that he never fully recognized the viciousness of the victimization that was being perpetrated on nongang members.

In addition to the eight types of economic victimization that I have discussed in this chapter, prison gangs may also manage prostitution rings. If the prices charged are not exorbitantly high, these rings are not necessarily victimizing for the customers. They become victimizing only for the prostitutes themselves and, even then, only when the prostitutes are forced into the trade or coerced to handle more clients than they prefer under threat of victimization by gang members should their generation of income fall off. One may wonder how it is possible for a prostitute to operate in a prison under the eyes of the correctional officers. Guenther reprints a "snitch kite" that answers this question. The note refers to what is probably an individual operation rather than a gang-controlled prostitute, but the mechanics are otherwise the same.

> Inmate Brinkley 32619, D Cellhouse, have sex with inmates from time the doors open at 6:20 a.m. until 7:00 a.m. or after. The officers that in charge of D Cellhouse just sat in the office.
>
> It is getting very dangerous for the inmates that live on this side of the cellhouse. All the inmates walk up and down the gallery

waiting they time to have sex with Brinkley 32619 and before you know it someone will get kill. The inmate that jump on Brinkley live in C Cellhouse coming over to Brinkley cell at 6:20 a.m. to.

Will you please put a stop to this Hoe [whore] House once and for all. This Hoe House is going to get some one kill over it Sir.[21]

Under ideal conditions, the amount of homosexual prostitution that occurs in prison could be greatly reduced. It is unlikely that it could be completely eliminated without greatly increased levels of staffing. There are too many blind spots in prison architecture and too few correctional officers and other staff members assigned to each of the prison areas.

ECONOMIC VICTIMIZATION IN WOMEN'S PRISONS

Investigators of prison behavior in correctional institutions for women have been so busy looking at lesbianism and its correlates that they have been unable to find time to examine stealing and other forms of economic victimization in most of their studies. Heffernan found that stealing among prisoners or other economic violations of the inmate normative exchange system at Occoquan were negatively sanctioned in the prisoner subculture. Most of the women did not engage in this behavior, although nearly all of them were willing to steal from the prison administration. They were bitter in their comments about those fellow-prisoners who were without principles and those who had to be "out-slicked." Women who stole from other prisoners were subject to the widespread advertising of their misbehavior in the informal rumor network, as well as being excluded from further economic transactions and perhaps suffering direct verbal or physical aggression.[22]

Giallombardo's study at the Federal Reformatory for Women in Alderson is typical of studies in women's prisons in that she describes economic roles in some detail without giving the reader even a hint of the possibilities for victimization that are built into these roles.[23] At Frontera, Ward and Kassebaum found that the sharing tenet of the convict code was endorsed by only 56% of their inmate sample. The single code element receiving a lower level of endorsement was an item that divided the perceptual world into those "in the know and those who are suckers."[24] One might expect that economic victimization would be fairly high in an institution where the inmate endorsement of sharing among prisoners had deteriorated almost to the tipping point, but Ward and Kassebaum say nothing more about it. They do mention that there were very few "merchants" at Frontera, and offer the opinion that this was due both to the liberal prison rules that permitted a wide variety of material items to be legally possessed by the women and to the abundance of "snitches" who reported every illegal transaction to the administration.

Are we to believe that economic victimization is substantially lower in women's prisons than in men's prisons? The evidence is not strong, but it is consistent in suggesting a surprisingly low level of economic victimization in women's prisons. Since Ward and Kassebaum were extremely successful in obtaining data on homosexual behavior at Frontera, and since they clearly made an effort to obtain information on the economic system, it is reasonable to conclude that their failure to identify extensive economic victimization accurately reflects conditions in the prisoner social system. Field investigations of female prisoner subcultures generally report higher degrees of prisoner social organization than are found in men's prisons. We know that economic victimization was minimized in men's prisons in the days of the traditional convict code, so it makes sense to assume that the continuation of these traditional attitudes in women's prisons has been associated with low to moderate rates of economic victimization. Another factor contributing to this is the small size of women's prisons, which limits the possibilities for organized gang activities. The fact that very few female prisoners have been members of organized crime groups in their preprison lives means that they are unlikely to duplicate this form of social organization behind the walls. It is my impression, based on a number of field visits to women's institutions, that the level of social organization in jails is much lower than it is in prisons, and that there is consequently a higher degree of economic victimization experienced in these short-term facilities.

NOTES

1. S. P. Srivastava, The quality of basic necessities in prison, *The Indian Journal of Social Work* 33 (1973):337–346; *The Indian Prison Community* (Lucknow, India: Pustak Kendra, 1977).
2. Donald Clemmer, *The Prison Community* (New York: Holt, Rinehart and Winston, 1940), p. 159.
3. Ibid., p. 160.
4. Gresham M. Sykes, *The Society of Captives* (New York: Atheneum, 1966), p. 105.

5. Srivastava (1977).
6. Terence Morris and Pauline Morris, *Pentonville, A Sociological Study of an English Prison* (London: Routledge and Kegan Paul, 1963).
7. David Lamson, *We Who Are About to Die* (New York: Charles Scribner's Sons, 1936), p. 153, quoted in Vergil L. Williams and Mary Fish (Eds.), *Convicts, Codes, and Contraband: The Prison Life of Men and Women* (Cambridge, MA: Ballinger, 1974), p. 85.
8. A. Rudoff, "Prison Inmates: An Involuntary Association," Ph.D. dissertation, University of California—Berkley, 1964, pp. 184–185.
9. W. Mann, Socialization in a medium-security reformatory, *Canadian Review of Sociology and Anthropology* 1 (1964):153.
10. Anthony L. Guenther, Compensations in a total institution: The forms and functions of contraband, *Crime and Delinquency* 21 (1975):247.
11. Ibid., p. 248.
12. Clemens Bartollas, Stuart J. Miller and Simon Dinitz, *Juvenile Victimization: The Institutional Paradox* (New York: Wiley, 1976).
13. Mann (1964), p. 153.
14. Lamson (1936), pp. 227–228, quoted in Williams and Fish, (1974), p. 88.
15. Leo Carroll, *Hacks, Blacks, and Cons* (Lexington, MA: D.C. Heath, 1974).
16. Confessed killer gives Congress details on inmate murders at federal prison at Atlanta, *Corrections Digest* 4 (August 11, 1978):7–8.
17. Williams and Fish (1974).
18. James B. Jacobs, *Stateville: The Penitentiary in Mass Society* (Chicago: University of Chicago Press, 1977), p. 158.
19. Ibid., p. 159.
20. R. Theodore Davidson, *Chicano Prisoners: The Key to San Quentin*, (New York, Holt, Rinehart and Winston, 1974).
21. Guenther (1975), p. 247.
22. Esther Heffernan, *Making It in Prison: The Square, the Cool, and the Life* (New York: Wiley, 1972).
23. Rose Giallombardo, *Society of Women: A Study of Women's Prisons* (New York: Wiley, 1966).
24. David A. Ward and Gene G. Kassebaum, *Women's Prison: Sex and Social Structure* (Chicago: Aldine, 1965), p. 40.

Social Victimization
Among Prisoners

Social victimization refers to the victimization of a prisoner because he or she is a member of an identifiable social group. This group may be racial, ethnic, religious, ideological or offense related. The point is that in social victimization, it is not the actions of the individual prisoner that attract victimizers, but rather the prisoner's group membership. It is difficult to determine the social component of a given incident of prisoner victimization when only one case is at hand. The aggregation of individual incidents produces patterns that more clearly point to the presence of social victimization. We know very little about social victimization in the traditional maximum security prison except what is contained in literary reports such as biographies.

Historically, type of offense and race were the two most important dimensions along which social victimization proceeded. Certain offense patterns have always been good insurance against victimization, while others encourage it. Violent offenders are generally accorded higher status in the prisoner subculture than property offenders and suffer correspondingly lower rates of victimization. The prisoner who has raped an adult may be considered to be a respectable violent offender, but if his victim was around the age of puberty or below, he is disdained as a "baby raper." Child molesters are particularly vulnerable. King and Elliott report that when a child rapist was received at Albany prison in England, he was assaulted within minutes, probably by another prisoner who came in on the same "chain" (a shipment of new admittees in which all of them are handcuffed to the same chain for safe-keeping).[1] The offenders, along with certain other nonviolent sex offenders, snitches and "dings" (mentally ill prisoners), populate the bottom of the prisoner social system and are subject to repeated physical and verbal abuse by their fellow prisoners. It is ironic that most prisoners ignore their own deviance and have an extremely conservative opinion of baby rapers, arguing that these unfortunate misfits deserve additional punishment far beyond that assigned to them by the courts. It is common for some baby rapers to be victimized so extensively that they have to be confined in the prison's segregation unit for their own protection.[2]

Morris and Morris comment that there were only two types of offenders at Pentonville prison in England whose status in the prisoner subculture could be predicted before entrance into the institution. These were certain types of sex offenders and racial–ethnic minorities. The total minority population at Pentonville in about 1960 was small, amounting to no more than one in every 20 prisoners. Most of the minority prisoners were black, with Asians, Turks, Cypriots, Indians and Pakistanis in very limited numbers. Most of the blacks were incarcerated for offenses related to prostitution, which further depressed their status in the white-dominated prison social system. Prejudice was very high in Pentonville. The door of a storeroom in the Wood Shed was marked, "Smoking Lounge—No Black Bastard." This kind of prejudice was translated into physical victimization in a variety of forms, most of which did not involve actual fighting because the whites dominated the system so thoroughly that it was foolish for minority prisoners to fight back.[3]

Racial discrimination such as that described by Morris and Morris has not always been part of prison life. Sellin's brilliant treatment, *Slavery and the Penal System*, explains that through most of history, imprisonment and similar forms of punishment were reserved for slaves. One had to be a minority group member to be imprisoned. Down through the years, punishments that were once reserved only for slaves were generalized to majority group members from the lower classes, thus setting up racial and ethnic conflicts within prisoner populations.[4] We can see this process continuing today, in that middle- and upper-class majority group members are severely underrepresented in American prisons, much more so than one would expect from class-specific offense rates. Pentonville represents an intermediate step between the all-minority prison and the modern minority-dominated prison in which lower-class majority-group prisoners completely control the prisoner subculture and victimize minority-group members at will. It is this middle stage of the historical development of penal institutions that we refer to as the traditional American prison.

Until approximately 1962, blacks in the Stateville Penitentiary in Illinois were rigidly assigned to a low caste and forced to conduct themselves in a completely subservient manner. At that time, blacks began to be allowed to hold decent jobs in the prison's convict work force. Racial segregation continued for a few years longer, extending to living quarters, work crews and even movement through the halls.

> When moving through the prison in their lines, the whites always paired up together at the front of the lines and the blacks fell into place behind. Whites continued to hold the best jobs in the prison, particularly in the administration building, where the few black inmates were usually employed as janitors. While there were occasional mutterings of "white devil" and occasional instances of blacks breaking into the front of the lines, racial confrontation per se was avoided at least until 1969.[5]

In the California system, which was later to become the site of extremely high rates of prisoner violence, racial conflicts accounted for only 12% of the incidents of violence in 1963–1964.[6] Researchers working for the California Department of Corrections still saw prisoner violence in individualistic rather than collective terms.[7] Rudoff's study of the prisoner social system at Deuel Vocational Institution was the last major investigation to be carried out in a prison dominated by white prisoners. The first prison race riot[8] had already occurred in 1962, before Rudoff had completed the analysis of his data, and this heralded the beginning of the passing of the crown and scepter from whites to minority-group members in American prisons.

Whites, blacks and Chicanos generally tolerated each other at Deuel. As tension rose in the prison, one or more of the fairly large number of highly racist prisoners would perpetrate an act against another group and the conflict would rapidly escalate into a race riot. Many more prisoners participated in riots than were involved in the precipitation of the incidents. The riots were rarely spontaneous. Prisoners knew a riot would occur ahead of time, even knowing where it was planned to occur. Staff members also knew, thanks to the receipt of snitch kites. White prisoners "scheduled" a riot whenever they felt that the blacks were getting strong enough to challenge their authority. Prison holidays or incidents external to the prison, such as a black–white boxing match or reports of rioting in the Congo and American ghettos, were cited as the specific sources of the heightened tension among racial groups, but that was apparently more of an ideological smoke screen than an accurate description of the causal forces producing the riots.[9] What was happening meant that whites were beginning to lose their dominance of the prison subculture at Deuel and were doing everything they could to maintain it. Rudoff just happened to stumble onto the situation as the change-over began. More recent studies show a different pattern in which blacks (Chicanos in the case of some western prisons) have solidified their control, victimize lower-status whites at will, and rarely have their hegemony challenged by whites in an open race riot.

By 1980, the changeover in the racial control of prisoner sub-cultures, with its attendant consequences for prisoner victimiza-tion phenomena, has taken place in all prisons serving states with large urban populations. Site visits to prisons in rural states, such as Montana and Wyoming, confirm that these changes, which are universally reported in the literature, have not yet had impact on many rural prisons. The percentage of minority group citizens in rural states outside of the South is much too small to produce enough felons to carry out the takeover of prisoner subcultures. However, these institutions, along with some "white collar" institutions in the federal prison system, have not attracted the interest of criminologists or the attention of reporters, lawyers and other investigators who might study and publicize intergroup relations in those institutions. In a rural state, a small prison that contains only 700 prisoners and has never had a major race riot offers little encouragement for academic research or exposés in national magazines. For this reason, we can do little more than note the existence of these exceptions to the rule.

RACIALLY BASED VICTIMIZATION

Readers of earlier chapters will have already discerned the outline of intergroup relations in contemporary American prisons. Since Rudoff's study, investigations in North Carolina, California, Pennsylvania, Ohio, Rhode Island and Illinois have all found that whites are more likely to be victimized by blacks in correctional institutions than the reverse, and this is confirmed for other prison systems in many of the more literary accounts that have been published in recent years. The demographic racial balance has already shifted in almost all urban correctional systems. By 1974, 47% of all prisoners in state correctional facilities were black. Although whites were listed as 51% (with 2% being from other racial groups), this figure is misleading because ethnic minorities such as Chicanos were included in the 51%.[10] In many of the prisons that have less than a majority of blacks, the superior social organization of the blacks allows them to dominate a larger number of whites. The same thing can be said for Chicano–Anglo relations in California and a number of other prisons located in the southwest.

The immediate consequence of this is higher victimization rates for whites than for minority group members. Davis,[11] Bartollas et al.[12] Carroll,[13] and Lockwood[14] are among those who have reported that prison homosexual rapes are predominantly interracial in nature, with whites being the victims in almost every instance. Goldfarb extends this analysis to short-term prisoners in the nation's jails, saying that ". . . at least in isolated cases, gang rapes of inmates are conducted as a special manifestation of deep racial antagonisms that exist in society at large and which are exacerbated in jails."[15] A study in the North Carolina prison systems quantifies racial differences in victimization, showing that the black victimization rate was approximately 45% lower than the white victimization rate. Approximately four out of every ten incidents were interracial, of which 82% involved a black aggressor and a white victim.[16]

Showing that whites are more likely to be victimized than blacks is not the same as proving that this victimization pattern is due primarily to racial animosity. To show that requires that we first establish a high level of racial animosity in correctional institutions and that we then find a way to link that animosity to actual victimization incidents. Here are some comments made about blacks by white prisoners.

> We just stick in our own groups. Like we don't bother with the other kids, especially the colored kids, and they don't want to have much to do with us. So they let us go our way, and we let them go theirs.[17]

■ ■ ■

I was never prejudiced on the streets and there was this black family—only one black family where I come from—and I used to hang around with them. And when I got in Elmira, man, I started getting prejudiced. Now I don't talk to niggers.[18]

■ ■ ■

All the time, all I could think about was killing them niggers because of their attitude towards the white dudes. Everytime a nigger sees a white dude, they say, "I am going to make him my kid." That kind of stuff really makes me sick. I just want to kill them all.[19]

On the streets I never was a racist. I was never down on the blacks. But here I have been forced to be a racist. I was told the first rule was that, "You never talk with a black off the job." If you talk with a black, you would be isolated by the rest of the whites and then attacked.[20]

■ ■ ■

Most of the blacks at San Quentin are mentally defective, lazy and vicious. I know that you disagree with me, but all you have to do is open your eyes and you will see. All that they want to do is play a game on whitey, live off of our backs. When I first got here ten years ago there was a real Nazi party with a real political outlook. If the spooks started anything, the Nazi's went out and took care of things. They would stab a few spooks and get things under control so no real troubles would develop.[21]

It is clear that some of these negative white attitudes were the result of interracial conflict rather than the cause of it. We need evidence about how imprisoned blacks feel about whites, and this is more difficult to obtain. It is disturbing that the plethora of white quotes on interracial relations is matched by only a handful of quotes from black prisoners. Summaries of black attitudes often present them in an extremely negative light. For example, Bunker says that the psychological effects of institutionalized racism have left black prisoners with nothing but hate. "They have no desire—no motivation—for anything except revenge and license for whatever they desire."[22] When blacks speak for themselves, their racism is muted.

Every can I been in that's the way it is. . . . It's gettin' even I guess. . . . You guys been cuttin' our b___s off ever since we been in this country. Now we're just gettin' even.[23]

■ ■ ■

The black man's just waking up to what's been going on. Now that he's awake, he's gonna be mean. He's been raped—politically, economically, morally raped. He sees this now, but his mind's still small so he's getting back this way. But it's just a beginning.[24]

• • •

If there is a white sissy who hangs out with blacks, he gets it from the whites. The same goes for blacks. If they see a brother hanging around the whites they call him an Uncle Tom.[25]

Theorists writing about interracial victimization have not hesitated to link it to black racism. Because most of them are white males, their rapport with black victimizers may have been severely attentuated and racial identification may have added to the sympathy they felt for the white victims. Speaking of sexual assaults, Davis says, "They are expressions of anger and aggression prompted by the same basic frustrations that exist in the community, and which very probably were significant factors in producing the rapes, robberies, and other violent offenses for which the bulk of the aggressors were convicted."[26] Scacco's interviews with black aggressors led him to believe, "There are definite socioracial overtones in the act of sexual victimization."[27] Irwin, whose qualifications as an observer of prison affairs are unparalleled, has theorized that it is the deep-seated resentment that lower-class blacks have toward middle-class whites that leads to aggressive gang rapes.[28] Finally, Buffum suggests,

The motivation of the Negro prisoner to have homosexual contact is more directed by dominance needs and sexual access than by strong needs for affective investment. Indeed these needs may tend to involve the Negro in prison in the aggressor role in homosexual rape more often than the white prisoner.[29]

In Carroll's opinion, "The prison is merely an arena within which blacks may direct aggression developed through 300 years of oppression against individuals perceived to be representatives of the oppressors."[30] The black prisoners that he interviewed in an eastern penitentiary indicated that although a few blacks were "rippers" who engaged heavily in homosexual attacks, nearly all black prisoners had participated in these attacks from time to time. This is strong evidence in support of the relationship between racism and at least sexual forms of prisoner victimization. Alan, a white victim with whom we have become acquainted at several other points in this book, quotes a black aggressor as repeatedly calling him a "white punk," a "white bitch," and asking questions like, "How does it feel to have a black p___k in you, white boy?"[31] Quotes such as these establish a direct link between racism and sexual victimization in Alan's case, although this does not mean that all interracial victimization has similar motivational roots.

Several other theorists minimize the influence of racism in interracial victimization. In an early article, "Sex Deviation in a Prison Community," Huffman characterizes black homosexual participators as primitive, responding according to stimulus and response. He quotes an obviously white prisoner as saying, "The Negro homosexual (particularly the aggressive one) is a comparatively simple mechanism and moves in a straight line to satisfy his sexual desires."[32] It appears that Huffman would have us believe that the only reason black prisoners attack white prisoners is because they are more easily pressed into service than their black brothers. A more convincing argument is made by Lockwood, who concludes that

> Beyond the existence of the victim–aggressor race pattern itself, however, we encountered little empirical evidence to support this position. Neither aggressors nor their peers emphasized racial antagonism in interviews. This idea also fails to explain the significant number of blacks becoming targets and victims of aggressors. We should also consider that most rape victims of black aggressors in the street are black. If sexual aggression were primarily motivated by racial animosity, we would expect to find the same victim–aggressor ethnic pattern on the street as we find in prison.[33]

Putting all of these observations together, it seems reasonable to conclude that racism is a major cause of some of the interracial victimization that occurs in prison, but it is not the only cause. Some interracial victimizations are probably devoid of racist motivation whereas others occur only for racist reasons. We do not know the relative percentages of different motivational patterns in prison victimizations. However, it is safe to say that these proportions probably vary greatly from setting to setting, according to the characteristics of the institution, elements derived from the prisoners subculture within the institution, and the attitudes and experiences that white and black prisoners import into the institution with them.

RACE, GANGS AND VICTIMIZATION

The *Freeworld Times* printed the following item in its section of obituaries in 1973.

24-year old inmate sustained fatal stab wounds at the California State Prison on Aug. 30. Lynwood Bell reportedly died about 30 minutes after he was chased across the exercise yard at the institution and stabbed in the chest.

Authorities found a foot-long piece of sharpened steel at the scene.

Two inmates, both members of the "Mexican Mafia," are suspected in the attack. One alleged assailant was wounded in the leg by a tower guard. Warning shots had reportedly been fired but the assailant ignored them.

On Aug. 29 two inmates were wounded, one critically, when a tower guard shot between them in an attempt to break up their fight. A black inmate was stabbed in that incident.

A Corrections Department spokesman stated that the two incidents "Certainly fit the pattern of the gang attacks."[34]

Interracial (or interethnic) victimization takes on a new meaning when it occurs as part of the deliberate policies of large gangs that are organized along racial and ethnic dimensions. We have already seen in Chapter 5 how the gangs at Stateville in Illinois took the sub rosa economic system away from the individual white prisoners in the late 1960s. None of these gangs was white. Three of them were black and the other was Latino, all with extensive bases on the street in Chicago. Minority group members entering Stateville were strongly pressured to join one or more of these gangs—the Stones, Disciples, Vice Lords and Latin Kings. Newly admitted prisoners who had been associated with one of these gangs before conviction were welcomed with open arms and immediately made at home. White men were unable to defend themselves against ethnic groups operating with such a high degree of social organization. After a few years of gang domination, white prisoners began to duplicate their tactics by forming gangs, such as the Ku Klux Klan and the House of the Golden Dragon, but these white racist gangs had only a minor impact on the dominance of the nonwhite gangs.[35]

There is some degree of disagreement as to the extent of the contribution by prisoner gangs to victimization phenomena in the California prison system. State prison officials are quick to emphasize the role that the Mexican Mafia and Nuestra Familia have made to prison violence.[36] Vignettes taken from official records by Toch give us the flavor of this interracial violence.

Three months before, a "racial disturbance" had occurred between

Negro inmates and inmates of Mexican origin, in another institution. One member of the "Mexican" group (6), had been killed, and the suspicion fell on L, a member of the Negro clique. After this incident, several members of both factions were transferred to their current location. Then, in succession, (1) S, a close friend of L, is stabbed while passing through a group of "Mexicans"; inmate C is known to be responsible for this stabbing; (2) C is stabbed to death by unknown assailants.[37]

● ● ●

During a period of racial tension, a clique of white prisoners had issued an ultimatum to blacks, prohibiting them from entering the T.V. room. Black inmate T resolved to "lead his people" (against everyone's advice) by watching television. and C enter the T. V. room, and are immediately assaulted with some homemade blackjacks by a group of whites. Staff prevents the murder of the two men.[38]

Moore, while not disagreeing with the official characterization of violence perpetrated by the Mexican Mafia and Nuestra Familia, points out that these gangs are primarily composed of "state-raised" youths who are following styles of leadership that they were exposed to in their earlier years in state youth institutions that were even more violent than maximum security adult institutions such as San Quentin. Moore sees both groups as "strong-armed gangs that use extreme violence in pursuit of power and economic control."[39] At the same time, she is careful to separate the behavior of these gang members from constructive Chicano self-help groups that exist side by side with the violent gangs in the California prison system.

The conflict between the Mexican Mafia and Nuestra Familia became so severe that it was allegedly responsible for half of the 34 murders of prisoners in the California prison system during 1972.[40] In addition to this intergroup conflict, there was additional violence involving black and white prison gangs that emerged in the late 1960s and early 1970s. These were known as the Black Guerilla Family and the Aryan Brothers. The Black Guerilla Family was made up primarily of black militants and the Aryan Brothers was a white neo-Nazi group. In prisons that have experienced the development of powerful gangs, it is no longer adequate to conceptualize the prisoner subculture in individualist terms. Jacobs recommends that we view these modern prisons as arenas in which large power blocks of highly organized prisoners whose Jacobs recommends that we view these modern prisons as arenas in which large power blocks of highly organized prisoners whose organization is supplemented and sustained by racial, political and religious symbols compete for dominance on the group rather than the individual level.[41] Individual prisoners who are not affiliated with one of these supergangs cannot possibly withstand the pressure that these gangs may bring to bear and therefore become easy victims of all kinds of mistreatment and abuse.

RACISM AS AN ADMINISTRATIVE SOCIAL CONTROL DEVICE

"Divide and conquer" has always been good advice for prison administrators. If the prisoner population can be divided into factions that are then set upon each other, they are less likely to unite in their opposition to the policies of the prison administration. This is a delicate line to walk, for if the strategy is overused, it can result in intergroup violence of such severity that it tears the prison apart. California State Senator Mervyn Dymally investigated Soledad Prison and concluded that prison guards were able to "divert hostility from themselves by encouraging the racist tendencies of the white and Chicano inmates and playing them off against the blacks."[42] The letters of George Jackson offer additional evidence in support of this analysis of race relations at Soledad.[43] There is a considerable amount of evidence suggesting the similar use of prisoner racism as a social control device by prison staff members at San Quentin. Wright concludes that racist attitudes are positively encouraged by correctional officers who directly reward racist behavior. Furthermore, the white prisoner who is openly antiracist is branded as a radical by the prison administration and is "likely to be harassed by the guards as well as by the other white prisoners."[44] Pallas and Barber testify about the use of similar techniques at Attica in New York.[45]

A more benign version of this strategy is reported from a women's prison in the midwest by Spencer, who carried out an extensive participant observation study in this institution over a period of two years. The usual spontaneous racial conflicts that occurred between black and white women in this institution were supplemented by discriminatory practices in work assignments, living quarters and pay incentives for the prisoners, which subtly perpetuated the myth of white superiority. In addition, the administration deliberately heightened racial consciousness among the prisoners as a way of keeping them from developing a unified front. Nonracial incidents or events were often redefined by staff members as having racial overtones so as to contribute to the level of racial tension in the institution. White staff members who became too friendly with black prisoners were ostracized and harassed by their fellow staff members. If the racial tension became so high that the administration felt there was a danger of a mass riot that would naturally reflect negatively upon the prison, they would give favors to several of the blacks to "prove" that they were willing to give equal treatment to all prisoners, which would siphon off the excess tension that might have led to a black rebellion.[46]

It would be unfair to suggest that all prison administrators play the game of encouraging racial conflict to undermine prisoner unity, even though my observations from site visits and participant observation in a western maximum security institution are consistent with this conclusion. It is enough to conclude that a sizeable number of administrators and correctional staff members sometimes behave in such a way as to encourage wittingly or unwittingly racial conflict. This in itself demonstrates the complexity of prison victimization, for it exposes a situation in which what appears to be the victimization of whites by blacks or perhaps the reverse is at least partially due to manipulation by staff members and unwritten policies followed by prison administrators. Once we have assimilated this insight, we realize how foolish it would be to attempt to solve prison problems of race relations by intergroup awareness sessions and similar social-psychological techniques that ignore the impact of structural factors on conflicts between racial and ethnic groups, both individually and collectively.

NOTES

1. Roy D. King and Kenneth W. Eliott, *Albany: Birth of a Prison—End of an Era* (London: Routledge and Kegan Paul, 1977).
2. Lee H. Bowker, Victimization in correctional institutions: An interdisciplinary analysis, in John A. Conley (Ed.), *Theory and Research in Criminal Justice: Current Perspectives* (Cincinnati: Anderson, 1979), pp. 109–124.
3. Terence Morris and Pauline Morris, *Pentonville: A Sociological Study of an English Prison* (London: Routledge and Kegan Paul, 1963).
4. Thorsten Sellin, *Slavery and the Penal System* (New York: Elsevier, 1976).
5. James B. Jacobs, *Stateville: The Penitentiary in Mass Society* (Chicago: University of Chicago Press, 1977), p. 69.
6. Lawrence A. Bennett, The study of violence in California prisons: A review with policy implications, in Albert K. Cohen, George F. Cole and Robert G. Bailey (Eds.), *Prison Violence* (Lexington, MA: D. C. Heath, 1976), pp. 149–168.
7. Dorothy R. Jaman, Patricia Coburn, Jackie Goodard and Paul F. C. Mueller,

"Characteristics of Violent Prisoners (San Quentin-1960)," Research Report Number 22, California Department of Corrections, Sacramento, 1966; Dorothy R. Jaman, "Behavior During the First Year in Prison, Report III—Background Characteristics as Predictors of Behavior and Misbehavior," Research Report Number 43, California Department of Corrections, Sacramento, 1972.

8. Vernon Fox, Analysis of prison disciplinary problems, *Journal of Criminal Law, Criminology and Police Science* 49 (1972): 321–326.

9. Alvin Rudoff, "Prison Inmates: An Involuntary Association," Ph.D. dissertation, University of California at Berkeley, 1964.

10. James J. Stephen, *Survey of Inmates of State Correctional Facilities, 1974,* Advance Report (Washington, DC: National Criminal Justice Information and Statistics Service, 1976).

11. Alan J. Davis, Sexual assaults in the Philadelphia prison system and sheriff's vans, *Transaction* 6 (December 1968): 8–16.

12. Clemens Bartollas, Stuart J. Miller and Simon Dinitz, *Juvenile Victimization: The Institutional Paradox* (New York: Wiley, 1976).

13. Leo Carroll, *Hacks, Blacks, and Cons* (Lexington, MA: D.C. Heath, 1974).

14. Daniel Lockwood, *Prison Sexual Violence* (New York: Elsevier, 1980).

15. Ronald Goldfarb, *Jails: The Ultimate Ghetto of the Criminal Justice System* (Garden City, NY: Doubleday, 1976), p. 96.

16. Dan A. Fuller, Thomas Orsagh and David Raber, "Violence and Victimization Within the North Carolina Prison System," paper presented at the annual meeting of the Academy of Criminal Justice Sciences, 1977.

17. Barry C. Feld, *Neutralizing Inmate Violence* (Cambridge, MA: Ballinger, 1977), p. 183.

18. Lockwood (1980), p. 79.

19. Ibid., p. 79.

20. Erik Olin Wright, *The Politics of Punishment: A Critical Analysis of Prisons in America* (New York: Harper and Row, 1973), p. 120.

21. Ibid., p. 120.

22. Edward Bunker, War behind walls, in Burton M. Atkins and Henry R. Glick (Eds.), *Prisons, Protests, and Politics* (Englewood Cliffs, NJ: Prentice-Hall, 1972), p. 66.

23. Carroll (1974), p. 184.

24. Ibid., p. 185.

25. Wright (1973), p. 120.

26. Davis (1968), p. 16.

27. Anthony M. Scacco, Jr., *Rape in Prison* (Springfield, IL: C. C. Thomas, 1975), p. 48.

28. John Irwin, "Some Research Questions on Homosexuality in Jails and Prisons," working paper presented to the Conference on Prison Homosexuality, cited in Peter C. Buffum, *Homosexuality in Prisons* (Washington, DC: U.S. Government Printing Office, 1972), p. 23.

29. Buffum (1972), p. 22.

30. Carroll (1974), p. 184.

31. Ibid., p. 183.

32. Arthur V. Huffman, Sex deviation in a prision community, *Journal of Social Therapy* 6 (1960):174.

33. Lockwood (1980), p. 106.

34. *The Freeworld Times* 2(7) (August–September 1973):13.

35. Jacobs (1977).

36. See for example James W. L. Park, The organization of prison violence, In Bailey (1976), pp. 89–96.
37. Hans Toch, *Police, Prisons and the Problem of Violence* (Washington, DC: U.S. Government Printing Office, 1977), p. 59.
38. Ibid., p. 60.
39. Joan W. Moore, *Home Boys: Gangs, Drugs, and Prison in the Barrios of Los Angeles* (Philadelphia: Temple University Press, 1978), p. 114.
40. *The Freeworld Times* 2(2) (February 1973):5.
41. Jacobs (1977), p. 6.
42. Quoted in Jessica Mitford, *Kind and Usual Punishment* (New York: Random House, 1971), p. 254.
43. George Jackson, *Soledad Brother: The Prison Letters of George Jackson* (New York: Bantam Books, 1970).
44. Wright (1973), p. 123.
45. J. Pallas and B. Barber, From riot to revolution, in R. Quinney (Ed.), *Criminal Justice in America* (Boston: Little Brown, 1973), cited in Robert Johnson and Dennis D. Dorin, Dysfunctional ideology: The black revolutionary in prison, in Denis Szabo and Susan Katzenelson (Eds.), *Offenders and Corrections* (New York: Praeger, 1978), pp. 31–52.
46. Elouise J. Spencer, "The Social System of a Medium Security Women's Prison," Ph.D. dissertation, University of Kansas, 1977.

The Victimization
of Prisoners by Staff Members

 The documentation on staff–prisoner victimization in America's prisons is extensive but shallow. Most of this material describes victimization in prisons for men, with a smaller amount of documentation for institutions containing delinquent boys and very little information on staff–prisoner victimization in institutions for females. The treatment of the subject is superficial in that incidents tend to be mentioned only in passing (or as part of a polemical piece of writing), and they are not presented or analyzed in any great detail. Like other prison victimization reports, they tend to be recorded factually and not related to any general theoretical framework. Another general problem with documentation on staff–prisoner victimization is that the quality of the reporting of incidents is often difficult to determine. Reports are almost always limited to the views of one of the participants or observers, with no corroboration from others. Even when reports are written by social scientists, they usually consist of second- and third-person accounts derived from interviews rather than direct observation by the scientists.

Material on the victimization of prisoners by staff members is also beset by definitional problems. How does one separate the victimization of prisoners by individual staff members from the "fair" application of institutional policies by correctional officers?

This problem is particularly severe when dealing with historical material for which institutional standards of appropriate treatment are not available. Victimization is generally thought of as consisting of acts committed by individuals and groups that go beyond the conditions imposed upon prisoners by official institutional policies and state laws. In the modern prison, this definitional problem is not such a serious one because the official policies of the state and federal correctional systems are generally quite humane. Excessively victimizing behavior by staff members is usually clearly against the regulations of the institution. This is not the same as saying that offenders against these institutional regulations will be punished. In many correctional systems, it is probable that a careful staff member can engage in extensive victimizing behavior toward prisoners before he or she will be officially reprimanded for it. Even then, it is extremely unlikely that a staff member will ever be terminated for such behavior.

Definitional problems still exist in those jurisdictions that continue to use physically harsh means of punishing prisoners, and also in any correctional institutions where "goon squads" are used. The goon squads are groups of physically powerful correctional officers who "enjoy a good fight" and who are called upon to rush to any area of the prison where it is felt that muscle power will restore the status quo. If a prisoner is ripping up things in his cell and refuses to be quiet, the goon squad may be called and three or four of these correctional officers will forcibly quiet him, administering a number of damaging blows to the head and body. If there is a fight between two prisoners, the goon squad may break it up. Should a prisoner refuse to report to the hospital when he is ordered to do so, he may be dragged from his cell and deposited in the hospital waiting room. Mentally ill prisoners who are acting out are almost always initially dealt with by goon squads rather than by qualified therapeutic personnel or even by orderlies under the direction of such personnel. It is difficult to draw the line between the necessary application of force where human life or the social order are extensively threatened, and the misuse of violence by goon squad members.

Aside from goon squads and the few states that officially permit physically harsh means of punishment, we can define the behavior of a correctional officer as victimizing or nonvictimizing by comparing questionable incidents with the body of official regulations and policies that is usually summarized in a handook distributed to all correctional officers. If the behavior goes beyond the regulations and policies, then it is victimizing. If it does not, then it is difficult to accuse the officer of being an aggressor in all but the most extreme cases.

However clear we may be able to make the definition of victimization by line staff members, there is no way to create a similarly precise definition for wardens and other top-level correctional administrators. When they implement a policy or regulation that is victimizing or potentially victimizing, they must take responsibility for having created a definition of the situation within which correctional officers may carry out what amounts to victimizing behavior as they perform their duties in conformance with institutional regulations. Few of these regulations are proclaimed by correctional administrators simply out of sadism. Instead, these administrators balance one evil against another, and decide to implement a potentially victimizing regulation because they feel that this regulation will solve more problems than it creates. This means that, except for cases at the periphery of reasonable judgment, we cannot easily judge an administrative action to be victimizing unless we know the rationale behind that action and have some objective set of data about conditions in the institution that informed the administrative decision. Since this kind of information is almost never available, we are left with a murky situation in which administrative responsibility for prisoner victimization can usually be assigned in only the most tentative fashion. With these qualifications in mind, we will proceed to examine the documentation on staff–prisoner victimization in correctional institutions.

PHYSICAL VICTIMIZATION

However unpleasant prisons may be today, historical materials make it clear that they were infinitely worse in the past. Clemmer tells us that it was once common for correctional officers to assault prisoners with clubs and their fists, but by the late 1930s, perhaps in response to a new state law, the frequency of these attacks had declined to the point at which they occurred "only rarely."[1] Conley shows how the emphasis on custody and industrial productivity encouraged brutality and corruption in the Oklahoma prison system from the early 1900s through the 1960s. In addition to the usual beatings, officers used deliberate tortures such as forcing the men to eat in the hot sun during the summer when shade was nearby and handcuffing prisoners to the bars in their cells (with knotted rags in their mouths) so that when their legs collapsed, their body was suspended only by the handcuffs. When wardens ordered that physical victimization of prisoners by correctional officers be suspended, these officers adapted by moving to techniques of psychological victimization.[2]

The decrease in brutality by correctional officers that Clemmer describes as having occurred in Illinois in the 1930s did not reach some southern prisons until the 1970s. The mistreatment of prisoners in the Arkansas prison system has been documented in books such as *Killing Time, Life in the Arkansas Penitentiary*[3] and *Inside Prison U.S.A.*[4] The latter includes a description of the infamous "Tucker telephone," as well as blow-by-blow accounts of beatings. In the Tucker telephone, a naked prisoner was strapped to a table and electrodes were attached to his big toe and his penis. Electrical charges were then sent through his body which, in "long distance calls," were timed to cease just before the prisoner became unconscious. Murton and Hyams state that in some cases, "the sustained current not only caused the inmate to lose consciousness but resulted in irreparable damage to his testicles. Some men were literally driven out of their minds."[5] In testimony under oath, a 15-year-old prisoner accused the superintendent of an Arkansas institution of kicking and hitting him in the back and stomach while another staff member held him on the ground. The superintendent did not confirm this allegation, but he admitted driving a truck at 40 miles per hour with three prisoners draped over the hood and then jamming on the brakes to catapult them to the ground as a unique method of punishment.[6]

Reports from Louisiana,[7] Mississippi,[8] Virginia[9] and Florida[10] confirm that the habitual mistreatment of prisoners is not limited to the Arkansas prison system. The brutalization of prisoners by correctional officers outside of the south seems to be less extensive and also less sadistically innovative. Some of the incidents reported from northern prisons make little sense, such as the prisoner who was killed by the use of chemical gassing weapons when he was locked in a solitary security cell[11] or the three prisoners who were handcuffed to overhead pipes as punishment for being too "noisy" during sleeping hours.[12] Most of the incidents reported from these facilities seem to be associated with unusual occurrences such as prison riots, protests and punitive transfers. These incidents all involve some sort of prisoner challenge to the authority of prison staff members, and the challenge is sometimes met with violence as a way of reestablishing administrative authority. For example, prisoners being transferred from one Ohio penitentiary to another after a period of considerable unrest alleged severe guard brutality. One prisoner asserted that he was handcuffed and chained, taken into a bus, and then beaten on the head by a correctional officer with a blackjack and left unconscious. Another prisoner alleged that while handcuffed, he was dragged into the bus where he suffered kicks and other blows about the back, legs, hips and groin. The worst incident described by the prisoners told the story of a prisoner who first had Mace sprayed in his face while he was still in his cell, and then was beaten with chains, blackjacks and fists by five correctional officers who then spit on him, slammed his head against the cell door, and took him to the bus, where he was subjected to further assault.[13]

When 500 prisoners at the Pendleton Reformatory in Indiana refused to return to their cells on a winter day in 1972, the correctional officers used tear gas and shotguns to force them back. None of the prisoners was shot because the shotguns were discharged into the air rather than at the prisoners. This change in policy was probably due to an earlier incident at the Reformatory in which "46 men [prisoners] were wounded, many critically, from shots in the head, in the back, through the chest, in the legs, feet, thigh, through the groin, in the side—in fact some who tried to throw up their hands in the traditional gesture of surrender had their hands shattered and are minus fingers."[14] In a related incident, a group of black prisoners refused to return to their cells, and one black prisoner raised his hand in the black power salute. A guard was heard to say, "That one is mine!" and the young man was fatally riddled with five bullets. Testimony before the United States Senate later revealed that approximately 50% of the correctional officers involved in the incident belonged to the Ku Klux Klan.[15]

Excessive violence used during a prisoner altercation may not be legitimate, but it is understandable. There are few parents who have not gone too far in punishing their children when they were angry. A more serious problem occurs when prisoners are brutalized for an extended period of time after a riot as punishment for having participated. A classic example of this occurred after the disaster at Attica in New York. Correctional administrators, in violation of a court order, refused to admit a group of doctors and lawyers to the prison as observers on the pretext that they needed to have an opportunity to assess the prison's condition. During the time that the observers were deliberately excluded, extreme violence occurred, involving the vanquished prisoners. The Second Court of Appeals finally issued an injunction against further reprisals and physical abuse and found that in the four days beginning with the recapture of Attica, the state troopers and correctional personnel struck, prodded and assaulted injured prisoners, some of whom were on stretchers. Other prisoners were stripped naked and then forced to run between lines of correctional officers who beat them with clubs, spat upon them, burned them with matches, and poked them in the genitals—among other things.[16]

The Attica reprisals are well documented, but Toch is generally skeptical of other prisoner reports of organized brutality by correctional officers. He takes a different approach, looking at official records of officer–prisoner violence in New York State for the year 1973. A total of 386 incidents were recorded in the official file, and these involved 547 prisoners and 1,288 employees. The relative number of officers and prisoners in these incidents is meaningful in itself in that it indicates the more than two-to-one odds that prisoners face in these altercations. One might argue that with odds such as these, there is little excuse for causing excessive injury to the prisoners. In fact, there were no injuries at all in one-third of the reports. The most common action cited was a "hold," which included such maneuvers as half-nelsons, pulls and choking. Toch believes that correctional officer violence is routinely justified by formulas similar to those used to justify police brutality, and that it is really based on correctional officer subcultural norms favoring violence against prisoners. These norms develop because of the pervasive fear of prisoners that is part of the correctional officer subculture. This same subcultural phenomenon makes it almost impossible to convince a correctional officer to testify against one of his fellow employees, so corroborating testimony is rarely obtained in investigations of officer brutality, except from other prisoners. Toch also links officer violence to official regulations that forbid the forming of meaningful interpersonal relationships between officers and prisoners. Such regulations leave officers with only naked force as a way of enforcing order and also create what Toch characterizes as a "trench warfare climate" in prisons.[17] Whether one concentrates on the day-to-day routinized violence or the extreme brutality that is sometimes associated with prison disturbances and transfers, the conclusion is the same. It is that although most correctional officers in most prisons do not engage in any form of brutality and are only concerned with defending themselves against attack, there are enough officers who have values and beliefs that favor brutality and enough incidents that seem to require some sort of a show of force by officers so that there is a steady stream of minor unnecessary or excessive acts of violence in America's prisons, punctuated by occasional acts in which officers go far beyond any reasonable standard of the application of necessary force.

If an officer who favors the brutalization of prisoners is careful, he or she can limit the application of excessive force to incidents that fit the prison's definition of the appropriate use of force to maintain prison discipline or prevent escapes. Complaints lodged against such a correctional officer will invariably be dismissed by the warden who will rule that the violence was appropriately applied within institutional regulations. In fact, it may be claimed that had officers not used violence in the incident, they would have been delinquent in the performance of stated duties and subject to dismissal. This kind of rationale also makes it difficult for a prisoner to receive a fair hearing in court, where the warden's testimony carries considerable weight with judges and juries. As an example of this, I was close to a case in which a mentally ill prisoner was climbing a fence separating two prison yards and was fatally shot in the head by a prison officer who had commanded him to stop. The officer, who was stationed in a tower, probably was unaware of the mental condition of the prisoner and might not have taken that into account in any case. More importantly, he did not need to shoot the prisoner, as going from one prison yard to another does not constitute a risk of escape. Since the prisoner was unarmed, a shot in the leg rather than the head would have been more than sufficient even had he been climbing a fence on the boundary of the prison compound. The warden chose to ignore these arguments and immediately supported the action of the officer, saying that it was appropriate and required by institutional regulations. The local officials outside of the prison also accepted the judgment of the warden and declined prosecution in the case. There is nothing more serious than murder, and if this can be so easily justified by correctional officials one can appreciate the wide variety of possibly victimizing acts that are similarly justified annually in the United States.

The Involvement of Correctional Officers in Sexual Aggression

There are three ways that correctional officers can be involved in sexual aggression against prisoners. The first is to carry out the aggression themselves. This is occasionally hinted at, but has been well documented only for isolated cases that involved female and adolescent male victims. The second type of involvement is for correctional officers to permit a sexual attack in their presence and then to enjoy the spectacle. Although occasionally mentioned in passing, the best example of this sort of behavior in the literature comes from an institution for the retarded rather than from a prison.[18] The final form of correctional officer involvement in sexual attacks on prisoners is passive participation by deliberately failing to carry out one's custodial responsibilities. In this behavior, the officer does not adequately control an area or deliberately stays away from a site in which it is known that sexual assaults regularly occur. Although seemingly less severe than the first two forms of staff participation in sexual assaults, this third type is the most important because its occurrence is much more common than the first two types. As Sagarin and MacNamara conclude, prison rapes hardly seem possible "without the connivance, or at least deliberate inattention, of prison authorities.[19]

Cole[20] and Wooden[21] site numerous examples of sexual assaults on juveniles by correctional officers. Boys and girls may be forced to submit to sexual advances by threats of violence or they may be manipulated to cooperate by promises of favors. Bartollas et al. quote a youthful prisoner:

> He had some intercourse with me about every two weeks. I did not want to do it, but he talked about getting me out of [here] faster and I wanted to get out because I had been here a long time. I think the reason I did it was I just came back from AWOL and I thought I had a long time to go so I thought I would get out of here.[22]

These authors also show how a staff member can subtly approach the topic of participation in sexual relations with a prisoner so that they can not be quoted as having made a direct overture or threat. Another prisoner that they interviewed told them how a staff member began to talk to him about people they knew in common and then switched to the prisoner's homosexuality in what appeared at first to be an attempt to help him. Then the staff member began to talk about the sexual acts that he enjoyed himself and linked that to sexual acts that the prisoner enjoyed. At this point it was clear to the prisoner that he was being manipulated into committing homosexual acts although the staff member had not made a specific quotable overture.[23]

The occasional reports of sexual assaults carried out against girls and women by jailers, sheriffs, deputies and other correctional officials[24] were taken more seriously after the national publicity given to the case of Joanne Little.[25] Like many other county jails and understaffed correctional facilities, the Beaufort County Jail in North Carolina employed no female staff members to care for its occasional female prisoners. The autopsy report of the Beaufort County Medical Examiner made clear that the 62-year-old jailer had been killed by Ms. Little while he was forcing her to engage in sexual relations with him. Little stabbed him seven times with an icepick and then escaped, only to turn herself in to the police at a later date.[26] It is unlikely that Little was the first prisoner to be sexually approached by this jailer. Unfortunately, professional standards in rural local jails are so variable and documentation so completely lacking that it is impossible to make even "a ball park estimate" of the national incidence of this form of sexual victimization.

The only documented case of a correctional staff member forcing prisoners to engage in sexual behavior with one another is contained in Cole's book, *Our Children's Keepers*. He quotes a 15-year-old boy as saying that two counselors forced a friend of his to go into another room and have sexual intercourse with a known homosexual prisoner. When the friend refused to do so, he was taken into another room and beaten. The counselors then came out and brought in the homosexual prisoner, following which the two prisoners had sexual relations for the amusement of the counselors. In the words of the observer, "They get a kick out of somebody going through it—then they make fun of him in front of everybody else."[27] We cannot give too much credence to this report in view of the way in which it was obtained. It is included here merely as an example of how such events may occur in correctional institutions.

The contribution to sexual assaults between prisoners that is made by correctional officers who fail to carry out adequately their duties is legendary. There are relatively few prisons that are so poorly constructed and so greatly understaffed that it is absolutely impossible to staff members to keep prisoners under sufficient surveillance to prohibit sexual aggression. When Davis asked 26 correctional employees to take polygraph tests, 25 refused, presumably because they felt they were guilty of failing to carry out their assigned duties in situations that led directly to the sexual assault of prisoners in documented cases. Davis describes sexual assaults that were made possible because the officers in charge did not adequately patrol their areas. It is easy for skeptics to dismiss many of the reports of correctional officer complicity in prisoner sexual assaults, but the kind of documentation provided by Davis convinces us of this complicity beyond the shadow of a doubt. In one incident, a prisoner was reported as having screamed for over an hour while he was being gang-raped in his cell within hearing distance of a correctional officer who not only ignored the screams but who laughed at the victim afterward. Prisoners who reported this incident passed polygraph examinations while the accused officer refused to take the test.[28]

Extreme examples of officer involvement in inmate sexual behavior include a southern institution in which a prisoner could buy a homosexual partner from a correctional officer or even from the deputy warden[29] and the use of homosexual prisoners as "gifts" from staff members to prisoner leaders who helped them keep the institution quiet.[30] One ex-prisoner claims to have been presented to "an entire wing of the prison, as a bonus to the convicts for their good behavior. In this wing, any prisoner who wanted his services, at any time and for any purposes, was given it; the guards opened doors, passed him from one cell to another, provided lubricants, permitted an orgy of simultaneous oral and anal entry, and even arranged privacy."[31]

It is easy to see why some authors place heavy blame on correctional officers for their contribution to prison sexual assaults.[32] The only objective observer who defends them is Lockwood, who feels that the combination of sexually aggressive prisoners, overcrowded conditions, management and program needs that require prisoners to intermingle, and legal limitations imposed by the courts creates a situation in which the ability of correctional officers to prevent sexual victimization is sharply attentuated.[33]

Brutality in Children's Institutions

Professional standards in institutions for delinquent youth appear to be much more variable than professional standards in state correctional systems for adults. Although there are many exemplary institutions in which not even the slightest hint of staff brutality would ever be tolerated, these exist close by other institutions in which a wide range of staff aggression toward prisoners is not only tolerated but encouraged. It is impossible to estimate accurately a national rate of staff–prisoner victimization in juvenile institutions, but the impression one gets from reading the literature is that this form of victimization is probably more prevalent in juvenile institutions than in adult institutions. Cole tells about a staff member in a Louisiana institution who assaulted prisoners with a hosepipe and big sticks. The staff member combined the beatings with economic victimization when he extracted a portion of all the gifts received by prisoners through the mail.[34] Quoting descriptions of beatings derived from accounts collected by James,[35] Chase concludes that there are more American children being mistreated in institutions than in their homes.[36] The severity of this indictment is accentuated by the most recent report on American child abuse, which presents 507,494 incidents of child abuse reported to official agencies in 1977, a reporting rate of 2.3 cases per 1,000 population.[37]

The John Howard Association's report on the Illinois Youth Centers at St. Charles and Geneva provides rare detail on the physical abuse of youngsters by staff members. Of 46 youths between the ages of 14 and 19 whom they interviewed at St. Charles, 23 stated that they had been slapped, kicked, punched, had their arms twisted or were struck with an object by a staff member. About half of the youths stated that they had witnessed staff members committing such acts against other youngsters. Many of the staff members also admitted the use of extensive corporal punishment, and there were several staff members who were consistently named as physical abusers of children. One staff member admitted striking youngsters on different occasions with a stick, a fishing pole and his hands. These situations did not involve the use of necessary restraint to subdue a youth who was attacking a staff member or another youth. Instead, it was a matter of general brutality when staff members were in bad moods.[38] This kind of gratuitous punishment differs in degree, but not in kind, from the vicious brutality suffered by youngsters in reformatories more than a century ago.[39]

Reports of beating of institutionalized children are from all parts of the nation, from the deep south[40] to the relatively well-funded institutions that are found in Massachusetts. A Harvard student posing as a delinquent at a Massachusetts institution observed an incident in which a younster's hair was used to mop up urine from the floor.[41] Feld showed that staff brutality was higher in custody-oriented institutions than in treatment-oriented institutions. The former institutions were characterized by acts such as choking and physical beatings, whereas the more benign treatment-oriented staff members limited themselves to beatings with a plastic baseball bat and other minor physical punishments.[42]

The most detailed analysis of staff–prisoner victimization in juvenile institutions was carried out by Bartollas et al. in their study of an Ohio reformatory. A number of forms of staff–prisoner victimization at this institution were actually supported by the informal staff normative code, a code analogous to the convict code among the prisoners. The "acceptable" forms of staff exploitation were psychological and social in nature, although physical victimization was not supported by the staff normative code. For example, direct physical brutality was defined as unacceptable when a leader was intoxicated, upset because of a personal problem, using weapons against the youth or deliberately trying to seriously injure a youngster. It was also unacceptable to encourage directly (as opposed to passively) the victimization of one prisoner by another, to aid escapes (which led to increased punishment for the escapee when he was caught), and to sexually exploit the boys for one's own pleasure. The tie-in of homosexual gratification to rewards such as cigarettes, protection from peers, or promise of early release was defined as particularly offensive behavior under the staff normative code and was dealt with informally by staff members whenever a rumor about sexual exploitation was substantiated. Informal sanctions usually led to the resignation of the offending staff member.[43]

PSYCHOLOGICAL VICTIMIZATION

We have already mentioned Conley's observation that correctional officers in the Oklahoma State Penitentiary who were temporarily forbidden to physically brutalize prisoners switched to psychological forms of victimization. For example, officers conducting shakedowns would deliberately break open little boxes that contained a prisoner's personal trinkets instead of asking him for the key. They would also harass the prisoners by "making noise in the cell house so they couldn't sleep, refusing personal requests, failing to respond to an inmate's call for help if he was ill or a victim of an assault, and otherwise constantly hounding the individuals."[44] These forms of psychological victimization can be perpetrated on individual prisoners who have been marked for special mistreatment or on all prisoners as a matter of personal policy.

The author once observed the classic example of psychological victimization in which the sergeant placed letters to a prisoner where the prisoner could see them but not reach them, and then claimed that there were no letters for that prisoner. The prisoner became quite agitated as a result and eventually developed considerable paranoia about his mail. In each incident, the officer tormented him throughout the day and then gave him the letters in the evening saying that he had just discovered them. Eventually, the prisoner lost control completely and was cited for a disciplinary infraction, which may well have been the officer's goal in the manipulation. A more elegant from of the same game is described by Heise as "The Therapeutic 'No.' " In this game, staff members deliberately say "no" to a prisoner who has come with a legitimate request in an attempt to force an explosive or angry response.[45]

A very sophisticated form of the psychological victimization of prisoners by staff members occurs when correctional officers use their special knowledge of the outside world to heighten prisoner anxieties about their loved ones, their release date or other subjects of paramount importance. An example of this, reported from a women's institution, involved a prisoner whose son was in foster care while she was incarcerated. The officer she worked for would wait until she was within hearing distance and then begin a conversation with a second correctional officer about how commonly foster children were mistreated. These discussions went on endlessly, concentrating on subjects such as starvation, corporal punishment and sexual victimization. The prisoner was not allowed to speak, nor could she report the incidents to the administration. How could she prove that the officers were deliberately practicing psychological victimization against her? These incidents, along with the mishandling of a medical condition by the prison physician, almost agitated her enough to attempt an escape.[46]

Staff members are also privy to another source of potentially victimizing information about prisoners—the data in their central files. Information in these files contains not only the complete criminal records of prisoners but also material from social investigations, institutional reports and other items revealing the most intimate details of their lives—details that are often irrelevant to any criminal prosecution. It is common in some institutions for correctional officers to uncover this material to embarrass prisoners. Homosexual behavior, low-status crimes such as sexual offenses against minors, self-destructive acts and bouts with mental illness are examples of the kinds of subjects that officers sometimes extract from central files to use against prisoners. This method of psychological victimization is not confined to correctional institutions, for Goffman also observed it in a mental hospital.[47] A variation on the game occurs when officers pass on derogatory labels that have been affixed to unlucky prisoners by their colleagues in crime, such as "rat," "snitch" and "punk."[48]

The number of forms that psychological victimization of prisoners by staff members can take is almost limitless. New examples are constantly being reported in the literature or revealed in testimony given in the nation's courts. In Nevada, a warden put a pistol to the neck of a prisoner and said, "Move or I'll kill you," when it was not necessary for him to do so because the deputy warden was already walking the prisoner down the corridor to solitary confinement.[49] An officer in a California penitentiary who had been asked for help by a prisoner who was coughing blood gave him a note that said, "Yell for help when the blood is an inch thick, all over the floor, and don't call before that."[50] It is likely that if the officer had judged the prisoner's condition to be serious, he would have summoned medical help. The psychological victimization in this incident occurs because the officer deliberately pretends that he will never summon help while the prisoner is alive. An injunction was granted in New York State against the assignment of male guards at a women's prison, which occurred as a result of testimony that these officers deliberately came into shower rooms to watch the women as they were naked and also deliberately watched them when they were on the toilet.[51] In one of the most gruesome incidents revealed in a Senate subcommittee hearing, an Ohio correctional officer collected pet cats from the prisoners and then "dashed their brains out in sight of the whole prison population."[52] Being deprived of their children, prisoners often invest fatherly and motherly emotion in their pets so that this act of brutality symbolized multiple infanticide to many of the prisoners who could not avoid seeing it.

In the history of prisons in America, groups of prisoners sometimes mutilated themselves in protest against mistreatment by staff members. The mass cuttings of heel tendons described by Keve[53] are no longer common on the American prison scene. Likewise, the self-mutilations accomplished by Peruvian prisoners as a result of severe beatings administered by criminal justice personnel are not replicated in this country.[54] Today, self-destructive behavior by prisoners is much more likely to be an individual act than an act of group protest. Mattick is probably correct that self-destructive behavior is declining as a percentage of all prison violence.[55] The highest rate of self-mutilations known in contemporary American prisons occurred at Angola Prison in Louisiana in a ten-month period in 1974. A total of 107 self-mutilation cases were heard by the disciplinary board during this period, an average of about ten per month.[56] The despair felt by prisoners who damaged themselves has been well documented in the literature.[57] This has been linked to physical victimization by correctional officers,[58] but there has been little recognition in the literature of the ways in which psychological victimization by prison officers can also contribute to suicidal and other self-damaging acts. One occasionally hears comments to the effect that psychologically disturbed and inadequate prisoners are more likely to be "picked on" by staff members than well-adjusted, highly prisonized inmates. In institutions where this is true, the deliberate mistreatment by staff members of prisoners who are already highly disturbed may be sufficient to precipitate self-destructive incidents.

Occasions in which prisoners harm themselves primarily because of psychological victimization by correctional officers are probably relatively rare in the United States. A more common contribution to prisoner self-destruction that is made by correctional officers is the lack of sensitivity to the needs of prisoners who are approaching potentially self-destructive personal crises. Because correctional officers are usually poorly trained in interpersonal relations, most of them neither recognize nor are sufficiently motivated to assist prisoners undergoing psychological breakdowns. For every officer who sadistically torments such

115

prisoners, there are hundreds who fail to give adequate support or to call in qualified medical personnel in a situation that is gradually deteriorating. This is not a matter of victimization at the individual level but is instead a reflection of policies and funding priorities in state legislatures and other funding bodies.

ECONOMIC VICTIMIZATION

Prisoner officers and other staff members in correctional institutions may be involved in economic victimization of a very direct sort, such as eating a prisoner's food or wearing his or her clothing. Most institutions guard against this sort of direct economic victimization. It is probably more common for prisoner officers to victimize economically their charges *indirectly* by being involved in contraband operations and loansharking. For example, the director of the Omaha Urban League alleged in 1974 that prisoner officers were regularly bringing in drugs and reaping profits from the drug traffic in a midwestern penitentiary.[59] The warden of the federal penitentiary in Atlanta said that nothing could be done to halt the alleged staff corruption in that institution unless the culprits were actually caught in the act. At the same hearing, one of his prisoners testified that 95% of all marijuana in the prison was provided by staff members.[60] A Tampa newspaper, investigating the homosexual attack and murder of a 19-year-old prisoner, mentioned that the prisoners who assaulted the victim were middlemen for a loan racket run by the officer who was supervising the area in which the prisoner was raped and killed. Testimony revealed that the victim had been subjected to sexual assault before his death as punishment because the correctional officer believed that he was "snitching" on him for selling ham from the kitchen for private profit. In addition to the assault by prisoners, it was alleged that the victim had been beaten by several correctional officers four days before he died and had begged to be placed in the isolation unit but that his request was denied.[61]

When a staff member is involved in a sub rosa economic system of the prison, it is possible to "burn" prisoners with impunity because they cannot possibly report the crime to the administration without revealing their own involvement in the illegal activity. If the prisoner is a member of a powerful gang or clique, pressures can be brought to bear on correctional officers to keep them from this sort of economic victimization. On the other hand, sophisticated officers are careful never to burn any prisoner who has this kind of backing. Instead, they victimize only the isolated prisoners who enlist their help in sub rosa economic transactions. Such a prisoner, who gives an officer some money to smuggle out of the prison for his wife, may find out that the officer has pocketed it instead of delivering it, or perhaps that a portion of it was subtracted as an additional payment for delivery beyond the amount already agreed upon.

The definition of victimization becomes contorted out of all recognition in the case of the officer who regularly participates in sub rosa smuggling activites with prisoners but who keeps his record clean by occasionally reporting unsophisticated prisoners to the administration for attempting to bribe him. Victimization in this instance consists of enforcing the regulations that the officer should *have been enforcing* in a setting in which the regulations were habitually ignored. One officer who allegedly charged up to $300 a trip to "pack" contraband in and out of the prison made enough money over his career to establish an independent business in the free community. This "horse" (a slang term for prison officers who smuggle contraband into the institution) was probably able "to stay in business" for such a long time because he only "packed" for powerful, trustworthy prisoners and systematically wrote infraction tickets on every other prisoner who approached him.

We cannot leave the subject of the economic victimization of prisoners by staff members without mentioning drug testing, industrial victimization and the suppression of prisoner unions. These topics do not fit our definition of victimization because they refer to institutional policy and, in some cases, enacted law. Many prison industries are operated under less than safe conditions in order to maximize productivity. Once a major problem in America's prisons,[62] this lingers on today in industrial programs that continue to use equipment that is antiquated and unsafe.

The testing of dangerous drugs by prisoners, which has been rapidly declining in recent years, is another form of institutional victimization that is outside our technical definition. Beginning with a 1904 study of bubonic plague by Colonel R. P. Strong,[63] prisoners were paid a pittance (if anything) but offered minor administrative favors in return for participating in highly dangerous experiments. Even these small rewards were more than sufficient motivation to recruit prisoners for medical- and drug-testing experiments because the prisoners were artifically economically disadvantaged by policies and laws that forbade them to be paid more than a few cents an hour. Was it really necessary to apply radiation to the testicles of prisoners so that later they would become sterile? Prisoners, whom I know personally, were involved in such an experiment, claiming they were not adequately informed of the consequences at the time that they agreed to participate. Some of them would now like to lead normal married lives and have children, but their criminal records largely rule out adoption and their participation in the radiation experiment leaves them unable to conceive their own children. In an excellent treatment of the subject, Meyer shows how the pharmaceutical companies and the general public have benefited over the years from low-cost prisoner experiments. The victimizing nature of these experiments has been given credence by their abolition under contemporary federal standards for drug-testing experiments.[64]

The substandard wages that are generally paid to men and women working in prison industries are also economically victimizing, although such wages do not constitute victimization under our definition of the subject. However, technical victimization creeps into this situation when prisoners attempt to organize unions, following the model that is accepted in free society, and they are prevented from doing so when administrative actions such as punitive transfers, punitive segregation and unjust parole board "flops" (parole board decisions to increase sentence length) are used to suppress the formation of prisoner unions.[65] Although prisoner unions are permitted in some European nations (such as KRUM, organized in Sweden in 1966), the only way for prisoner unions to survive in the United States is if they have a power base outside of the institution. The San Francisco-based Prisoners' Union, which was co-founded by John Irwin, is an example of this kind of an organization. Whether it will have any significant national impact remains to be seen.

SOCIAL VICTIMIZATION

The most blatant form of social victimization carried out against prisoners by correctional officers is racial discrimination. Two other forms of victimization that are essentially social in nature are the nonperformance of stated duties and the deliberate handing over of supervisory responsibilities to prisoners who then use their staff-sanctioned power to abuse others. Reports of correctional officer discrimination against black prisoners abound in the literature.[66] These reports include evidence of discrimination in job assignments[67] and disciplinary hearings.[68] Racial discrimination becomes mixed with religious discrimination when groups such as the Black Muslims are denied their religious rights.[69] Carroll describes an incident in which kissing between a prisoner and a visitor, which was officially prohibited but always permitted for uniracial couples, resulted in the abrupt termination of a visit when a black prisoner kissed his white visitor.[70] Carroll also observed correctional officers admitting white visitors to inmate organizations without searches, but systematically searching visitors to black organizations and conducting bodily postvisit searches of black prisoners three times as often as similar searches of white prisoners.[71] All of these reports pale in comparison with the allegations of virulent racism by correctional officers at Soledad prison in California.[72]

When a staff member turns over supervisory activities to a prisoner, all of the other prisoners in that jurisdiction are subject to a potential victimization. We have already seen some examples of sexual victimization that occurred because of this form of staff behavior. I cite only two additional examples here. Testimony in a federal court alleged that a prisoner in a Texas institution had been set up as a "prison enforcer" for which he was rewarded with special privileges such as a homosexual in his cell to service his sexual needs and the authority to assault other prisoners at any time in the service of maintaining institutional order.[73] The other example comes from the juvenile institution studied by Bartollas et al. Staff members in this institution often catered to the needs of "heavy" (physically powerful) prisoners in return for their cooperation in running the reformatory. These favored prisoners were permitted to unlock the doors of their fellow prisoners with the staff's keys. This gave the "heavies" license to victimize other prisoners in return for their allegiance to staff members.[74]

The social victimization of prisoners as a class of individuals occurs when correctional officers and other staff members neglect to carry out their stated duties. Bartollas and his associates described staff members who stayed in their offices, perhaps taking naps, thus leaving the weaker prisoners open to all sorts of victimization by their peers. Other staff members discriminated directly against scapegoats by giving them all the menial work details in the cottage, seldom talking with them, or permitted other youths to victimize them openly in the presence of staff.[75]

Prisoners are beginning to realize that they can file legal actions against correctional staff members who refrain from carrying out their duties in ways that lead to prisoner victimization. A recent issue of *Corrections Compendium* reports several such cases filed under 42 U.S.C. 1983. One of the complainants had suffered sexual abuse and alleged a history of incidents over a period of two years because of inadequate supervision by institutional staff members. The other alleged that one prisoner had been killed and another injured by a fire that broke out in an Arkansas jail while the sheriff had gone to a basketball game, leaving the jail unattended.[76] There is increasing recognition that such actions by correctional staff members constitute a serious form of victimization.

Two theoretical explanations for the victimization of prisoners by correctional officers have been advanced in the literature. These are the total institutions theory and the role theory. Actually there is very little difference between these two approaches. Total institutions theory looks at institutions as a whole and emphasizes the similarities between prisons, mental hospitals and other total institutions. In contrast, role theory emphasizes the role played by correctional officers and argues that citizens can be rapidly socialized to play the role of correctional officer.

The creation of total institutions theory is generally credited to Goffman in his book, *Asylums,* in which he discusses social and psychological assaults upon inmates by staff members. In Goffman's conception, the psychological victimization of inmates by staff members is part of the overall process of mortification, in which the inmates' attachment to civilian life is stripped away. The exasperating thing about much of the unnecessary psychological victimization that goes on is that the staff justifies the victimization in terms of institutional needs.[77] Following this same line of analysis, Hartmann has identified the existence of the staff role of the "key jingler" for persons who deliberately use power in a manner that is debilitating to the inmates. These individuals are concerned with "throwing their weight around" rather than promoting the welfare of the inmates under their control.[78]

The maximum security prison is conceptualized as a miniature totalitarian state by Burns. The six basic features of a totalitarian regime—totalitarian ideology, a single party typically led by one person, a terroristic police, a communications monopoly, a weapons monopoly and a centrally directed economy—are systematically applied to maximum security prisons in Burns' analysis. In this model, staff members who are in a position of great authority will be sorely tempted to practice brutality, blackmail, bribery and favoritism. Terroristic police practices are part of the social control mechanism for keeping inmates in line.[79] If Burns' conception of the maximum security prison as a totalitarian regime is correct, then we would expect that those correctional officers who are better integrated with the culture of the prison and more socially involved in it would be more brutal and totalitarian than those officers who exist at the periphery of the staff subculture. An exploratory investigation by Shoemaker and Hillery suggests that this may be true in some institutions. However, the correlations they found were significant in only one of three institutions (and that was a boarding school rather than a maximum security prison),[80] so their evidence does not lend more than minimal support to the theory advanced by Burns.

Role theory as applied to the victimization of prisoners by officers received support from the Stanford Prison Experiment conducted by Haney et al.[81] In this experiment, college students who had been authenticated as psychologically normal were paid to role-play guards and inmates in a pseudoprison in the basement of a Stanford building. Everyone involved was aware of the fact that the experiment was artificial, although it was very well staged. Commenting on this experiment, Zimbardo says:

At the end of six days we had to close down our mock prison because what we saw was frightening. It was no longer apparent to most of the subjects (or to us) where reality ended and the roles began. The majority had indeed become prisoners or guards, no longer able to clearly differentiate between role-playing and self. There were dramatic changes in virtually every aspect of their behavior, thinking, and feeling. In less than a week the experience of imprisonment undid (temporarily) a lifetime of learning: human values were suspended, self-concepts were challenged and the ugliest, most base, pathological side of human nature surfaced. We were horrified because we saw some boys (guards) treat others as if they were despicable animals, taking pleasure in cruelty, while other boys (prisoners) became servile, dehumanized robots who thought only of escape, of their own individual survival and of their mounting hatred for the guards.[82]

In the Stanford experiment, approximately one-third of the staff members became tyrannical in their arbitrary use of power over the inmates. They developed creative ways of breaking the spirit of the prisoners who were in their charge. Although the other two-thirds of the staff members were not tyrannical, there was never a case in which one of them interfered with a command given by any of the tyrannical guards. They never even tried to pressure the other staff members into behaving more reasonably. The experiment was called off because of the possibility that some of the subjects were being severely damaged by their experiences. Three of them had had to be released in the first four days because they had severe situational traumatic reactions, such as confusion in thinking, severe depression and hysterical crying.

This experiment devastates the constitutional sadism theory of staff brutality, which is, in any case, not represented in the serious literature on staff–inmate victimization. The realization that any normal human being can take on the negative character-istics commonly associated with the worst of prison officers leads us to look more carefully at how roles are structured in the prison situation. A study of mine shows that even civilian volunteers who become quasistaff members of a correctional institution can engage in types of behavior that are psychologically victimizing. In a volunteer program administered by me in which all but two of the staff members were volunteers from the external commu-nity, there were many cases of power-tripping and sexual entice-ment by the staff members, with power-tripping being primarily engaged in by males, and sexual enticement by females, although the reverse was true in some cases. The power-tripper enjoys a feeling of control over the lives of prisoners and manipulates them in therapy groups and in administrative situations so as to make them more dependent and more anxious than they would otherwise be. Power-trippers are sure that inmates should do what they are told, and they imply that they have a great deal more power over the inmates' release date than is actually the case.

Sexual enticement occurs when the volunteer staff member dresses, talks and acts in a sexually suggestive way while within the prison. Pseudoromances are encouraged in which the pris-oners are led to believe that the staff members have a real interest in them, while the staff members in actuality are merely gratifying themselves by being admired and sought after. When the relationship goes too far, the prisoners are often subjected to disciplinary actions because the victimizing staff member claims that it was "all the prisoner's fault." In addition, some prisoners become so emotionally involved that when the relationship falls apart, they become suicidal. Others come looking for their "lovers" when they are released from prison, only to find out that these staff members have no intention of following up on the promises they made while the prisoners were safe behind bars.[83]

Is the role of the prison guard so compulsive that a certain percentage of people who play it will be invariably motivated to abuse prisoners in one way or another? The comments by Zimbardo and my experiences say yes, and this idea is also consistent with a report by Jacobs and Kraft, that suggests the possibility that racial differences among guards are suppressed by the "master status" of the prison officer.[84] However, an obscure publication on correctional institutions in Wisconsin offers contrary evidence. This report by Rose describes what happened during a 16-day period when members of the Wisconsin State Employees Union went on strike and National Guard Units took over the administration of the prisons. The National Guardsmen were in the prisons for more than twice the period of time of Zimbardo's experiment, yet they were not institutionalized by the experience. Instead of becoming brutal and mistreating the inmates, they treated them like decent human beings. They relaxed the disciplinary regime and at the same time reduced the number of incidents of violence among inmates.[85]

It is probable that the reason the National Guardsmen's behavior did not deteriorate during their time as correctional officers was that they never conceived of themselves as playing the role of prison officers. They had a different role to play—the role of National Guardsmen acting in an emergency. In addition, they had a network of relations with each other that existed before they had entered the prison and that strengthened their resistance to the negative process of institutionalization. With these kinds of social supports, it is possible that the National Guardsmen could have had tours of duty of one or two years in length without ever adopting the more negative aspects of the role of the prison officer. International studies of prison camps in which the prisoners are able to live rather normal lives under the supervision of military units also offer some evidence in support of the idea that the military role can take precedence over the prison officer role and minimize the appeal of engaging in behavior that is at least psychologically victimizing if not physically brutal.

NOTES

1. Donald Clemmer, *The Prison Community* (New York: Holt, Rinehart and Winston, 1940), p. 204.
2. John A. Conley, "A History of the Oklahoma Penal System, 1907–1967," Ph.D. dissertation, Michigan State University, 1977.
3. Bruce Jackson, *Killing Time, Life in the Arkansas Penitentiary* (Ithaca, NY: Cornell University Press, 1977).
4. Tom Murton and Joe Hyams, *Inside Prison, U.S.A.* (New York: Grove Press, 1969).
5. Ibid., p. 7.
6. Prison brutality revealed during the federal hearing, *The Freeworld Times* 1 (January 1972):2.
7. Fear, Angola's punishment camp terrorizes prisoners, *Southern Coalition Report on Jails and Prisons* 5 (Spring 1978):3.
8. Stephen Gettinger, Mississippi: Has come a long way but it had a long way to come, *Corrections Magazine* 5 (June 1979):8; *Corrections Digest* 4 (December 12, 1973):3.
9. Philip J. Hirschkop and Michael A. Millemann, The prison life of Leroy Jones, in Burton M. Atkins and Henry R. Glick (Eds.), *Prisons, Protest, and Politics* (Englewood Cliffs, NJ: Prentice-Hall, 1972), pp. 55–59.
10. Jessica Mitford, *Kind and Usual Punishment* (New York: Random House, 1971), pp. 41–42.
11. Oklahoma prison guards indicted for inmate gassing incident, *Corrections Digest* 6 (February 5, 1975):2.
12. Federal jury convicts prison guards of brutality, *Corrections Digest* 5 (March 6, 1974):2–3.
13. 'Dedicated' with violence, *The Freeworld Times* 1 (August 1972):8–9.
14. Rioters killed, *The Freeworld Times* 1 (February 1972):6,9.
15. Ibid., p. 6.
16. Mitford (1971), p. 290.
17. Hans Toch, *Police, Prisons, and the Problem of Violence* (Washington, DC: U.S. Government Printing Office, 1977), pp. 65–67.
18. Robert Bogdan and Steven J. Taylor, *Introduction to Qualitative Research Methods* (New York: Wiley, 1975).
19. Edward Sagarin and Donal E. J. MacNamara, The homosexual as a crime victim, *International Journal of Criminology and Penology* 3 (1975):21.
20. Larry Cole, *Our Children's Keepers: Inside America's Kid Prisons* (New York: Grossman, 1972).
21. Kenneth Wooden, *Weeping in the Playtime of Others: America's Incarcerated Children* (New York: McGraw-Hill, 1976).
22. Clemens Bartollas, Stuart J. Miller and Simon Dinitz, *Juvenile Victimization: The Institutional Paradox* (New York: Wiley, 1976), p. 214.
23. Ibid., p. 214.

24. Gene Kassebaum, Sex in prison, violence, homosexuality, and intimidation are everyday occurrences, *Sexual Behavior* 2 (January 1972):39–45.
25. The case of Joanne Little, *Crime and Social Justice* 3 (Summer 1975):42–45. For a more recent case, see Women press for change at Tutwiler, *Southern Coalition Report on Jails and Prisons* 5 (Fall 1978):3.
26. Woman's killing of jailer raises inmate abuse questions, *Corrections Digest* 5 (December 11, 1974):11–12.
27. Cole (1972), p. 8.
28. Alan J. Davis, Sexual assaults in the Philadelphia prison system and sheriff's vans, *Trans-Action* 6 (December 1968):11.
29. Jack Griswold, Mike Misenheimer and Art Powers, *An Eye for an Eye* (New York: Holt, Rinehart and Winston, 1970), pp. 42–43, cited in Anthony M. Scacco Jr., *Rape in Prison* (Springfield IL: C.C. Thomas, 1975), p. 32.
30. Sagarin and MacNamara (1975).
31. Ibid., pp. 21–22.
32. See, for example, Davis (1968) and Scacco (1975).
33. Daniel Lockwood, *Prison Sexual Violence* (New York: Elsevier, 1980), p.140.
34. Cole (1972), p. 64.
35. Howard James, Children in trouble, *Christian Science Monitor* (April 5, 12, 19, 26, and May 10, 24, 1969), cited in Naomi F. Chase, *A Child Is Being Beaten* (New York: McGraw-Hill, 1976), pp. 154, 160.
36. Chase (1976), p. 151.
37. *National Analysis of Official Child Abuse and Neglect Reporting* (Washington, DC: Government Printing Office, 1969).
38. John Howard Association, *Illinois Youth Centers at St. Charles and Geneva* (Chicago: John Howard Association, 1974).
39. See, for example, Cliff Judge and Roma Emmerson, Some children at risk in Victoria in the 19th century, *Medical Journal of Australia* 1 (1974):490–495.
40. John Vodicka, Louisiana warden indicted for beatings of juveniles, *Southern Coalition Report on Jails and Prisons* 5 (Summer 1978):1.
41. Wooden (1976), p. 108.
42. Barry C. Feld, *Neutralizing Inmate Violence* (Cambridge, MA: Ballinger, 1977).
43. Bartollas et al. (1976).
44. Conley (1977), p. 237.
45. Robert E. Heise, *Prison Games* (Fort Worth: privately published, 1976).
46. Kenneth Dimick, *Ladies in Waiting Behind Prison Walls* (Muncie, IN: Accelerated Development, 1977), pp. 46–47.
47. Erving Goffman, *Asylums* (Garden City, NY: Doubleday, 1961).
48. Heise (1976).
49. *Corrections Digest* 3 (November 1, 1972), pp. 11–12.
50. Mitford (1971), p. 148.
51. Injunction granted against assignment of male guards at Bedford Hills, *Corrections Compendium* 2 (October 1977), p. 3.
52. Mitford (1971), pp. 268–269.
53. Paul W. Keve, *Prison Life and Human Worth* (Minneapolis: University of Minnesota Press, 1974).
54. H. H. A. Cooper, Self-mutilation by Peruvian prisoners, *International Journal of Offender Therapy* 15 (1971):180–188.
55. Hans Mattick, The prosaic sources of prison violence, in Jackwell Susman, *Crime and Justice, 1971–1972* (New York: A.M.S. Press, 1974):179–187.

56. A. Astrachan, Profile/Louisiana, *Corrections Magazine* 2 (September–October 1975):9–14.

57. See, for example, R. S. Esparza, Attempted and committed suicide in county jails, in Bruce Danto (Ed.), *Jailhouse Blues* (Orchard Lake, MI: Epic Publications, 1973), pp. 27–46; James L. Claghorn and Dan R. Beto, Self-mutilation in a prison hospital, *Corrective Psychiatry and Journal of Social Therapy* 13 (1967):133–141; Robert Johnson, *Culture and Crisis in Confinement* (Lexington, MA: D. C. Heath, 1976); Hans Toch, *Men in Crisis* (Chicago: Aldine, 1975); *Living in Prison: The Ecology of Survival* (New York: Free Press, 1977).

58. R. J. Wicks, Suicide prevention—A brief for corrections officers, *Federal Probation* 36 (September 1972):29–31.

59. Nebraska prisoners speak-out, *The Freeworld Times* 3 (January–February 1974):7.

60. Danger, death, corruption at Atlanta federal prison detailed in Senate testimony, *Corrections Digest* 9 (October 6, 1978):3–4.

61. Inmate death linked to guard rackets, *The Freeworld Times* 2 (May 1973):15.

62. See Conley (1977) for historical examples of excessive industrial accidents caused by deliberate administrative inattention to matters of safety.

63. Gilbert F. McMahon, The normal prisoner in medical research, *Journal of Clinical Pharmacology* 71 (February–March 1972):72.

64. Peter B. Meyer, *Drug Experiments on Prisoners, Ethical, Economic, or Exploitative?* (Lexington, MA: D. C. Heath, 1976).

65. C. Ronald Huff, Unionization behind the walls, *Criminology* 12 (1974):175–193; Prisoners' union: A challenge for state corrections, *State Government* 48 (1975):145–149.

66. Haywood Burns, The black prisoner as victim, in Michele G. Hermann and Marilyn G. Haft (Eds.), *Prisoners' Rights Sourcebook* (New York: Clark Boardman, 1973), pp. 25–31.

67. Ronald Goldfarb, *Jails: The Ultimate Ghetto of the Criminal Justice System* (Garden City, NY: Doubleday, 1976), p. 405.

68. Erik O. Wright, *The Politics of Punishment: A Critical Analysis of Prisons in America* (New York: Harper and Row, 1973), p. 127.

69. James B. Jacobs, *Stateville: The Penitentiary in Mass Society* (Chicago: University of Chicago Press, 1977), p. 59.

70. Leo Carroll, *Hacks, Blacks, and Cons* (Lexington, MA: D. C. Heath, 1974), pp. 123–124.

71. Ibid., pp. 127–128.

72. George Jackson, *Soledad Brother: The Prison Letters of George Jackson* (New York: Bantam, 1970).

73. This week: Texas prison faces federal court test, *Corrections Digest* 9 (October 6, 1978):2–3.

74. Bartollas et al. (1976), pp. 208–209.

75. Ibid., pp. 207–209.

76. Sheriff may be liable for acts of his subordinates, and Leaving prisoners unattended can lead to civil rights violation, *Corrections Compendium* 2 (June 1978):5.

77. Goffman (1961).

78. Carl Hartman, The key jingler, *Community Mental Health Journal* 5 (1969): 199–205.

79. Henry Burns, Jr., A miniature totalitarian state: Maximum security prison, *Canadian Journal of Criminology and Corrections* 11 (July 1969):153–164.
80. Donald J. Shoemaker and George A. Hillery, Jr., "Violence and Commitment in Custodial Settings," paper presented at the annual meeting of the American Sociological Association, 1978.
81. Craig Haney, Curtis Banks and Philip Zimbardo, Interpersonal dynamics in a simulated prison, in Robert G. Leger and John R. Stratton (Eds.), *The Sociology of Corrections* (New York: Wiley, 1977), pp. 65–92.
82. Philip Zimbardo, Pathology of imprisonment, *Society* 9 (6) (1972):4.
83. Lee H. Bowker, Volunteers in correctional settings: Benefits, problems, and solutions, in *Proceedings of the American Correctional Association* (Washington, DC: American Correctional Association, 1973), pp. 298–303.
84. James B. Jacobs and Lawrence J. Kraft, Integrating the keepers: A comparison of black and white prison guards in Illinois, *Social Problems* 25 (1978):304–318.
85. Beth Ross, *Changing of the Guard: Citizen Soldiers in Wisconsin Correctional Institutions* (Madison: League of Women Voters of Wisconsin, 1979).

Prison Staff Members as Victims

 Line staff in correctional institutions were once reasonably safe from victimization. This is no longer true. The contemporary correctional officer is subject to five analytically distinguishable types of risks. These are riots, patterned spontaneous attacks, unexpected attacks, the daily grind and victimization by their fellow staff members. Prisoners in a riot often take correctional officers as hostages and are increasingly likely to torture or kill them. Every correctional officer has reason to fear the rapid switch of control from the administration to the prisoners that occurs in a "successful" riot. The fear is great enough so that many correctional officers are careful to stay on the side of those prisoners who would be most likely to defend them in a riot situation.

Patterned spontaneous attacks and unexpected attacks are the other two forms of prisoner–prisoner physical victimization. Putting the terms patterned and spontaneous together in one rubric may appear contradictory, but it is not. Some spontaneous attacks in prisons are patterned in that there are certain high-risk activities engaged in by correctional officers during which the likelihood of their being assaulted is perhaps 50 or 100 times as great as it is in an average day's work. Examples of officer activities involving high risks are breaking up prisoner fights, arranging a transfer from one cell to another for a recalcitrant

prisoner, escorting prisoners to punitive segregation and conducting shakedowns under certain conditions. Prisoners who
strike out at officers in situations such as these are doing so
spontaneously—much as auto accidents occur spontaneously—
but both of these phenomena are patterned and can be predicted
ahead of time to some degree. The number of people to be killed
in automobile accidents on holiday weekends is normally predicted with considerable accuracy and given wide publicity in
hopes of having a deterrent effect. No similar predictions are
formally made in correctional institutions, but the correctional
officers know when they are being assigned to perform dangerous
tasks, and some of them do their best to avoid such tasks to
minimize their risk of being assaulted. Unexpected attacks differ
from patterned spontaneous attacks only in that they occur in a
completely unpatterned fashion. (An officer is walking down the
tier and a prisoner who thinks he has been unfairly discriminated
against jumps on him and assaults him with a lead pipe.) While
correctional officers can at least do something to try and minimize
the risk of patterned spontaneous attacks, the only way to minimize unexpected attacks is to have little or no contact with
prisoners, and this occurs only for those officers who remain in
enclosed glass booths all day, who work "out front," or who
"pull" tower duty. Although unexpected attacks are less frequent
than patterned spontaneous attacks, their unpredictable nature
causes them to have a disproportionately large effect on the fear
and apprehension experienced by correctional officers.

Assaults on staff members by prisoners constitute no more than
0.1% of the victimizing activities carried out against correctional
officers by prisoners. The other victimizations are part of the
daily routine to which officers are subjected unless they are in
positions that have minimal contact with prisoners. Except for
occasional economic or social victimization, the victimizing incidents that comprise the daily grind are psychological in nature.
They range from the corruption of authority to veiled threats
made against the lives or families of correctional officers. Psychological victimization is omnipresent in the professional lives of
correctional officers. Any conversation with a prisoner may turn
out to be a manipulation in disguise, and correctional officers are
all too well aware that they probably never get to the bottom of
half of the manipulations that are practiced against them.

In addition to these forms of victimization by prisoners, correctional officers may also be attacked from their blind side. That

is to say, staff–staff victimization may also occur in correctional institutions. It may occur among correctional officers, or the officers may be victimized by administrators. In this latter case, it is often difficult to know whether the administrators are victimizing a staff member or just carrying out their duties according to institution policy. The correctional officer who is black, liberal or better educated than average is in definite danger of being victimized by fellow staff members. Anyone who dares to be too friendly with prisoners is suspect in a rigid caste system, and correctional officers and administrators are quick to apply informal and perhaps even formal sanctions against the offender. Paradoxically, the person being victimized in these situations is probably being punished for having performed his or her job in a manner that is more consistent with rehabilitative standards and with Federal civil rights legislation than the day-to-day occupational behavior of the other staff members in the institution.

THE PREVALENCE OF
PRISONER–OFFICER ASSAULTS

Many prisoners have attitudes toward correctional officers that are intensely negative[1]—negative enough to support overt action against those whom they consider to be their oppressors. Control in the traditional American prison was so tight that these negative attitudes were almost never translated into victimizing behavior. Besides, the rhetoric of militancy and oppression was never used to heighten hatred and justify aggression by prisoners in those days. Mattick says that since 1960 the proportion of assaults by prisoners on officers as a fraction of all prison violence has increased.[2] We cannot be sure that he is correct, since comparable data are not available for all time periods. However, putting together what little is known, his assertion seems to be a fair description of what has been happening in correctional institutions as they have become increasingly overcrowded and under-controlled.

Before examining the details of prisoner–staff assaults, we should try to get an idea of the prevalence of these assaults. The early surveys by Akman and Sellin have been supplemented by recent reports on prisoner–staff assaults from California, Illinois, Michigan, New York, North Carolina and Virginia. The Akman survey of Canadian penitentiaries during 1964 and 1965 identified 32 incidents in which 37 correctional officers were assaulted by prisoners. Most of the offenses consisted of bodily attacks without weapons. Stabbing or cutting weapons were used in 12 of the assaults. The odds of being attacked were .0068 in 1964 and .0046 in 1965 for Canadian correctional officers, figures that were considerably lower than the assault victimization rates for the prisoners. The majority of the 37 victimized officers were not seriously harmed; ten of them sustained no injury at all and 11 suffered only minor injuries that required no more than first-aid treatment.[3]

Sellin identified eight correctional staff members who had been killed by prisoners in American state prisons during 1965,[4] but none had been killed during the previous year.[5] Other reports of prisoner–staff homicides were compiled by Thomas, Buffum and Sylvester et al. Thomas relates the astonishing finding that there has not been a murder of a correctional officer in a British national prison in more than 100 years.[6] In Pennsylvania, five prison officers were killed between 1954 and 1973, on the basis of which Buffum has calculated a homicide victimization rate of 1.8 per 10,000 officers per year.[7] A national study of prison homicides by Sylvester et al. found 11 prisoner–staff homicides in 1973, which constituted a rate of 2.62 per 10,000 staff members. If we project this figure over a career of 20 years of service as a correctional officer, the officer would face a one in 200 possibility of being slain in the line of duty.[8]

Returning to the Sellin studies, we find that 1964 data collected from 13 states and the District of Columbia contained only 22 assaults on prison staff members. Sellin's description of the incidents allows us to categorize 21 of them as patterned spontaneous attacks and only 1 of them as an unexpected attack. The patterned spontaneous attacks occurred when officers were taking prisoners into custody for rule violations or when they attempted to break up altercations between prisoners. The single unexpected attack occurred in a Utah penitentiary when an officer was hit on the head with a lead pipe by a prisoner who was serving an extended term for aggravated assault. The relative prevalence of prisoner–staff and prisoner–prisoner assaults can be gauged from the 1964 figures reported by the Kentucky State Penitentiary, in which 138 prisoners were assaulted as compared with only four prison officers.[9] The Akman and Sellin studies suggest that the rate of prisoner violence directed toward correctional officers in the 1960s was not particularly high, at least as compared with what followed in the 1970s.

Park reports that there were 59 incidents of prison staff members being assaulted by prisoners in the California prison system in 1970. This number increased slightly in 1971, then decreased in 1972, but increased sharply to 84 incidents in 1973 and 93 incidents in 1974. He comments that this increasing violence has been associated with greater deliberateness and ideological rhetoric on the part of the prisoners.[10] Data on prisoner attacks against correctional officers at Stateville and Joliet prisons in Illinois were abstracted from accident reports by Jacobs. These reports are almost certainly an understatement of the true incidence of prisoner–staff assaults, since only those assaults resulting in injuries would be likely to be contained in the accident report files. With this qualification in mind, we note only one or two incidents per year between 1966 and 1970 followed by ten in 1971, 20 in 1972, 13 in 1973 and 12 in 1974.[11] Prisoner assaults on staff members showed a similar increase in the New York State Prison System. A total of 110 officers and six civilian personnel were assaulted by prisoners in 1974, an increase of 47% over the 1973 statistics.[12] The officers in the Michigan State Prison System also suffered an increased risk of inmate assault in a two-year study of accident reports and critical incident files. The accident reports, which are more comprehensive than the critical incident files, showed 69 prisoner assaults on correctional personnel during 1972 and 86 assaults in 1973—an increase of 25%. When the accident reports were analyzed in detail, it was found that 17% of the incidents were what we would call unexpected attacks and 83% were what we would call patterned spontaneous attacks, attacks which were "clearly related to incidents of shakedowns, disciplinary tickets, breaking up inmate fights, transferring or transporting inmates from one location to another, etc."[13]

These limited time series data suggest that prisoner violence against staff members is rising in all regions of the nation. The single apparent exception to this trend is found in an unpublished report by Guenther on violence in two federal correctional institutions. Reanalyzing his data, we find that the number of incidents of violence against staff members in the two institutions was approximately the same in 1971–1973 as it had been in 1968–1970. However, these data are somewhat misleading, for, although the number of assaults was constant, the seriousness of the assaults apparently increased greatly, since the percentage of assaults carried out with weapons rose from 17% in 1968–1970 to 39% in 1971–1973.[14]

The studies carried out in North Carolina and Virginia prisons did not compare rates over time, but they are valuable for a different reason. The collected data on prisoner and staff victimization represent the same time frame, permitting a direct comparison between these two forms of prison violence. In Virginia, there were 44 assaults against staff members in four correctional institutions over a period of 32 months, as compared with 586 assaults against prisoners in these institutions. This means that only 7% of the known assaults in these Virginia prisons were carried out against staff members.[15] The percentage of assaults that had staff members as victims in the North Carolina Prison System was similar, constituting ten of 126 incidents recorded during a three-month period in 1975. Approximately 10% of the assaults occurring in the ten institutions studied were carried out against correctional officers. Although Fuller et al. calculate a staff victimization rate that is higher than the prisoner victimization rate, they do so by inflating the staff rate to account for staff time not spent in direct contact with prisoners and deflating the prisoner assault victimization rate by adjusting for victim precipitated assault and by choosing to focus on officially recorded data instead of the prisoner self-report data that they had collected.[16] It seems hardly fair to adjust assaults on prisoners for victim precipitation and to refrain from making a similar adjustment for assaults on staff members. Are we to believe that the behavior of staff members is always perfect, and that they never contribute to their own victimization through unwise or inappropriate treatment of prisoners? Even the unadjusted official report rate of assaults among prisoners is much higher than the prisoner–staff assault rate, and the unadjusted prisoner self-report rate is 17 times as high as the unadjusted official officer rate. It therefore seems appropriate to conclude that in North Carolina, as well as Virginia, the prisoner–officer assault rate is much lower than the prisoner–prisoner assault rate, although both rates are quite high by civilian standards.

WHAT HAPPENS IN A
PRISONER–OFFICER ASSAULT?

Practically any kind of weapon can be used in an assault on a correctional officer. The recorded assaults on prison officers at Stateville in 1974 included being hit with a baseball bat or a pipe, being punched by a prisoner, kicked, smashed with an iron bar, struck with earphones, scratched and knifed.[17] Some prisoners even used their own feces as weapons against correctional officers—the object being more to humiliate them than to injure them.[18] Most maximum security prisons are constructed in tiers that overlook large indoor open spaces, so it is easy for prisoners to throw objects down on officers while they are walking on their rounds. At Stateville, objects such as steel bearings, bed springs and paper clips are thrown or shot with the aid of rubber bands or spring devices at officers during the night shift when the lights are out, and it is impossible for the officers to identify the aggressors.[19] In the most vigorous example of this technique, a prisoner dropped a 60-pound motor from the top tier onto the office enclosure of one cell block. It crashed through the metal roof of the office and struck the officer's desk, barely missing the officer, who would have been severely injured or killed had the motor hit him directly.[20] The dangerousness of cell block work for correctional officers is illustrated by the fact that two-thirds of all fatal assaults on officers in prisons during 1973 occurred in cell blocks.[21]

Reports of recent prison riots indicate the danger of assault and even homicide that occurs during these riots. In a riot at the U.S. Penitentiary in Leavenworth, Kansas in 1973 five officers were injured, one was killed, and four prison employees were taken hostage.[22] When the superintendent of an Alabama institution entered a cell block during a riot to negotiate the release of guards who were being held hostage, the prisoners refused to negotiate and began stabbing the officers in front of him.[23] Seven hostages were taken by rioting prisoners at the Maryland Penitentiary in 1973. The prisoners had a discussion in which they attempted to decide whether to burn, hang or behead one of the officers. They decided to burn him but could not find any lighter fluid and, rejecting the suggestion of one prisoner to behead him, they finally decided to hang him. Just as he was being hanged, another prisoner came and saved him. Two of the officers who were taken hostage were protected by friendly prisoners who secured prison clothing for them and placed them in cells apart from the other prisoners. They were not discovered until the tier was retaken by the officials, who conducted a cell-by-cell search.[24]

The attempt by some prisoners to protect correctional officers during riots is not uncommon. Unfortunately, they are often overruled by the leaders of the riot, who are willing to enforce their opinions with violence directed toward any prisoners who do not accept their leadership. As an example of this, prisoners in an Arizona riot allegedly stabbed one officer to death and then went into the shower to decide what they were going to do with the second officer. They decided to kill him to prevent their identification and then began to beat him to death. Two prisoners attempted to get them stop and were beaten themselves. At this point, almost all of the other prisoners in that section of the cell block participated in beating the officer to death.[25]

The examples go on forever, and the script is almost always the same. In July, 1978, one officer was killed in a Georgia prison riot, and three more were stabbed to death in an Illinois riot.[26] The ten staff members who were taken hostage in a Walla Walla prison riot in May, 1979, were luckier, perhaps because only one of them was a guard. Eight others were counselors and the remaining hostage was a paralegal worker for Institutional Legal Services. The closest that any of the hostages came to suffering any violence occurred when a prisoner held a knife to the throat of the correctional officer. However, the prisoners made clear that they would kill all of the hostages if prison officers attempted to rush the building.[27] In addition to assaults and murders, hostages in prison riots may be subjected to sexual attacks, and they almost always suffer severe psychological trauma. In some cases, officers who were not physically damaged to any great degree were sufficiently traumatized that they were forced to take an early retirement from the prison service for medical reasons.

We will limit our discussion of patterned spontaneous assaults to a few examples. Jacobs relates a patterned spontaneous assault on prison officers that occurred in the Stateville Penitentiary during a baseball game. In this incident, "Two black inmates began to fight on the ball diamond. When the officers came in to break it up, inmates poured out of the stands. They knocked seven guards to the ground, kicked and beat them, and then dispersed."[28]

Here are three other patterned spontaneous incidents abstracted from official records by Guenther. The first occurred at a youth center and the other two incidents were at federal prisons.

Three boys attacked a Supervisor (male). When investigating an unusual gathering of boys in the North Wing at 8:05 a.m. Mr. —— had a blanket thrown over his head, and was struck numerous times. The perpetrators were readily identified.[29]

■ ■ ■

(Prisoner X) began choking an officer, Mr. ——, when he approached the inmate to inquire about his erratic behavior. Prisoner

X, after being subdued by two inmates, admitted taking a "tab" of LSD in the Visiting Room that day.[30]

• • •

(Prisoner Y), under the influence of drugs, inflicted wounds on his left arm and left leg. When an attempt was made to remove him to the hospital, he created a disturbance and had to be subdued with a strait-jacket, handcuffs, and leg irons.

One officer, Mr. ———, was injured.[31]

The officers involved in the patterned spontaneous incidents knew that they were in a dangerous situation, but they had to carry out their assigned duties. In contrast, the officers in unexpected attacks have no warning until the moment that the attack occurs. For example, one captain in the Western Pennsylvania Penitentiary was allegedly beaten to death by four long-term prisoners in the exercise room of the behavior adjustment unit.[32] An officer, on a routine check in the Arizona State Prison, walked into a shower room and was seriously injured by a booby-trap that exploded, breaking his right wrist and causing multiple cuts on his face and chest. A month later, three prisoners stripped five officers at gun point, tied them up and attempted to escape.[33] Once an incident such as these occurs in the penitentiary, it has an immediate effect on the morale of all the other officers. They become much more careful in the performance of their duties, and there is an immediate rise in the absentee rate. Some of the absentees are probably suffering legitimate psychosomatic reactions to the fear of victimization while others have made a conscious decision to minimize the risk to body and mind by staying home until things settle down in the prison.

Physical victimization among staff members is almost never mentioned in prison studies. Mitford reports the case of Dr. Rundle, which contains minor physical victimization as well as elements of psychological and economic victimization. In this case, which occurred at Soledad prison in California, Dr. Rundle was subpoenaed to give evidence in the case of a prisoner who was accused of killing a correctional officer. He described the adjustment center as a miserable, filthy place where prisoners did not get a shower for weeks. He also mentioned tear-gassings and beatings that he had witnessed there. He was called in by the warden as soon as he returned to the prison and told that, although his answers were true and he was under oath, it was inappropriate for him to have made these comments in court. When Rundle refused to turn over the confidential psychiatric file of a prisoner-patient to the warden in a later case, he was cornered and surrounded by approximately 20 prison officers who forcibly seized his briefcase and took the confidential file away from him. They then forced him to the warden's office, at which point he was fired and immediately removed from the prison grounds.[34] It is easy to infer from this episode that the same or even harsher treatment might be meted out to line staff members who offended the warden by exercising their constitutional rights or carrying out their duties according to professional standards. This would be consistent with the observation made by Burns that the methods used on prisoners in correctional institutions are also used to keep line staff well under control.[35]

Administrative victimization of staff members based on official displeasure is probably less common than the victimization that occurs among line staff members. Most of this everyday victimization is psychological in nature. It becomes physical only on those occasions when the keepers of staff norms find it necessary to emphasize heavily their verbal explanations of appropriate behavior to new or otherwise recalcitrant staff members. It is likely that this form of victimization occurs much like the victimization reported by Homans in "Output Restrictions Norms and Social Sanctions." He found that one of the social control devices used among the workers he studied was "binging." Under the norms of the work group, if one of the employees did anything considered to be inappropriate, a fellow worker had the right to "bing" him. This meant that he could be smashed on the upper arm with a blow of considerable force, to which the victim was not allowed to respond. When combined with the use of sarcasm and personal invective, these social control mechanisms were very effective in minimizing the amount of employee deviance from the norms of the employee group, which were in many ways antithetical to the norms of the management.[36] Following this line of reasoning, we would expect that liberal or well-educated prison officers, as well as those who are particularly favorable toward prisoners and treatment programs, would be subjected to psychological and occasionally even physical victimization of the "binging" variety by their fellow staff members.

PSYCHOLOGICAL VICTIMIZATION OF STAFF MEMBERS

Spencer describes the use of derogatory labeling to keep staff members in line in a midwestern women's prison. Staff members who become too close to prisoners are given the derogatory label—"true flunky." It may even be implied that the staff member is homosexually interested in the prisoners she befriends.[37] A report from a men's prison in Texas suggests the same kind of psychological victimization. Officers in this institution were forced to maintain rigid loyalty to the staff's normative code. It was expected that counselors and other treatment personnel would be more proprisoner than officers, so they were permitted to display somewhat more positive attitudes in their dealings with prisoners without suffering negative sanctions. However, if they went too far, they would find out that call tickets that they made out for prisoners were not being answered or that prisoners were coming at incorrect times for appointments because the officers were deliberately harassing them.[38]

If officers are careful to maintain an adequate degree of conformity to staff behavior norms, they will probably not suffer any kind of victimization by fellow staff members. This could never be said with regard to prisoner–staff psychological victimization, for there is nothing an officer can do to avoid this except to have no contact with prisoners at all. Rothbart collected data on prisoner protests to explain why this is so. He found in his fieldwork that protesting prisoners tried to give as much verbal abuse as possible to officers without going so far as to bring negative consequences on themselves. He uncovered a war of nerves in which the prisoners were constantly gaming the officers and at the same time staying on the right side of the invisible boundary at which official sanctions could be taken against them.[39]

The confrontiveness described by Rothbart is not practiced equally by all ethnic groups in prison. Carroll argues that confrontiveness is used by aggressive minority groups whereas censoriousness is more characteristic of white prisoners. In censoriousness, the prisoner claims that what an officer has done is inappropriate in terms of institutional regulations rather than threatening the officer with bodily harm or verbal insults. Confrontiveness has an even greater impact when it is supported by organized gangs or groups of prisoners.[40] For example, an officer at Stateville explained that a gang member who had been ordered to go along with the officer could respond by saying, "Fuck you Jack, I'm not going," and then a group of gang members would surround the officer and the aggressor.[41] Few officers would stand up to a group of gang members in a situation such as this. Most would call for reenforcements or allow the incident to pass if a face-saving mechanism could be found. An officer who was interviewed by Carroll expressed his feelings about this sort of confrontiveness.

> "It's a frightening effect. Here you are all alone surrounded by ten or fifteen blacks and it's your problem, you know. Good luck! What are they gonna do to me? Or they gonna drive me into the ground? Or is one gonna come at me with a razor blade and slash my throat? Or are they gonna beat the shit outta me? Believe me, all this is possible. . . . Well whenever possible, I don't book 'em.[42]

While confrontiveness apparently allows minority group members to avoid infraction reports in some institutions, the same confrontiveness may produce a higher number of infraction reports at other institutions where staff members feel they are still in control of the situation. Black prisoners in one state prison rated themselves as being no more aggressive than white prisoners, and yet they were rated by correctional officers as being more aggressive, receiving substantially more infraction reports than the white prisoners. The researchers in this study concluded that the largely white prison officers were discriminating against the black prisoners, but an alternative explanation of their results is that the reason the more subjective infractions, such as disobeying a direct order and verbal aggression, were disproportionately written on black prisoners is that the prisoners engaged in much higher levels of confrontive behavior toward correctional officers than their white colleagues. If this is true, than we can conceptualize the higher rate of subjective tags as an appropriate institutional response rather than as racial victimization. It is interesting that there were few racial differences in disciplinary infraction tickets written for offenses such as escape or attempted escape, sexual offenses and theft.[43]

It is not clear whether the censoriousness/confrontiveness racial difference in male prisoner tactics is replicated in female correctional institutions. A considerable amount of confrontiveness occurs and is carried out by "bullies" at Occoquan[44] and "hostile bitches" at the Indiana Women's Prison.[45] "Loud talking" was also used against staff members at the women's prison, studied by Spencer, along with lying, remarking on the officers' faults, applying negative labels to them and blackmailing them.[46] It is possible that these three studies were carried out in institutions and at times when the racial difference in the psychological victimization of officers had not yet developed.

There are two classic accounts of prisoner–staff psychological victimization in the literature in which the authors go beyond the description of individual incidents to form interpretive typologies. The most recent of these typologies was developed by Bartollas et al. in their study of a juvenile institution. New staff members at this institution were particularly vulnerable to psychological games. In one game, the prisoner would physically threaten the staff member by saying that he would "get his" after the boy was released or escaped. The prisoner then would begin to cultivate the friendship of the threatened staff member, who was confused but gratified at the same time, and who tended to react by giving the offender excessive privileges. In another example of psychological victimization, threatening inmates intimidated female staff members by staring at them in ways that suggested they desired them sexually. They would concentrate on their breasts, hips and legs, finally making them so uncomfortable that their job performance was affected.[47] In these and other forms of psychological victimization, prisoners were the winners in that they gained greater freedom to break the rules, increased their material level of living, and expressed their belligerence toward staff members without receiving any negative sanctions for their behavior.

The other typological treatment of psychological victimization in correctional institutions is more theoretical than descriptive. It was first stated by Sykes in his article, "The Corruption of Authority and Rehabilitation,"[48] where he described three forms of psychological victimization in male maximum security prisons: corruption through friendship, corruption through reciprocity and corruption through default. In corruption through friendship, the prisoner takes particular pains to be nice to an officer whose need for human kindness makes him vulnerable to the technique. Once they are good enough friends, the prisoner asks for illegitimate favors, and the officer feels obligated to provide these favors to avoid losing a friend. Corruption through reciprocity occurs when prisoners do favors for officers and then ask for favors in return. Since the officer is generally evaluated in terms of how orderly his area is kept, the prisoners can make or break his reputation according to whether they cooperate or make trouble. The officer is forced to dispense illegitimate favors to coerce prison leaders to help him control his area of responsibility. The job of the correctional officer is tedious and repetitive. When an officer makes mistakes in a prisoner count, an entire institution could be held up for hours until the count is corrected. Counts are made over and over again, day in and day out. Searches of cells and all kinds of minor secretarial tasks are also part of the daily routine. When an officer has a prisoner for a secretary, there is much appeal in allowing the secretary to take over some of these mundane tasks. In return for this, of course, there will be favors given under the principle of reciprocity.

Corruption through default is often mixed up with corruption by reciprocity. It occurs because the officer who permits a prisoner to do part of his work eventually loses the authority he has over that area of work. The prisoner secretary becomes the authority on that task and uses that authority to gain favors for himself from other prisoners. Once authority has been given up in this fashion by correctional officers, it is very difficult to regain it. Prisons tend to operate on custom rather than law, which gives a considerable degree of legitimacy to the continuation of patterns in which prisoners perform certain tasks that are officially to be done by staff members.

Through these three methods of corruption, the authoritarian power of prison officers is gradually whittled away. They constitute psychological victimization in that many prisoners consciously use these tactics to manipulate officers to gain illegal ends. The psychological victimization shades off into economic victimization in that officers may be fired from their jobs as a result of some of these manipulations, especially if they do not cooperate with the prisoners.

OTHER FORMS OF STAFF VICTIMIZATION

The evidence on the social and economic victimization of staff members is extremely limited. There is some indication of social victimization among staff members that occurs when racial minority correctional officers are subtly discriminated against or mistreated by their white supervisors. For example, a report on the Stateville and Joliet prisons in Illinois suggested that administrators were quicker to fire black employees than white employees for the same offenses and that negative staff attitudes toward black prisoners were carried over to black employees.[49] There is also evidence of racial discrimination in the hiring and promotion of black correctional officers in the south.[50] However, correctional administrators in a number of states have made special efforts to hire minority staff members and to provide them with the kinds of working conditions that will motivate them to continue their employment in prison service over an extended period of time. It may be that there is more discrimination within the unions that represent correctional officers than on the part of correctional administrators. It is difficult to separate the normal aloofness, with which seasoned officers greet new recruits, from racial discrimination.[51] Since there is a paucity of evidence on the matter, there is nothing else to be said about it.

I have already mentioned that the psychological victimization of staff members by prisoners can turn into economic victimization when they engineer enough upsets in an officer's working area so that he or she is suspended or terminated. Explaining how prisoners in a women's institution can control the termination of correctional officers, Dimick says that, "Ten or twenty complaints about a guard would bring an inquiry, ten more a dismissal. Maude (the leader of the prisoners) could arrange that in a matter of minutes."[52] An alternative form of prisoner–staff economic victimization at the Indiana Women's Prison is blackmail against staff members who have been seduced into homosexual relationships with prisoners.[53] Jacobs and Retsky describe a more subtle way of getting at an officer's job.

> [The prisoners] may attempt to elude the counting officer by hiding in their cell or shuffling back and forth if the count is taken while the inmates are in line entering the cell house. In either case, the delay and disruption of the prison routine will be attributed to the guard who is responsible, and he will earn both formal censure and informal derision from his colleagues.[54]

In the women's facility at Occoquan, many officers were "held in line" by prisoners who did no more than threaten to report these officers for actions they had taken that were in violation of administrative regulations.[55] There are so many conflicting regulations in almost all correctional institutions that it is a rare officer who can avoid being put in this sort of position.

The technique of having an officer terminated by generating artificial complaints can also be used by fellow officers who are displeased with the attitude or behavior of a colleague. Conley recounts the story of an officer who watched three other officers assault a prisoner and then fired a shot over the prisoner's head when he grasped a rock with intent to defend himself. The three officers were incensed at their colleague for not having shot to kill and immediately began to agitate against him. Within three months they had accumulated sufficient complaints so that the offending officer was terminated.[56]

Even more severe victimization can occur when an officer offends administrators as well as other officers. In several cases described in detail by Murton, correctional officers suffered grievously because of their unwillingness to ignore the brutalization of prisoners. One of the officers was told by the institution's superintendent that he would beat him up and that he would probably would not get home alive. His offense was that he had dared to submit a confidential report on brutality to a state representative. The victim in this incident was immediately suspended, terminated two days later, and shortly after that was arrested, handcuffed and placed in jail. He was not permitted to post bail at first, and then finally released on bail after four days. He was charged with four counts of a felony (defaming public officials) as his reward for having exposed officer brutality. Although the charges were eventually dismissed, he was never reinstated in the state correctional service.[57] Stories such as this one are as unusual as they are outrageous. Prisoners have many defenders who are quick to publicize any hint of brutality, but there is no similar cadre of supporters for the victimized correctional officer. If we take a total institutions approach to victimization phenomena,[58] we can expect to find much more than is currently documented in the literature.

CAUSES OF PRISONER VICTIMIZATION OF
STAFF MEMBERS

Most treatments of prison violence talk about general causes and do not separate out the causes of violence against officers from violence among prisoners. The most general factor in these discussions is usually what is characteristic of prisons as total institutions. More specific attention has been given to the causes of prison violence in riots. The American Correctional Association has taken a leading role in gathering together understandings of the causes of prison riots. In the report, *Causes, Preventive Measures, and Methods of Controlling Riots and Disturbances in Correctional Institutions*, the ACA summarized the literature into two general causes, five institution-related causes and five noninstitution-related causes of prison riots. The general causes were the

unnatural institutional environment and the antisocial characteristics of the inmates. Institution-related causes were inept management, inadequate personnel practices, inadequate facilities,
insufficient constructive and meaningful activity, and insufficient
legitimate rewards. Those causes that were unrelated to the
institution were basic social attitudes, unrest in a larger community, inadequate finances, lack of meaningful rewards, and
inequities and complexities in the criminal justice system.[59]

In a more recent study of the causes of prison riots, Wilsnack
and Ohlin examined riots in all of the major state penal institutions plus the District of Columbia between January 1971 and
June 1972. During this 18-month period, there was no specific
factor that was always followed by a prison disturbance. At the
same time, there were a number of differences between those
prisons that experienced riots and those prisons that experienced
nonriot forms of resistance to authority. Both rioting and nonriot
resistance were more likely to occur in maximum security facilities
in which inmates were overcrowded and idle than in other
prisons. It appears that stress and deprivation in the lives of the
prisoners promote the occurrence of collective violence. Procedures for tightening up security, which are potentially depriving
for inmates, and the instituting of liberalizing reforms did not
have a clear relationship to rioting or to nonriot resistance. When
disorganization and conflict occur in the prisoner population and
in the prison administration, this may lead to a riot. Social
disorganization among prisoners is indexed by variables such as
assaults among prisoners, assaults by inmates on staff members,
and heterogeneity among prisoners in terms of age, offense and
criminal career. Another factor in the occurrence of riots is that
prison problems are often given considerable attention in the
popular press. All the riots studied by Ohlin and Wilsack were
preceded by actions of both legislators and citizen groups to
influence the operation of the prison.[60]

Individual violence directed at correctional officers by prisoners
may be a function of the participation of those prisoners in
informal prisoner groups. I have already noted Carroll's finding
that white prisoners used censoriousness to attempt to force staff
members to live by their own particular rules, while black
prisoners used direct confrontation tactics. Blacks were able to do
this because they had a higher degree of social organization in
their ethnic group. Whites, on the other hand, had very weak

social organization and so did not have enough group support to put any direct aggressive pressure on staff members.[61] What is known about the relationship between rising violence against prison officers in California and Illinois and the rise of gangs in those prison systems is also consistent with this thesis.

There is one other study that deals with the causes of violence against staff members in a roundabout way. Bidna (1975) studied the effects of increased security procedures in the California Prison System on a variety of measures of prisoner violence, one of which was the rate of assaults by prisoners on staff members. Assaults by prisoners on staff members declined after the new security procedures were introduced. Stabbings in general by prisoner gang members as a matter of gang policy seemed to decrease substantially while stabbings performed by individuals for individual reasons increased. This particular finding of the study was not broken down as to whether the stabbings were of prisoners or staff members.[62] Because the decline in total prisoner assaults on staff members was not large enough to be statistically significant, we cannot formally say that tightened security procedures produced a significantly lower rate of prisoner–staff assaults. However, it may be that statistical significance would have been achieved had the study covered a longer period of time, or else that California did not utilize the most effective security procedures. The long-term results of the California experiment could turn out to be either better or worse than is indicated by Bidna's results.

SOME EFFECTS OF PRISONER–STAFF VICTIMIZATION

Correctional officers are unlikely to commit suicide as a result of victimization by prisoners. In this respect, they are very different from the self-destructive prisoners, discussed earlier. They are more likely to experience personal stress over a long period of years, which probably results in a number of medical illnesses. There has been no American study to date that examines this area, although the subject has been broached with respect to police officers.[63] In a study of Illinois correctional officers, 89% of the subjects agreed with the statement, "Inmates try to take advantage of officers whenever they can," and just under 40% felt that the job of the correctional officer was extremely dangerous. Very few officers believed that their jobs were not danger-ous.[64]

Cedric G. Bullard in Australia provides some evidence on this topic in an unpublished doctoral dissertation. He combines self-theory and role-theory with particular emphasis on role conflict in an analysis of the linkage between physiological and psychological activities and work stress. Maximum security prisons have higher sickness absence rates than minimum security prisons, which indicates that they inflict a higher level of stress on the officers who work there. Variations in sickness rates by officers in the United States would probably be an excellent index of the degree of psychological victimization of officers by prisoners in American correctional institutions.[65]

NOTES

1. Rebecca Leonard, "Communication in the Total Institution: An Investigation of Prisoner–Guard Interaction in a State Penitentiary," Ph.D. dissertation, Purdue University, 1976.
2. Hans Mattick, The prosaic sources of prison violence, in Jackwell Susman (Ed.), *Crime and Justice, 1971–1972* (New York: A.M.S. Press, 1974), pp. 179–187.
3. Dogan D. Akman, Homicides and assaults in Canadian penitentiaries, *Canadian Journal of Corrections* 8 (1966): 284–299.
4. Thorsten Sellin, Prison homicides, in Thorsten Sellin (Ed.), *Capital Punishment* (New York: Harper and Row, 1967), pp. 154–160.
5. Thorsten Sellin, Homicides and assaults in American prisons, 1964, *Acta Criminologica Medicalis Legalis Japonica* 31 (1965): 139–143.
6. J. E. Thomas, Killed on duty, an analysis of murders of English prison service staff since 1850, *Prison Service Journal* 7 (1972): 9–10.
7. Peter Buffum, Homicides in Pennsylvania prisons, 1964–1973: A preliminary research note, in *Report of the Governor's Study Commission on Capital Punishment* (Harrisburg: Commonwealth of Pennsylvania, 1973), pp. 111–114.
8. Sawyer F. Sylvester, John H. Reed and David O. Nelson, *Prison Homicide* (New York: Wiley, 1977).
9. Sellin (1965).
10. James W. L. Park, The organization of prison violence, in Albert K. Cohen, George F. Cole and Robert G. Bailey (Eds.), *Prison Violence* (Lexington, MA: D.C. Heath, 1976), pp, 89–96.
11. James B. Jacobs, *Stateville: The Penitentiary in Mass Society* (Chicago: University of Chicago Press, 1977).
12. Agenor L. Castro, Violence in the urban prison, in Vernon Fox (Ed.), *Proceedings, 20th Annual Southern Conference on Corrections* (Tallahassee: Division of Continuing Education, Florida State University, 1975), pp, 8–21.
13. Michigan Department of Corrections Program Bureau, "Analysis of Inmate Assaults on Officers, 1972–1973," Lansing, MI, 1974, p. 1.

14. Anthony L. Guenther, "Violence in Correctional Institutions: A Study of Assaults," unpublished paper, College of William and Mary, 1974.
15. Linda Grasewicz, *A Study of Inmate Assaults in Major Institutions* (Richmond: Virginia Department of Corrections, 1977).
16. Dan A. Fuller, Thomas Orsagh, and David Raber, "Violence and Victimization Within the North Carolina Prison System," paper presented at the annual meeting of the Academy of Criminal Justice Sciences, 1977.
17. Jacobs (1977), p. 243.
18. Hans Toch, *Police, Prisons, and the Problem of Violence* (Washington, DC: Government Printing Office, 1977).
19. James B. Jacobs and Harold G. Retsky, Prison guards, *Urban Life* 4 (1975): 5–27.
20. Anthony L. Guenther and Mary Q. Guenther, Screws vs. thugs, *Society* 11 (July–August 1974): 42–50.
21. Wendy P. Wolfson, "The Patterns of Prison Homicide," Ph.D. dissertation, University of Pennsylvania, 1978.
22. Leavenworth riot leaves one guard dead, five injured, *The Freeworld Times* 2 (August–September 1973): 7.
23. Obituaries, *The Freeworld Times* 3 (January–February 1974): 7.
24. Maryland inmates hang two guards, *The Freeworld Times* 2 (April 1973): 1, 3.
25. Arizona murders remain unsolved, *The Freeworld Times* 2 (August–September, 1973): 14, 20.
26. Riots in Georgia and Illinois leave four guards, two inmates dead, *Corrections Digest* 9 (July 28, 1978): 7–8.
27. Michael Prager, Prison ordeal ends peacefully, *Walla Walla Union-Bulletin* (May 10, 1979).
28. Jacobs (1977), p. 163.
29. Guenther (1974), p. 37.
30. Ibid., p. 46.
31. Ibid., p. 51.
32. Obituaries, *The Freeworld Times* 3 (January–February 1974), p. 7.
33. Unrest continues in Arizona prison, *The Freeworld Times* 1 (September–October, 1972): 2.
34. Jessica Mitford, *Kind and Usual Punishment* (New York: Random House, 1971), pp. 115–118.
35. Henry Burns, Jr., A miniature totalitarian state: Maximum security prison, *Canadian Journal of Corrections* 11 (July 1969): 153–164.
36. George C. Homans, Output restrictions, norms and social sanctions, in William A. Rushing (Ed.), *Deviant Behavior and Social Process,* 2nd ed. (Chicago: Rand McNally, 1975), pp. 10–15.
37. Elouise J. Spencer, "The Social System of a Medium Security Women's Prison," Ph.D. dissertation, University of Kansas, 1977, p. 153.
38. G. L. Webb and David G. Morris, *Prison Guards: The Culture and Perspective of an Occupational Group* (San Marcos, TX: Coker Books, 1978).
39. George S. Rothbart, "Social Conflict in Prison Organization," Ph.D. dissertation, University of Washington, 1964.
40. Leo Carroll, "Race and Three Forms of Prisoner Power: Confrontation, Censoriousness, and the Corruption of Authority," paper given at the annual meeting of the American Society of Criminology, 1976.

41. Jacobs, p. 161.
42. Leo Carroll, *Hacks, Blacks, and Cons* (Lexington, MA: D. C. Heath, 1974), p. 136.
43. Barbara S. Held, David Levine and Virginia D. Swartz, Interpersonal aspects of dangerousness, *Criminal Justice and Behavior* 6 (1979): 49–58.
44. Esther Heffernan, *Making It in Prison: The Square, the Cool, and the Life* (New York: Wiley, 1972).
45. Kenneth Dimick, *Ladies in Waiting Behind Prison Walls* (Muncie, IN: Accelerated Development, 1979).
46. Spencer (1977).
47. Clemens Bartollas, Stuart J. Miller and Simon Dinitz, *Juvenile Victimization: The Institutional Paradox* (New York: Wiley, 1976).
48. Gresham M. Sykes, The corruption of authority and rehabilitation, *Social Forces* 34 (1956): 257–262.
49. Stateville and Joliet racist, understaffed, inhumane, unclean, according to in-house report, *Corrections Digest* 9 (May 5, 1978): 6.
50. Ronald Goldfarb, *Jails, The Ultimate Ghetto of the Criminal Justice System* (Garden City, NY, Doubleday, 1976), pp. 404–405.
51. Jacobs and Retsky (1975).
52. Dimick (1979), p. 84.
53. Ibid., p. 90.
54. Jacobs and Retsky (1975), p. 15.
55. Heffernan (1972), p. 182.
56. John A. Conley, "A History of the Oklahoma Penal System, 1907–1967," Ph.D. dissertation, Michigan State University, 1977, p. 239.
57. Thomas Murton, *The Dilemma of Prison Reform* (New York: Holt, Rinehart and Winston, 1976), pp. 66–69.
58. For summary of the total institutions approach to correctional institutions, see Lee H. Bowker, *Prisoner Subcultures* (Lexington, MA: D. C. Heath, 1977), pp. 23–25, 39–41, 60, 61.
59. American Correctional Association, *Causes, Preventive Measures, and Methods of Controlling Riots and Disturbances in Correctional Institutions* (Washington, DC: American Correctional Association, 1970).
60. Reported in Richard W. Wilsnack, Explaining collective violence in prisons: Problems and possibilities, in Albert K. Cohen, George F. Cole and Robert G. Bailey (Eds.), *Prison Violence* (Lexington, MA: D. C. Heath, 1976) pp. 61–78.
61. Carroll (1976).
62. Howard Bidna, Effects of increased security on prison violence, *Journal of Criminal Justice* 3 (1975): 33–46.
63. In fall 1978, the International Law Enforcement Stress Association began publication of the quarterly journal, *Police Stress.*
64. James B. Jacobs and Lawrence J. Kraft, Integrating the keepers: A comparison of black and white guards in Illinois, *Social Problem* 25 (1978): 304–318.
65. Cedric G. Bullard, "A Psychological Study of Prison Officers in New South Wales: A Stressful Occupation," Ph.D. dissertation, University of New South Wales, 1977.

The Place of Officially Sanctioned Victimization in a Nation Under God

 In Chapters 1 through 8, I have presented data that documented the extent and nature of the victimization of prisoners and staff members in correctional institutions for men, women and juveniles. With this foundation, I will now consider the causes, responsibilities, and solutions that are associated with prison victimization.

A PRELIMINARY TAXONOMY OF THE CAUSES OF PRISON VICTIMIZATION

It is difficult to survey the causes of prison victimization without producing a list of prison problems that is too general to be efficiently applied in any effort to reduce prison victimization.[1] It is true that practically all of the myriad problems that plague America's prisons are connected in some way to prison victimization, but limitations in human energy make certain that if we diffuse the causes of prison victimization too widely, we will create the impression that is is impossible to do anything to diminish the rate of prison victimization without completely redesigning our correctional system. In the preliminary taxonomy of causes that follows, we have listed only selected high points in the causal complex that undergirds prison victimization, and we have organized those causes into six general categories: general importation, individual background, subcultural institutional, situational, structural institutional and general policy.

General Importation Causes

General importation causes are broad factors contributing to prisoner victimization that are brought into the prison by prisoners and staff members from the free world. They represent certain general cultural conditions that are present in American society and, as such, cannot be greatly changed by any effort aimed primarily at reducing prison victimization. The four examples of general importation causes included here are the subculture of violence, gender-role definitions, racism and fears associated with homosexuality.

The Subculture of Violence. The thesis of the subculture of violence as originally developed by Wolfgang and Ferracuti refers to subcultural norms, values and beliefs that favor the use of overt criminal violence. The subculture is located in the lower class, and its value system "views violence as tolerable, expected, or required."[2] There is no question about the accuracy of the Wolfgang–Ferracuti characterization of the subculture of violence. However, claiming that norms, values and beliefs favoring violence exist only in the lower class obscures the more general American tendency toward violence that is revealed in our devotion to excessively violent sport spectacles reminiscent of the performances of the Roman gladiators, the widespread holding of proviolence opinions by American males,[3] and the overall rates of national violence that are far beyond the levels experienced in most of the nations of the world.[4] Importing many of the most violent American citizens into correctional institutions virtually assures that only the most stringent preventive efforts on the part of staff members could minimize violence rates in these institutions.

Gender-Role Definitions. Americans seem to experience significant difficulties in the area of gender-role identification. The culturally accepted mechanism for dealing with gender-role insecurities is to forge discrete rather than continuous and overlapping gender roles. That is to say, men must define their masculinity in ways that permit no overlap with the definition of feminity. In practice, this requirement leads to exaggerated masculine behavior in general and violence in particular. The more insecure the individual male, the greater the pressure toward exaggerated masculine behavior as sort of a cultural reaction formation against fears of femininity. Men from the lower classes, which supply the largest part of prison residents, are subject to extremely high levels of masculinity threats and tend to react to this problem with similarly high levels of exaggerated masculine behavior and violence, consistent with the theory of the subculture of violence. This general gender-role problem is the primary factor in the difference in physical victimization rates between male and female correctional institutions.

Racism. I have already discussed racism in considerably detail at several points, and I will not repeat these discussions here. Suffice it to say that the general racism that is present in the free society is imported into the institution, concentrated there, and exacerbated by the "pressure cooker atmosphere" of prison life. The changes in race relations that have occurred in American society since 1950 hold out hope that racism will not always be a major causal factor in prison victimization, but it is likely to continue to be so for several decades to come.

Fears Associated with Homosexuality. It follows from our foregoing discussion that anything that threatens the gender-role identification of prisoners or staff members will be sharply suppressed. A special case of this general process is the reaction that greets homosexual behavior or fantasized homosexual behavior by prisoners. Although homosexuality is quite common in correctional institutions, its implications for gender-role identification are sufficient to limit many prisoners to a sexless or masturbatory life. Homosexual fears relate to prison victimization in that they supercharge not only sexual aggression but also sexual seduction and the reaction to both of these classes of events by staff members. The reaction to homosexual overtures and pressures was so strong in the institutions studied by Lockwood that violence committed by victims in self-defense was even greater than violence perpetrated by sexual aggressors.[5] Staff members who have dysfunctionally high levels of homosexuality fears may also contribute to sex-related violence when they are too quick to separate alleged homosexual lovers, thus contributing to the formation of lovers' triangles and to the violence that decomposes the triangles into dyads.[6]

Individual Background

In addition to the general cultural variables that are imported into the prison with prisoners and staff members, there are specific imported background variables that impact prison victimization. Four examples of this class of causes of prison victimization are presented in this section: age, preinstitutional violence, drug culture participation and previous prison experience. As with other importation variables, the correctional system cannot control the mix of importation variables that occurs in residential institutions, except to the extent made possible by classifying certain types of inmates into separate institutions.

Age. Younger offenders are overrepresented among both aggressors and victims in prison victimizing incidents. The average age of incarcerated men and women has lowered for many years, with the result that the median age category of American prisoners is now age 20 to 24. Not much more than a third of the prisoners have completed their third decade of life, and a great many of them have not yet completed their second decade.[7] The decline in the average age of American prisoners is a major reason for the increase in prison violence rates.

Criminal Careers. Not too long ago, the majority of adults incarcerated in maximum security facilities had never committed a violent offense in their entire criminal careers. This is no longer true. The diversion of many property offenders to less severe punishments than incarceration has left most correctional institutions with a heavy concentration of prisoners who have preinstitutional records, including felonious violence. By 1974, 52% of all offenders in state prisons had been convicted of one of five violent crimes: sexual assault, robbery, assault, homicide and kidnapping.[8] That percentage is almost certainly higher now. People who have committed crimes such as these on the streets are unlikely to feel greatly deterred from committing them in a correctional institution where the likelihood of punishment is known to be slight. If the commission of street violence was as part of a delinquent gang that has a branch within the correctional institution, then it is even more likely to be repeated within the institution.

Drug Culture Participation. The traditional use of "pruno" (homemade alcoholic beverages) in correctional institutions has been completely outdistanced by the flood of powerful stimulants, depressants and hallucinogens that has permeated correctional institutions in the past decade. While it is true that objective evidence on the matter is in short supply, there is unanimous opinion by correctional administrators, line staff and prisoners that drug subculture participation is associated with high levels of institutional violence. Some violent incidents are directly stimulated by the use of violence-encouraging drugs such as speed. Other drug-related prison violence occurs as a result of irregularities in the economic and political transactions that surround the flow of drugs into the institution and from prisoner to prisoner within the institution. Since there is some evidence that custody-oriented institutions have higher drug use rates than treatment-oriented institutions,[9] it is likely that maximum security correctional institutions have higher drug-related violence rates than other institutions.

Previous Experience in Correctional Institutions. There is an inverse relationship between institutional experience and the likelihood of prison victimization that holds for staff members as well as prisoners. "Fish" are always fair game in correctional institutions, and the mixing of these inexperienced prisoners with prisoners who have already spent a number of years behind bars, perhaps on a number of separate commitments, heightens the junglelike quality of prison life. The level of victimization, particularly psychological victimization, suffered by rookie correctional officers is so high that its expectation has been institutionalized in the correctional officer subculture.[10]

In practice, it is difficult to separate different background variables because they are invariably intertwined. Prisoners who have preinstitutional violence on their records tend to have had previous periods of incarceration and so forth. Of one thing there can be no doubt, when such prisoners are introduced into a correctional institution as they were into Albany in England, there will be a rapid increase in the prison victimization rate.[11]

Subcultural Institutional Factors

This group of causal factors influencing prison victimization consists of subcultural phenomena arising among both staff and prisoners. Subcultures have the same characteristics as cultures except that they are different from the dominant cultures in the content of their norms, values, beliefs and material artifacts. Correctional institutions are dominated by their prisoner subcultures, and are also strongly influenced by subcultures that develop among staff members. Victimization phenomena in correctional institutions are greatly influenced by these subcultures, and it follows that modifications in correctional subcultures could be a strategic way of reducing prison victimization.

The Struggle for Political Dominance. The individual struggle for political dominance in the prisoner subculture has been replaced by battles among organized groups of prisoners. Prison life is now characterized by much of the same power-block confrontation that exists in national politics. This phenomenon is most fully developed in urban states where street gangs have powerful branches in each state prison. Once the dominance of a prison has been solidified by a gang or gangs, expressive violence will decrease and instrumental violence in the service of rational gang goals will increase. The overall prisoner victimization rate may not greatly increase except during the period when the gangs are struggling to achieve dominance. When that dominance has become unchallengeable, the total victimization rate can be expected to decrease somewhat, and the composition of prison victimization can be expected to be modified so that there is a regular round of economic victimization—reinforced by psychological victimization and physical victimization when necessary. At the same time, the amount of individually oriented victimization will decrease and the patterning and predictibility of victimization will increase.

Victimization in the Sub Rosa Economic System. The larger the sub rosa economic system in the prisoner subculture, the greater the extent of prisoner victimization—all other things being equal. In addition to outright frauds and other intentional victimizations that occur in the sub rosa economic system, there are also a great many victimizations that occur because of misunderstandings in the informal market system. These misunderstandings are much more common in a sub rosa economy than in a legitimate economy because there is no force of law to standardize exchange principles and to enforce appropriate sanctions for noncompliance with the rules of the system. Since sub rosa economic systems expand in an inverse relationship with the level of material items permitted under the legitimate economic system of the prison, we may state that those prisons that are the most physically depriving will have the highest victimization rates—all other things being equal. Most significant among those elements that are not equal between institutions is the level of security enforcement. Institutions that impose extremely strict security rules can succeed in depressing the flow of sub rosa economic goods to some degree, thus weakening the relationship between deprivation and victimization.

Prisoner Militancy. The recent increase in prisoner militancy has been documented by a number of observers.[12] This militancy impacts prison victimization, particularly the victimization of correctional officers by prisoners, both directly and indirectly. In some cases, militant groups and individuals demand that specific officers be victimized, but it is much more common for the generally confrontive attitudes produced by prisoner militancy to set off victimizing incidents that were not planned ahead of time or specifically directed toward named targets. Prisoner militancy also has an importation element in that it has been greatly influenced by the civil rights movement, black militant groups such as the Black Muslims, and the more recent radical activities of underground groups such as the Weathermen. Institutionalized radicals, who have had a variety of militant experiences on the streets, spread their radical attitudes to less militant prisoners, motivating them to adopt an increasingly militant stance in their conflicts with correctional officials and officers. The interesting thing about this process is that even the prisoners who were militant in the free society become more militant the longer they are incarcerated.[13] This dynamic suggests that prisons in which militancy achieves a foothold will tend to suffer a long-term spiraling increase of prisoner–staff victimization.

Victimization Arising from Staff Subcultures. We have described the role of staff subcultures in prison victimization earlier, following the insights contributed to the field by Bartollas et al., who are the only investigators to have devoted any significant amount of time to the relationship between staff subcultures and prisoner victimization.[14] It appears that staff subcultures encourage the victimization of prisoners (and often other staff members) in custody-oriented prisons more than in treatment-oriented prisons. We know little more than this about the distribution of the victimizing aspects of staff subcultures in American correctional systems. Like prisoner subcultures, staff subcultures can control victimization as well as promote it. It is encouraging that the staff subculture in the juvenile reformatory described by Bartollas, et al. inhibited certain severe forms of staff–prisoner victimization at the same time that it encouraged other less-vicious victimizing acts.

Situational Variables

Only with the rise of the study of the victimology of violent crimes in the past decade have we begun to understand the interaction between situational variables and victimization phenomena in the free society. Scientists who variously refer to themselves as social psychologists, psychologists, anthropologists, phenomenologists, microsociologists, symbolic interactionists and ethnomethodologists have the analytic tools to understand the interaction, but have rarely had any interest in the subject. In prison studies, the works of Toch,[15] Lockwood[16] and Johnson[17] that I have drawn so heavily upon in earlier chapters are the only concentration of knowledge on situational variables in victimization incidents, and even they do not try to fully explicate this subject. Toch and Johnson are interested in self-destructive prisoner breakdowns and treat victimization phenomena only in passing. Lockwood's research is limited to sexual assault and is thus too specialized to offer a general understanding of victimization processes in correctional institutions. Future research should be designed to reveal exactly how victimizing encounters develop, how they are defined by victims and aggressors, and the number and nature of the stages they go through. Particular attention should be given to the decision-points in the process at which the victimization might have been avoided by an action of one of the participants or an intervention by staff or prisoner observers. The methodological essays contained in Lockwood[18] and Carroll[19] provide excellent guidance as to how these studies might be carried out.

Structural Institutional Factors

The abovementioned factors in our preliminary taxonomy of the causes of prison victimization approach the victimization incident from the side of the actors in the incident, starting with general importation variables and then moving to individual background factors and finally to variables residing in institutional subcultures. Beginning with the next paragraph (below), we move away from the incident itself in the other direction, beginning with structural institutional factors and then moving on to elements of general policy. Structural institutional factors are those that originate in the organization of the prison—its administrative apparatus, architecture and so forth.

Undertrained, Mistrained and Undereducated Correctional Officers. Most correctional officers are insufficiently trained to perform their assigned duties and the human needs-related tasks that are inherent in these duties even if they are not expressly stated in job descriptions. Not all states have correctional academies, and many of the local training programs require little more than a memorization of the rule book. Mistraining occurs when there is a considerable amount of time and energy devoted to training new officers but that training includes little material on how to deal with the human dimension of relations with prisoners, how to protect prisoners from victimization by each other, and how to protect oneself from victimization by prisoners. Training sessions may dwell at length on mechanical requirements and devote only a few minutes to prisoner–staff victimization—with no time at all to prisoner–prisoner victimization. Finally, most correctional officers are undereducated in that they have no more than a high school education, which hardly prepares them for the delicate interpersonal negotiations and diagnostic assessments that they must made to carry out their duties adequately on a day-to-day basis. Many police departments, having suffered from similar deficiencies over the years, have instituted extensive training programs for new recruits and also require that these recruits have completed a four-year college education. It is hoped that similar moves will be made by correctional institutions in the future, and this will eliminate the lack of proper training as a significant cause of prisoner victimization.

Inadequate Architecture and Ecology. As Flynn has pointed out, many of the physical environments that have been perpetuated in correctional institutions are antithetical to the goals of correction and resocialization.[20] It is similarly true that physical correctional environments are usually inadequate to protect prisoners and staff members against the dangers of victimization. At least 95% of all correctional facilities currently in use were constructed before there was any awareness of the nature and extent of prison victimization. Even today, protection from victimization does not have a very high priority in the work of architects who design correctional facilities. We are still building prisons that contain blind spots in which victimization can occur outside of the view of staff members and which do not have adequate facilities for the maintenance of security between industrial areas in which weapons are manufactured and the prisoners' living areas. There is concern with line of sight as it relates to prison disturbances or escapes, but much less concern about line of sight with respect to incidents of individual victimization. If we plot the occurrences of victimization in a prison, we will find that they are heavily concentrated in those areas that are least conducive to proper supervision. Eliminating or modifying such areas would almost certainly reduce the total incidence of prison victimization.

Administrators who are burdened with the leadership of architecturally outmoded prison structures are unlikely to obtain funding for major architectural modifications. Instead, they must limit their activities to first studying the ecology of victimization within their institution and then making minor changes in the facility. For example, certain dead ends and blind spots in corridors and rooms should be sealed off. Covers may need to be removed from outdoor walkways so that tower officers can have an unobstructed view of every inch of the area through which prisoners move, and metal mirrors and remote control television cameras may have to be installed to provide supervision for areas that can not be directly observed by correctional officers at all times. Although some institutional modifications can be quite expensive, others can be accomplished with only materials that are on hand and require no capital addition to the budget.

Inadequate Classification Procedures. Classification procedures determine to what institution a prisoner is assigned in large correctional systems and, within institutions, in what living and working areas a prisoner must live out the term of his or her sentence. The initial housing of prisoners before they are classified also constitutes classification of a kind, for misassignment at this crucial point of a prisoner's career is probably more dangerous to the well-being of mind, body and possessions than any later classification procedure. The literature is replete with accounts of "fish" who were placed in cells, living areas or "tanks" with groups of experienced prisoners who proceeded to victimize them extensively without mercy. Other examples of the causal contribution to prison victimization made by poor classification procedures include giving a vulnerable person a single cell in a well-supervised area but simultaneously forcing him or her to work with prisoners who are heavy victimizers, and failing to give adequate protection to the aged, infirm, developmentally disabled or mentally ill offenders who are easy prey for prison "wolves," "gorillas" and other "ripoff artists."

Inexperienced prisoners should not, in general, be mixed with experienced prisoners, and violence-prone prisoners should not be mixed with nonviolent prisoners. In some cases, the violence potential of a small number of dangerous prisoners may be suppressed by mixing them with a relatively large body of nonviolent prisoners. The reverse situation in which a few non-violent prisoners are introduced into a violence-dominated setting is almost certain to produce a flurry of victimizing incidents. The mixing of young and old prisoners at El Reno seems to have reduced serious assaults in the institution, but we are not aware of its effects on other types of victimization phenomena. We know that management changes at El Reno may have contributed to the decrease in serious assaults there, so even that finding is subject to alternative explanation.[21]

Prison Deprivations. We have already mentioned that increased economic deprivation inflates the sub rosa economic system in the prisoner subculture and that this in turn increases the prison victimization rate. Similar arguments could be made about other prison deprivations, including the deprivation of heterosexuality, general sensory deprivation, and the deprivation of meaningful recreational and work involvements. This factor refers to the general characteristics of prisons as total institutions and to all of the opportunities and encouragements for victimization that total institutions habitually provide according to Goffman,[22] Zimbardo,[23] Burns[24] and others. The relative isolation of staff members in prisons contributes to their being institutionalized almost as much as the prisoners in many cases. The universality of many of these institutional effects suggests that it will be most difficult to suppress them without making radical changes in the structure of American correctional institutions.

Institutional Climate. This factor is closely related to prison deprivations. Institutions vary in their degree of totality, with some being much more oppressive than others. Prisons have never been adequately categorized on this dimension, but an approximation that has received attention is the custody–treatment continuum. Custody-oriented institutions are more totalistic than treatment-oriented institutions, having higher victimization rates as a result. The series of field studies on institutional climates by Moos[25] could also be linked to victimization phenomena in the same fashion as the custody-treatment dimension, although Moos has not attempted to do so.

The Corruption of Prisoner Authority by Staff Members. Correctional staff traditionally ensure the cooperation of prisoner leaders by granting them special privileges that are not extended to the entire prisoner population. Examples in which some of these privileges specifically entailed permission to victimize less fortunate prisoners were cited in earlier chapters. A more common pattern is to allow freedom from selected regulations for these prisoner leaders and then to have the leaders abuse the privilege and victimize others behind the backs (more-less) of the staff members. Either way, the process involves the corruption of prisoner authority rather than the corruption of staff power as in Sykes' famous essay on the corruption of authority in correctional institutions.[26] Fisher gave this process an apt label when he called it patronage in his study of Lomo, an institution for boys in California.[27]

Administrative Disorganization. Ohlin and Wilsnack found that riots and nonriot resistance were not associated with either tightening security (thus increasing prisoner deprivations) or instituting prison reforms (which are at least temporarily disorganizing). In short, institutional change of a deliberate sort did not lead to prison disturbances. In contrast, social disorganization of a more general nature did seem to be associated with collective violence. "Three-fourths of the prisons with riots had . . . experienced major administrative changes [in organization or personnel] or prolonged absences of key administrators, combined with public evidence of conflict within the prison staff."[28] Evidence of disorganization and conflict within the prisoner population was also strongly associated with prison disturbances. Two of the indices of disintegration used by Wilsnack and Ohlin in the prisoner population were themselves victimizing incidents. The only truly independent factor was a heterogeneous population in which prisoners of different ages, criminal histories and presenting offenses were mixed together rather than classified into separate facilities or units.[29]

It can be argued that these results have application to prison victimization beyond riots and nonriot collective resistance. It is likely that potential aggressors will take advantage of any loopholes in supervision and scheduling that are created by social disorganization and will quickly move to victimize their fellow prisoners or correctional officers in ways and at times that allow them to remain invisible to the supervisory structure. The greater the disorganization, the more possibilities there will be for opportunistic aggressors to victimize others. The positive side of the principle is that when change is carefully planned by sophisticated administrators who are familiar with social science research on organizational change, it can be accomplished without the extra added cost of increased victimization rates.

Conflict Among Staff Members. One of the indices used by Wilsnack and Ohlin should be elevated to a separate causal factor because of its importance in facilitating prison victimization. Conflict among staff members is a special form of prison disorganization that prison administrators can control and should always try to avoid. It can occur among administrators and line staff, treatment personnel and line staff, or different groups within the body of line staff members. Its genesis may be administrative incompetence, such as when administrators have mistreated their staff members so much that morale plunges, or it may be caused by demographic mixing. Demographic mixing occurs when there is an influx young liberal correctional officers into a line staff composed almost entirely of older conservative officers. Other demographic factors associated with staff conflict include racial differences and rural/urban differences. Demographic mixing cannot be avoided by careful administration in the same way as can the mistreatment of staff members. It is often forced upon prison units by external political forces and changes in a larger society. The only thing an intelligent administrator can do about it is to make special efforts to integrate the newcomers with the old-timers, with attitude changes on both sides, so that there is some degree of meeting of the minds in a neutral middle ground.

Conflicts between treatment staff and line staff are legendary in prison organizations. Differences in education and attitudes cannot be easily bridged. The administrative move most commonly associated with a heightening of treatment–custody staff conflict beyond controllable levels is the drastic changing of a custody-oriented program to a treatment-oriented program with a correlative increase in the status and power of treatment staff vis-à-vis correctional officers. The officers then feel that they have been betrayed and begin to devote all their efforts to undermining the new supervisory structure.

Regardless of how the staff conflict arises, it proceeds in the same way. Staff members begin to spend most of their time thinking about the conflict and plotting about how to gain an advantage in present and anticipated battles with the "other side." Staff members generally find allies against their foes among the prisoners, and this tends to break down some of the traditional social controls between staff members and prisoners, leading to increased corruption of authority. Supervision begins to deteriorate due to lack of attentiveness on the part of staff members, and this is followed by an increase of victimization among prisoners. The increased victimization rates may be hidden because there may be a simultaneous decrease in the number of infraction reports written by staff members due to both inattentiveness and the corruption of authority. There may even be a deliberate refusal to write such reports as a way of undermining the supervisory structure. A prison that has reached this point in the development of staff conflict needs to have martial law declared until the conflicts can be settled well enough for the normal prison routine to be reestablished. The alternative is for administrators to bide their time in hope that the problem will solve itself. It generally does, but only after a protracted period of conflict that often leads to a major prison disturbance and the replacement of the complacent administrators.

General Policy Factors

This final section of causes related to prison victimization has examples of general policy elements that are conducive to victimization in correctional institutions. Five factors are included: understaffing, underfunding, overinstitutionalization, overcrowding and the misplaced emphasis on rehabilitation.

Understaffing. The prisoner–staff ratio is directly associated with the rate of prison victimization.[30] When there are not enough correctional officers to supervise all of the areas of the prison, much prison victimization goes unnoticed. Correctional administrators faced with understaffing (almost all of them are) are forced to rob officers from one shift to put them on another and to transfer officers from positions involving prisoner contact so that adequate strength can be maintained in the towers and other positions that have the prevention of escapes as their primary responsibility. Stress-induced sick leave and absenteeism among line staff exacerbate this problem in almost all correctional institutions. When we see an officer–prisoner ratio of one to six, which is approximately the average in state correctional institutions for adults,[31] we must realize that these officers have to be spread over three separate shifts, with additional allowance made for weekends, vacations, absenteeism and sick leave. When all of these factors are considered, the officer–prisoner ratio is inflated between four and five times, and this figure is far too high for adequate supervision.

A final factor that contributes to the inflation of the officer–prisoner ratio is staff turnover. Low pay, as low as $6,240 to start, rigorous working conditions, fear of victimization and other negative factors all contribute to an extremely high turnover rate in most correctional systems. A recent article in *Corrections Magazine* reports annual state turnover rates as high as 74%. This astounding rate was achieved in Louisiana, and was followed by rates such as 65% in New Mexico, 63% in Vermont, 60% in Montana and 54% in Mississippi. Only 11 states plus the District of Columbia reported annual officer turnover rates below 20 percent.[32] When an officer resigns, he or she may first be absent for a number of days during which an ambiguous situation exists as to what to do about the position. Once the resignation becomes official, there is still the problem of the time lag that will occur before a new officer can be hired, trained and rushed into position. If the resigning officer's position was associated with a security function, then it will have to be covered immediately by a substitute who will be drawn from a less essential (less custody-oriented) position. As officers are moved around within the prison, a considerable amount of disorganization is created, and the supervision of prisoners is weakened.

Underfunding. Correctional administrators do not delight in understaffing their facilities. Their own careers are placed in constant danger by unfavorable officer–prisoner ratios. Many of them are forced to bear this condition because of severe unfunding from their state correctional system headquarters, which is, in turn, severely underfunded by state legislature, which is presumably carrying out the will of the general population. One of the few positive consequences of major prison disturbances is that these disturbances receive enough publicity so that legislators and citizens may shift their opinions and permit modest improvements in the officer–prisoner ratio in order to prevent future disturbances. All but a very few of the causal factors leading to prison victimization could be undermined if increased funding were to be provided to administrators who were well-versed in social science knowledge about prison administration and experienced enough to be able to apply this knowledge realistically instead of idealistically.

Overinstitutionalization. Studies of prisoner victimization are unanimous in agreeing that nonviolent property offenders are prime targets for prison "wolves" and other aggressors. These individuals are not very much of a threat to society since they confine their criminal behavior to minor property crimes and have never shown any tendency toward violence. For this very reason, they are unable to defend themselves in the prison jungle. It seems reasonable to argue that such offenders should never be placed in correctional institutions at all and to view their current incarceration level (more than a third of all incarcerated prisoners in the United States) as a case of overinstitutionalization that artificially inflates prison victimization rates at the same time that it cruelly victimizes offenders whose crimes hardly justify incarceration—to say nothing of the unremitting brutalization that many of them receive from their fellow prisoners.

Overcrowding. We have already discussed the extent to which the rapid rise in prisoner populations has exceeded institutional capacities in state after state. The overcrowding that is produced thereby is highly conducive to prison victimization.[33] A recent selected bibliography on overcrowding in correctional institutions published by the Law Enforcement Assistance Administration shows that the operational and academic communities have been concerned about the problem since the early 1970s.[34] Although it is important to understand how overcrowding impacts prison victimization, it is essential to realize that overcrowding is a residual variable. It is entirely controlled by sentencing policies, the general crime rate in the free society, release policies, policies on the construction of new correctional facilities or the modification of existing ones, and other general policy considerations.

Overcrowding impacts prison victimization through at least three distinct mechanisms. The first is by increasing general irritability, which is associated with an increase in negative attitudes and decreased tolerance of crowding.[35] The second is a decrease in the adequacy of supervision and physical protection afforded by architecture and ecology. Finally, there is evidence that violent prisoners have larger body buffer zones than nonviolent prisoners, so that when overcrowding occurs, they are constantly forced to be too close to their fellow prisoners, their body buffer zones are extensively violated, and the agitation that this produces leads to catharsis through violence.[36] Once we understand the viciousness and degradation that are part of prison victimization, the pictures of correctional facilities so overcrowded that beds are jammed end-to-end in corridors and recreation rooms take on new meaning.

A Misplaced Emphasis on Rehabilitation. How could an emphasis on rehabilitation be misplaced? Surely rehabilitation is a word that can never mean anything but good. Recent developments in the understanding of prison life have allowed us to see past this simple faith in rehabilitation and to realize that rehabilitation can have extremely negative results. For example, there is considerable evidence that the emphasis on rehabilitation and therapy in juvenile correctional institutions has resulted in the incarceration of many youngsters who have committed no criminal acts at all and sometimes in the assigning of longer sentences to status offenders than to serious criminal offenders.[37] In the case of adult correctional institutions, the emphasis on rehabilitation has been misplaced in that it has tended to obscure the necessity for devoting significant resources to the mundane goal of protecting the prisoners from each other. Thousands of studies of rehabilitative programs have made no mention of prison victimization and have diverted attention from badly needed investigations of the nature and extent of prison victimization. Treatment personnel have been hired in correctional institutions when there were not enough correctional officers to guarantee prisoner safety. Thus we see that even the best of intentions can ironically produce disastrous results in a topsy-turvy world of bars and buzzers.

RESPONSIBILITIES

There is something fundamentally misleading about the imagery of cause as applied to prison victimization. It implies that the forces producing the victimization are objective, external vectors that are at least partially beyond the control of human beings. The logical apparatus of causation is derived, of course, from the physical sciences, and there is considerable doubt as to how well this logical system applies to human behavior in any case. With regard to prison victimization, there is the more general problem that a discussion of cause is, at best, an indirect way of discussing responsibility for the problem—one that is misleading and potentially disorienting. It is therefore appropriate that I discuss the responsibility for prison victimization before moving on to a discussion of possible solutions to the problem.

There are at least seven levels of responsibility for prison victimization, proceeding from the most general to the most specific. These are voting citizens, legislators, state correctional administrators, local institutional administrators, immediate supervisors, the perpetrators of the victimization—and sometimes the victims themselves. The interesting thing about this chain of responsibility is that it can be broken at any point. Therefore, the continuation of high levels of prison victimization is dependent upon the acquiescence or active negativity of individuals at each of these levels. If the individuals at any single level of responsibility decided to move to significantly reduce the incidence of prison victimization, they could do so with dispatch. Passing the buck may be possible in the political arena, but it does not apply in this situation.

There is also something misleading about the model of the aggressor–victim relationship. The field of victimology has recognized that there is such a thing as victim-precipitated crime in which the victims have some degree of responsibility for their own victimization by virtue of their behavior prior to the commission of the crime. They may have encouraged a fight that led to their injury or encouraged their own victimization by willingly entering into abusive sexual relationships with homosexual or heterosexual partners. Not all prison victimizations involve "pure" victims and aggressors. In fact, a very sizeable number of victimizing experiences that occur behind the walls are so complex that we can only estimate differing percentages of responsibility between victims and aggressors, and we cannot always be sure which was which in a given incident. Except for these mixed cases, the immediate responsibility for prison victimization incidents is clearly held by the perpetrators of these acts.

At the next level of responsibility, correctional officers who are acting as supervisors of prisoners can prevent a high proportion of victimizing behaviors by fully carrying out their duties to the best of their ability. When they slack off on their work performance, do not properly patrol their assigned areas, give some prisoners power over others, play favorites in the distribution of privileges and so forth, they must take some degree of moral responsibility for the victimizations that result. Local prison administrators are in a similar position in that they can choose to develop institutional policies and to make minor modifications in the ecology of the institution that will greatly decrease the potential for prison victimization or they can ignore these factors and put their energies elsewhere. They can even choose to try to suppress records of prison victimization to maintain the status quo in the institution. They are never ordered to allow prison victimization to occur, and they may occasionally be encouraged to reduce it by their supervisors in the state and federal central correctional administration offices.

Many state correctional administrators may say that prison victimization is a terrible problem but there is nothing that they can do about it at their level. Nothing could be further from the truth. They can publicize the extent and nature of prison victimization to legislators and the public—as part of a campaign to increase prison budgets and to make special provision for the safety of prisoners in their charge. They can develop data-collection systems similar to the one now used in Wisconsin, so that they can present objective data on the incidence of prison victimization in their jurisdictions. They can give direct encouragement to institutional administrators in developing strategies for minimizing prison victimization, and they can exercise leadership in modifying training curricula and educational requirements for staff members so that these employees are better prepared to carry out their responsibilities in depressing the victimization rate.

Except for the rare occurrences of budget surpluses, there is never enough government money to go around. Therefore, the legislators must make choices and set priorities for budgetary items. Will there be a new prison or a new freeway? Should a criminal justice budget increment be primarily directed to law enforcement agencies, the courts or correctional institutions? Their job is not an easy one, and yet legislators clearly have legal and moral responsibilities for correctional matters. Even if public opinion is against increased funding for correctional institutions, legislators can take a courageous stand on the matter, and they can make efforts to educate the public about the need for safer prisons, showing them that the ultimate result of the brutalization of prisoners is an increased burden on the general public when these prisoners are released. They can also shame pressure groups who wish to undermine the correctional system by pointing out the dangers of following budgetary policies that, in essence, give official sanction to levels of violence and other forms of victimization that are significantly higher than existing levels in the free society.

Finally, citizens also share in the responsibility for the occurrence of prison victimization beyond minimum rates. Citizens tell legislators that they would prefer a freeway to a safer prison, that they want taxes to go down at any expense, that they want even minor property offenders to be incarcerated for long periods of time, and that they don't want to hear anything about what goes on in prisons except that the prisoners never escape. There seems to be an unspoken feeling that prisoners are somehow less than fully human and that they have lower intrinsic worth than street people. The finding of guilty is the final step in a symbolic transformation from citizenship to a Nibelung-like existence on the periphery of the moral community. We have no analogous mechanism for returning prisoners to fully human status, so their demotion has a tendency to become permanent. One of the consequences of this moral demotion is that most citizens are not very concerned about the safety of prisoners. They may say that if they didn't want to be victimized by their fellow prisoners, they shouldn't have broken the law in the first place. That is the same kind of reasoning that justified capital punishment for the stealing of a loaf of bread by starving children in medieval

England. If the general public were more strongly in support of attitudes toward prisons that were based on religious morality[38] or ethical humanism,[39] then it would be possible to quickly implement a number of the solutions to the problem of prison victimization.

SOLUTIONS

Every causal factor in prison victimization probably has a dozen possible solutions associated with it. My intent in this chapter is simply to offer examples of workable solutions rather than to provide an exhaustive treatment of the subject. The solutions are organized into three classes of actions, based on the degree of commitment and resources they require for implementation.

Solutions That Can Be Immediately Implemented with Minimal-to-Moderate Expense

These are solutions that do not require any major changes in existing correctional systems. All they require is careful planning and budget increases that are well within the capabilities of all legislative bodies. We have already examined some of the solutions that belong under this heading, including the development of statewide data-monitoring systems on prison victimization, making minor adjustments in the structure and utilization of correctional facilities so that their ecology is less conducive to victimization, improving classification procedures, and implementing higher security standards and procedures so that the flow of weapons and other contraband into the institution and between different areas in the institution is severely restricted. To these suggestions, we can add the implementation of an ombudsman system, an augmented reward system and increased family contacts.

The idea of using the prison ombudsman as one way of reducing prison violence has been convincingly proposed by Toch.[40] Ombudsmen must simultaneously gain the confidence of prisoners and staff members. Either subculture can so thoroughly undermine the performance of the ombudsman that there will be little positive effect realized from the position. Toch believes that ombudsmen who consistently demonstrate integrity in their dealings with both staff and prisoners can achieve the level of trust that is necessary to perform their tasks adequately, especially if they are not recruited from the ranks of prison staff members. From his viewpoint,

> Prison ombudsmen can reduce violence-enhancing pressures on inmates and staff because they are (or should be) free of the normative assumptions of prisons. They can thus help to solve problems which staff and inmates—caught in their respective sub-cultures—find it difficult to address in a constructive way.[41]

Toch also points out that prisoner subcultures need to have problem-solving mechanisms that are internal to their own caste in addition to the more overarching role of the ombudsman. Correctional officers need to experiment with new therapeutically oriented roles, and prisoners can benefit from participation in self-government. All of these suggestions represent ways of involving prisoners and staff members in the task of identifying and reducing the dangers of conditions that encourage or permit prison victimization. They enhance communication between the different parties in correctional institutions and they help to develop a sense of community as individuals put aside their personal interests to cooperate in the solution of common problems.

An augmented reward system can be implemented in a correctional institution in various ways and with a number of different components. Some therapeutic communities rationalize almost all rewards in terms of a token economy that rewards prisoners for acceptable behavior instead of punishing them for unacceptable behavior. It will probably be difficult to institute full-scale token economies in most correctional institutions because of their size and architecture. However, this can be part of a design to break up larger facilities into smaller operating units. Examples of augmented reward systems that fit more easily into traditional prison structures are conjugal visiting and work programs paying at least the minimum wage. Conjugal visiting is already in use in several American prisons, and has a long and successful history of use in many other nations.[42] Although there are problems in the implementation of conjugal visiting programs, such as what to do with prisoners who are not married or prisoners who have common-law relationships but no legal marriages, there are indications that the reward inherent in conjugal visits, particularly family visits as practiced in California and Canada, rather than merely permitting sexual intercourse between spouses as in Louisiana, is associated with a significant decrease in prison victimization. Prisoners are willing to go to considerable ends to keep their records clean when the reward for a clean record is a monthly visit with their spouse and children in a small apartment provided by the institution. The cost of constructing conjugal visit facilities on prison grounds may seem considerable at first, but it is a minor expense in comparison to total correctional expenditures.

It would be interesting to study the informal conjugal visit system that is currently in use at a number of American institutions. In this system, prisoners in minimum security settings are allowed to have "picnics" with their spouses (and often "friends") under conditions that permit some sort of sexual contact. At one institution, they were permitted to shelter themselves from public view by making tents of sorts out of blankets. When a new hard-nosed officer terminated permission for the practice, he immediately became the subject of numerous seemingly unrelated complaints to the prison administration. He was shortly removed and the custom was reinstituted. Since he had also offended a number of staff members by his rigid policies, it would not be fair to say that he was removed only because of his attitude toward the picnics, but this was certainly a major factor in his removal. There is some question as to the moral legitimacy of linking family or conjugal visits to the maintenance of a record free from proven participation in victimizing incidents, but if correctional institutions cannot implement more expensive alternatives for the reduction of prison victimization and if it can be objectively shown that this technique has significant results, it is worthy of serious consideration.

Another area of augmented rewards is in the field of employment. The systematic underpaying of prison workers, usually at the level of a few pennies an hour, ensures their continuing poverty and a distinct lack of involvement in their work. It also artificially depresses the level of material items legitimately made available within the prison. An increase in wages based on both good behavior and productivity by the prisoners and the open selling of prison-made goods in the free world would almost certainly reduce the importance of the sub rosa economic system— therefore the incidence of prison victimization. In addition to the indirect effect by suppressing the sub rosa economy, there would be a direct effect if prisoners were permitted to work at high-paying jobs only as long as they kept their records clean of victimizing, as opposed to inconsequential, infractions.

The final suggestion in this group of relatively inexpensive strategies is the increased facilitation of family contacts. Part of the reason why victimization is so fully institutionalized in prisons is the degree of isolation of prisoners from their families and other "free" people with whom they have (or might have) intense personal relationships. This isolation decreases the amount of social control exercised through these informal relationships and has the effect of largely abandoning prisoners to the norms, values and beliefs of the prisoner subculture. One way of keeping antiviolence norms alive is to promote much higher levels of family contacts than are normally permitted in prison settings. Costs associated with implementing this policy would range from increases in the capacity of visiting facilities to the running of special buses from large urban centers to correctional institutions and providing economic support for family members who have the need for child care or other support services in order to be able to visit their loved ones.

Solutions That Are Feasible Within The Present System, But Difficult or Very Expensive

One may say that the solutions proposed thus far are not very impressive. They do not involve major alterations of prisons as total institutions and many of them have links to the reduction of prison victimization that are only weakly suggested by the available evidence. If we want to make a greater impact or to be more certain of having a significant impact, we will have to make more extensive modifications in institutional arrangements and to increase correctional budgets more drastically. An obvious example of this is the need to make major modifications in many existing correctional facilities and to replace completely other correctional facilities in which the architecture facilitates continuously high levels of prison victimization. The research conducted by the National Clearinghouse for Criminal Justice Planning and Architecture has provided us with specific guidelines as to how correctional institutions can be constructed or modified so as to minimize their contribution to prison victimization.[43]

Another quite expensive option is to increase correctional budgets so drastically that adequate supervision can be provided in all facilities at all times. This means greatly increased training for correctional personnel as well as a 50–100% increase in the number of funded staff positions. It is cheaper in the long run to build new institutions that are specially constructed so that existing or slightly increased staffing levels can provide proper supervision than to drastically increase staff in the present facilities. The initial outlay in replacing architecturally outmoded institutions is greater, but the total expenditure over a 20-year period is likely to be considerably less.

Two other plans for the restructuring of correctional institutions that would almost certainly reduce the level of prison victimization are the widespread adoption of cocorrections and therapeutic communities. Smykla spent seven months of intensive paticipant observation at the cocorrectional Federal Institution at Pleasanton, California, during which he found almost the complete absence of the kind of predatory homosexual activity that is reported in male institutions. Other kinds of prisoner victimization were also apparently reduced by the cocorrectional atmosphere. This decrease in prisoner victimization was not due to overt sexual activity between the men and women. Although some sexual activity did occur, institutional efforts to control the activity succeeded in minimizing it. Instead, the decrease in victimization was due to fundamental alterations in the prisoner and staff subcultures that were caused by the presence of both genders. The correctional staff at the institution was sexually integrated to a much greater degree than the prisoners. The associate warden explained the effect produced by the introduction of women into the men's institution:

> The introduction of cocorrections makes you play cultural games not prison games. The game to play here is to show off in front of the other sex. When that gets out of hand, and you know it sometimes does, you just step in and say excuse me and that settles it.[44]

Generalizing from the Pleasanton experience, we may assume that sexually integrating all state correctional facilities would result in a considerable reduction in prison victimization. It would also require the modification of a number of the facilities. One major limiting factor would be that since no more than 5% of American correctional system residents are females, it would be impossible to balance any of the institutions with respect to gender. Having 50 women in a 1,000-bed prison might not have the same positive effects as a more balanced cocorrectional program.

Many of the prison characteristics that facilitate continuous victimization originate in the mass quality of the totalitarian regime. If all prisons were broken down into small therapeutic communities of no more than 30 to 50 residents, with intensive supervision provided, the victimization rate would be depressed immediately. The decrease in victimization due to the therapeutic communities would be at least as large as the difference between victimization rates in high-crime central cities and rural areas or small towns in the free society, and intensive supervision would assure that the decrease would be even greater. Therapeutic communities are organized on a completely different basis from traditional prisons in that they are structured so that the prisoner subculture is changed into a prosocial influence from the negative antisocial orientation of the convict code. Properly trained staff, facilities that have been modified to provide relative isolation among therapeutic communities, and the careful classification of prisoners into these communities would allow the slipover from antisocial to prosocial norms to occur.

Radical Solutions

Radical solutions are those solutions that fundamentally alter the present correctional system and perhaps also other related institutions. They may be financially expensive or they could actually be less expensive than current correctional arrangements. What distinguishes radical alternatives is not so much the budgetary modifications as the psychological costs and the possible social dislocations in the free world. These dislocations and costs are generally more than sufficient to discourage practitioners in the field of corrections from seriously considering radical alternatives. If such changes were to be implemented, the impetus for the changes would probably have to come from outside of the correctional establishment. In proposing radical alternatives to the present pattern of incarceration, I could allow my imagination to run wild, and perhaps I should. However, I will limit my suggestions in this forum to three modest proposals, all of which have already accumulated a modest amount of evidence in their favor.

The first of these three proposals is to lower incarceration rates by sentencing only violent offenders to correctional institutions. We have already pointed out how the adoption of this policy would depress prison victimization by decreasing the number of available victims within institutions. Observers of prisoner subcultures are unanimous in concluding that the strong rarely attack the strong. If only violent prisoners are housed together, and if there is additional classification within the violent group to separate the relatively strong and the relatively weak, then prison victimization would greatly decrease. Implementing this program would involve more than correctional institutions, since legislators would have to modify laws and judges would have to change their sentencing patterns. Additional changes would have to be made in noninstitutional corrections. Refusing to institutionalize property offenders would not mean that they would avoid punishment. There would instead be a mushrooming of community corrections programs involving service to the state, the repaying of victims and the drastic expansion of a number of other alternative correctional programs that are already in existence on a limited or trial basis.

An even more radical alternative would be to replace all correctional officers with national guardsmen or army privates, rotating them on a regular basis so that they never became excessively institutionalized. This sounds like an unreasonable proposal, but it was shown to be an practical one in a naturalistic experiment that occurred by chance in the Wisconsin prison system. When correctional officers went on strike, National Guard units took over Wisconsin prisons for a period of 16 days. It was expected that the prisoners would extensively victimize each other, as well as the guards, because of their inexperience in prison affairs. Quite the contrary, the performance of National Guard personnel was superior to the performance of the correctional officers they replaced in many ways. A study of the matter was carried out by Ross, who sent questionnaires to correctional officers, National Guard members, institutional residents and supervisory personnel in an effort to understand what happened during this period. Many of the guardsmen were understandably apprehensive about their safety when they first entered the institution, but they became less concerned with time. They treated the prisoners "like men" and these prisoners responded by behaving decently. The relaxation of general discipline and the human and rational enforcement of the rules resulted in improved morale rather than increased violence. The majority of the residents and supervisory personnel on duty reported that illegal or prohibited behavior either remained at usual levels or was reduced during the strike. Residents reported fewer sexual assaults, thefts, drug use and fights than usual.[45]

The import of this study is that the way in which correctional officers treat prisoners may be a significant factor in the level of prisoner violence that occurs in an institution. The staff subculture that the guardsmen brought into the prison with them was based on military norms and allowed them to resist the negative influences of institutionalization. We may argue that they would gradually deteriorate if they were permanently assigned to prisons, for which reason prison assignments should probably be limited to one year for most military personnel. Some might want to dismiss these findings, thinking that the prisoners deliberately behaved better to embarrass their keepers or that the positive effects of the experiment were due to the Hawthorne effect in which it is the fact of change, rather than the nature of the change, that is responsible for the improvement. We cannot refute these alternative interpretations, but there is also no reason to accept them, and none of the evidence presented by Ross favors these alternative interpretations. The message of the Wisconsin natural experiment is not that all correctional institutions should immediately adopt this new staffing pattern, but rather that an alternative form of staffing has been shown to have some value and that it should be tested on a larger scale instead of being disregarded. If more extensive testing continues to produce positive results, then it would be appropriate to suggest that it be universally adopted. Guarding prisoners with military personnel is not a new idea, and it is currently being used in a number of other countries. It would be unwise to move too quickly to a radical alternative such as this, since the total occupational dislocation associated with a full implementation of the plan would involve more than 125,000 correctional officers.[46]

The final proposal is the most radical of all and is taken from one of my articles that was originally written for the *International Journal of Offender Therapy and Comparative Criminology*.[47] This proposal involves the closing of all caging institutions, their replacement with open prison colonies, and the reduction of the number of colony inmates to minimum levels consistent with public safety. The prison camps would be self-contained cities located in isolated areas. They would be fenced and intensively patrolled to keep escapes as close to the zero point as possible. Within these enclaves, normal economic activity and family life would be encouraged. Prisoners could bring their families with them and would be allowed to earn normal wages in the limited number of prison industries permitted or to live at a subsistence level based on agriculture. Only long-term offenders would be admitted to these facilities since anyone having committed a less serious crime would repay society and their victims through noninstitutional correctional arrangements. This kind of prison camp system largely eliminates the effects of prisons as total institutions and might even have positive effects on prisoners by exposing them to a more socially acceptable lifestyle than they had before being sentenced.

A number of other countries have operated correctional colonies on this model with considerable success over the years. Reports from Mexico and the Philippines have appeared in the correctional literature.[48] India has adopted a policy of encouraging open colonies as much as possible and has published standards for these colonies in its *Model Prison Manual*.[49] Open colonies in India consist of huts organized on the basis of family units. They have adequate land and other facilities for agriculture and related activities. Family members can join prisoners in open colonies and can work with them in agricultural endeavors or various cottage industries. Wages paid for work accomplished for the state are set at the same level as wages in the free community and prisoners pay all their own expenses out of these wages. Although reports on prison colonies imply that this type of social organization decreases prison victimization, there is no direct evidence of this at present. It would be unwise to attempt to implement an open prison system without first creating a model program and carefully monitoring it to ascertain its impact on not only prison victimization but the other negative effects of imprisonment as well.

The solutions to prison victimization that have been sketched here have not been presented in any detail. No attempt has been made to construct a "how to" manual or even to flesh out any of the proposals for the reader. Instead, it is hoped that readers will be stimulated by these examples to think of solutions to prison victimization and to engage in intelligent conversations with other interested individuals, legislators and correctional officials about the possible implementation of these ideas. This process will eventually have much more positive effects on the correctional industry than any attempt to apply the same prescribed plan of action in every jurisdiction.

NOTES

1. See for example the list presented in Anthony M. Scacco, Jr., *Rape in Prison* (Springfield, IL: C. C. Thomas, 1975), pp. 92–116.
2. Marvin E. Wolfgang and Franco Ferracuti, *The Subculture of Violence* (London: Tavistock, 1967), p. 263.
3. Hans Toch, *Violent Men* (Chicago: Aldine, 1969); Monica D. Blumenthal, Robert L. Kahn, Frank M. Andrews and Kendra B. Head, *Justifying Violence: Attitudes of American Men* (Ann Arbor: Institute for Social Research, The University of Michigan, 1972).
4. A rough comparative view of the level of American violence may be gained by comparing homicide data from the Federal Bureau of Investigation's *Uniform Crime Reports* with statistics published by Interpol in the *International Crime Statistics*.
5. Daniel Lockwood, *Prison Sexual Violence* (New York: Elsevier, 1980).
6. Immogene L. Simmons, "Interaction and Leadership Among Female Prisoners," Ph.D. dissertation, University of Missouri, 1975.
7. The United States Department of Justice, Law Enforcement Assistance Administration, *Survey of Inmates of State Correctional Facilities 1974—Advance Report* (Washington, DC: U.S. Government Printing Office, 1976), pp. 24, 25.
8. Ibid., p. 28.
9. Ronald L. Akers, Normal S. Hayner and Werner Gruninger, Homosexual and drug behavior in prison: A test of the functional and importation models of the inmate system, *Social Problems* 21 (1974): 410–423.
10. G. L. Webb and David G. Morris, *Prison Guards: The Culture and Perspective of an Occupational Group* (San Marcos, TX: Coker Books, 1978).
11. Roy D. King and Kenneth W. Elliott, *Albany: Birth of a Prison—End of an Era* (London: Routledge and Kegan Paul, 1977).
12. For summary of this literature, see Lee H. Bowker, *Prisoner Subcultures* (Lexington, MA: D. C. Heath, 1977), pp. 106–109.
13. John R. Faine and Edward Bohlander, Jr., Prisoner radicalization and incipient violence, in C. Ronald Huff (Ed.), *Contemporary Corrections* (Beverley Hills: Sage, 1977), pp. 54–77.
14. Clemens Bartollas, Stuart J. Miller and Simon Dinitz, *Juvenile Victimization: The Institutional Paradox* (New York: Wiley, 1976).
15. Hans Toch, *Men in Crisis* (Chicago: Aldine, 1975); *Living in Prison: The Ecology of Survival* (New York: Free Press, 1977); *Police, Prisons, and the Problem of Violence* (Washington, DC: U.S. Government Printing Office, 1977).
16. Lockwood (1980).

17. Robert Johnson, *Culture and Crisis in Confinement* (Lexington, MA: D. C. Heath, 1976).
18. Lockwood (1980), pp. 8–16.
19. Leo Carroll, *Hacks, Blacks, and Cons* (Lexington, MA: D. C. Heath, 1974), pp. 11–21.
20. Edith Flynn, Sources of collective violence in correctional institutions, in Peter Lejins (Ed.), *Prevention of Violence in Correctional Institutions* (Washington, DC: U.S. Government Printing Office, 1973), p. 28.
21. Jerome Mabli, Charles Holley, Judy Patrick and Justina Walls, Age and prison violence: Increasing age heterogeneity as a violent-reducing strategy in prisons, *Criminal Justice and Behavior* 6 (1979): 175–186.
22. Erwing Goffman, *Asylums* (Garden City, NY: Doubleday, 1961).
23. Philip Zimbardo, Pathology of imprisonment, *Society* 9(6) (1972): 4–8.
24. Henry Burns, Jr., A miniature totalitarian state: Maximum security prison, *Canadian Journal of Corrections* 11 (1969): 153–164.
25. Rudolf H. Moos, *Evaluating Correctional and Community Settings* (New York: Wiley, 1975).
26. Gresham M. Sykes, The corruption of authority and rehabilitation, *Social Forces* 34 (1956): 257–262.
27. Sethard Fisher, Informal organization in a correctional setting, *Social Problems* 13 (1965): 214–222.
28. Richard W. Wilsnack, Explaining collective violence in prisons: Problems and possibilities, in Albert K. Cohen, George F. Cole and Robert G. Bailey (Eds.), *Prison Violence* (Lexington, MA: D. C. Heath, 1976), p. 71.
29. Ibid., pp. 70–71.
30. Linda Grasewicz, "A Study of Inmate Assaults in Major Institutions" (Richmond: Virginia Department of Corrections, 1977).
31. *Corrections Compendium* (May, 1977), p. 2, cited in Nicolette Parisi, Michael R. Gottfredson, Michael J. Hindelang and Timothy J. Flanagan, *Source Book of Criminal Justice Statistics—1978* (Washingdon, DC: U.S. Government Printing Office, 1979), p. 203.
32. Edgar May, Prison guards in America, *Corrections Magazine* 2 (December 1976), p. 35.
33. Wilsnack (1976); Edwin I. Megargee, Population density and disruptive behavior in a prison setting, in Cohen et al. (1976), pp. 135–144; Peter L. Nacci, Hugh E. Teitelbaum and Jerry Prather, Population density and inmate misconduct rates in the federal prison system, *Federal Probation* 41 (June 1977): 26–31.
34. Carolyn Johnson and Marjorie Kravitz, *Overcrowding in Correctional Institutions: A Selected Bibliography* (Washington, DC: U.S. Government Printing Office, 1978).
35. P. Paulus, V. Cox, G. McCain and J. Chandler, Some effects of crowding in a prison environment, *Journal of Applied Social Psychology* 5 (1975): 86–91.
36. Recent literature on body buffer zones includes A. F. Kinzel, Body buffer zone in violent prisoners, *American Journal of Psychiatry* 127 (1970):59–64; A. M. N. Hildreth, L. R. Derogatis, and K. McCusker, Body buffer zone and violence: A reassessment and confirmation, *American Journal of Psychiatry* 127 (1971): 1641–1645; Leslie M. Lothstein, "Personal Space in Assault-Prone Male Adolescent Prisoners," Ph.D. dissertation, Duke University, 1972; E. Rubinstein,

179

"Body Buffer Zones in Female Prisoners," Ph.D. dissertation, Long Island University, 1975; W. Saylor, "Identifying and Classifying Prison Inmate Social Role Types Utilizing a Measure of Personal Space," M.A. thesis, University of Maryland, 1978; S. Curran, R. Blatchley and T. Hanlon, The relationship between body buffer zone and violence as assessed by subjective and objective techniques, *Criminal Justice and Behavior* 5 (1978): 53–62.

37. Meda Chesney-Lind, Young women in the arms of the law, in Lee H. Bowker (Ed.), *Women, Crime, and the Criminal Justice System* (Lexington, MA: D. C. Heath, 1978), pp. 171–196.

38. For an example of this approach to prison affairs, see *Release,* a newsletter published by the Mennonite Central Committees of Canada and Pennsylvania.

39. A good example of this approach to prison affairs is *Jericho,* a newsletter published by The National Moritorium on Prison Construction, which is a project of the Unitarian–Universalist Service Committee.

40. Hans Toch, *Police, Prisons, and the Problem of Violence,* op. cit., pp. 76–79.

41. Ibid., p. 79.

42. For a brief overview of conjugal visiting, see Bowker (1977), pp. 116–117.

43. F. Warren Benton and Robert Obenland, *Prison and Jail Security* (Urbana, IL: National Clearinghouse for Criminal Justice Planning and Architecture, 1973).

44. John O. Smykla, "A Phenomenological Analysis of the Social Environment in a Coed Prison," Ph.D. dissertation, Michigan State University, 1977, p. 153.

45. Beth Ross, *Changing of the Guard, Citizen Soldiers in Wisconsin Correctional Institutions* (Madison: League of Women Voters, 1978).

46. Parisi et al. (1979), pp. 63, 195, 198, 202.

47. Lee H. Bowker, Exile, banishment and transportation, *International Journal of Offender Therapy and Comparative Criminology,* 24 (1980), in press.

48. Ruth S. Cavan and Eugene S. Zemans, Marital relationships of prisoners in twenty-eight countries, *Journal of Criminal Law, Criminology and Police Science* 49 (1958): 133–139; Bruce Zagaris, Finish penal system: Recent reforms, *New England Journal on Prison Law* 3 (1977): 437–486; Donald P. Jewell, Mexico's Tres Marias penal colony, *Journal of Criminal Law, Criminology and Police Science* 48 (1957): 410–413; Javier Pina y. Palacios, *La Colonia Penaldelas Islas Marias* (Mexico City: Ediciones Botas, 1970).

49. All India Jail Manual Committee, *Model Prison Manual* (Faridabad: Government of India Press, 1970).

Appendix
How Do We Find out
About Prison Victimization?

 I have argued that there are compelling reasons why we as citizens, social scientists and human service administrators should find out as much as we can about victimization in America's prisons. How does one go about collecting information on prison victimization? Various strategies have been used over the years to gain access to information about prison victimization, including the use of interviews, questionnnaires and participant observation, and the analysis of existing official records. These techniques are regularly used by social scientists, but the statistical analysis often presented in social science research reports does not always convey the complexity or the tragedy of prison victimization. For this reason, accounts of prison victimization by prisoners and comments by newspaper reporters, professional writers, prison administrators and other prison employees are also valuable additions to our knowledge about prison victimization. In the following sections, I will examine each of these methodological techniques, as well as a number of less commonly used strategies for gaining knowledge about victimization in America's prisons.

INTERVIEWS

In an interview, the investigator talks at length with prisoners, staff and other parties who are knowledgeable about prison victimization incidents. Interviews may be structured or unstructured. A structured interview consists of written questions that usually have specific answers to them and which are read to a respondent by the interviewer, who then writes the respondent's answers on the interview form. An unstructured interview is quite different, for it includes questions that are open-ended. The interviewer in an unstructured interview may have a topic guide but never has specifically worded questions to ask. Instead, each topic is introduced with a leading question and discussion continues until the topic has been completely explored. Structured interviews are advantageous for producing quantitative data that are then computerized, providing information such as victimization rates and objective factors related to victimization incidents. Researchers who are more interested in understanding how prisoners see the world and how they experience victimization are likely to prefer relatively unstructured interviews so that each point can be more fully explored. In both kinds of interviews, questions can be clarified for respondents who are unsure of their meaning; inconsistent responses can be discussed and reconciled before the interview is terminated; and the attitude and body language of the respondent can give the interviewer a great deal of additional information about the topic under investigation.

It is not easy to obtain honest responses to questions about prison victimization. Prisoners, guards, and administrators have reasons for wanting to disguise all or part of the victimization events that occur in their institution. Perhaps the most important factor in this reticence is the fear that what they say will be used against them by prison officials or that it will be leaked to friends and colleagues who might then label the interviewee a "snitch." The best way to deal with this problem is to guarantee anonymity to all interviewees. The trouble is that since interviews are conducted face-to-face, it is clear that interviewers may write down the names of their interviewees on the side, and thus violate the anonymity of the interview by creating a record that could cause great problems for the interviewee should it fall into the hands of either prisoners or administrators.

Interviews in a prison setting also have the problem that whatever is said by the interviewee must be filtered through the perceptions of the interviewer before it is written down on the interview form. This leads to misunderstandings that occur when interviewers are not fully cognizant of the details of prison life and in the introduction of systematic biases based on the prejudices and perceptual blind spots of the interviewers. Different interviewers may present the same questions in different ways—producing different answers. Structured interviews have less of a problem with these factors than unstructured interviews, and other biases can be greatly reduced by carefully training interviewers to be as objective as possible, by educating them about the nature of prison life, and by matching their race or ethnicity to the racial or ethnic group of the interviewees.

Newman[1] was one of the first prison investigators to write down the difficulties experienced in conducting interviews. Newman found that prison interviewing involved a number of problems that were not likely to be encountered in other research settings. For example, prisoners find it very difficult to distinguish between researchers and prison administrators. They are unlikely to cooperate in the research if they believe that the researchers are somehow connected to the prison's administration. Another problem is that prisons are not adequately equipped with interview rooms, and the few rooms that are set aside for interviews between prisoners and their lawyers are rumored to be "bugged." Interview settings should be quiet, comfortable and unquestionably confidential. A number of researchers have been successful by conducting their interviews in the chaplain's office because prisoners often believe that this is the only office in the prison that is not equipped with surveillance devices.

If researchers wear clothing or carry objects that clearly identify them with their university or other sponsoring organization, this will help to define their role to both prisoners and staff members. For example, a university researcher could carry a staff directory or university bulletin so that anyone with a question could look up his or her name in the official publication, or university cards identifying the researcher could be distributed to interviewees "in case they want to write to the researcher later to fill in something they forgot to say in the interview." These techniques are often sufficient to convince prisoners that the researcher is not an administrative spy. It will not do any good to establish an unambiguous role if there is not a believable level of honesty about the objectives of the research and the relationship between those objectives and the needs and interests of prisoners and staff members. Honesty is unquestionably the best policy whenever possible. Otherwise, there is the risk that everyone's confidence in the project will be destroyed when dishonest responses are exposed.

The quickest way to ruin an interviewing study is to interview unpopular or sexually deviant prisoners first. It is much safer to begin with interviews of individuals who are at the apex of the prisoner status hierarchy. Deviants and unpopular prisoners can always be interviewed last without damage and correctional officers can be interviewed after interviews of prisoners have been concluded. Whichever ethnic group is currently dominating the prisoner subculture should be fully mined before the researcher becomes too closely identified with subordinant ethnic groups.

The use of prison argot is so extensive that untrained interviewers will often be unable to follow what is being said. In addition, an inadequate understanding of the use of argot by prisoners may interfere with the development of rapport in interviews. There are many slang terms that are common in the criminal underworld on the streets as well as in the prison; these terms form the basis for the development of additional argot terminology that is specific to each institution and are used in one ethnic group but not others.

The problem of doing prison research without offending any of the subgroups within the prison was given an in-depth discussion by Giallombardo in 1966.[2] She recommended that field work with prisoners be completed before staff members are interviewed. By doing this, interviewers can minimize the risk that prisoners will define them as being on the side of staff members. When Giallombardo did a study of an eastern penitentiary for women, she was introduced to the staff and prisoners through a memorandum signed by the warden of the prison. This memorandum stated that she would be visiting the prison to make a scientific study of institutional living over a period of a year and that she was a social scientist from a prominent university. Cooperation with the study was requested from all staff members and prisoners, with the memorandum also guaranteeing their confidentiality. Staff members felt reassured by the memo and were willing to cooperate, but the memo was not even read by most prisoners and if it had been, the implied association between the research project and the warden might have sabotaged the entire study.

Because of the inadequacies of the method of introduction, Giallombardo was forced to spend three weeks walking around the prison grounds in an attempt to become familiar with the prisoners. The guards worked to define her role in such a way as to locate her in the social world of the prison and were very suspicious of her presence in their living area. Giallombardo solved the problem of how to present the objectives of the study by simply saying that it was intended to help women in trouble everywhere and to enable people to better understand the nature of institutional living. As she moved from group to group, she asked the prisoners if she might come to visit them sometime in their cottages, and although some tried to discourage her by saying that they really had nothing to offer, none of the prisoners refused her.

One easy way for prisoners to test the researcher's claim of confidentiality is to violate some minor regulation in front of the researcher and see if the administration finds out about it. In Giallombardo's case, some of the prisoners took food and coffee from the dining room in her presence, a clear violation of institutional regulations. Other prisoners asked her to do illegal favors for them. She steadfastly refused to be involved in any illegal activity, but she also did not report anything to the administration, so the prisoners gradually became convinced that she was independent of the prison's administration. Over the weeks, the testing decreased and the definition of her social role as a researcher was confirmed: she was well enough accepted by the prisoners so that she could enter a group and be ignored. Conversation continued as if she were just another prisoner, instead of immediately terminating any serious discussion and confining conversation to small talk until she left the room. Giallombardo was careful to be a good listener no matter what the prisoners wanted to talk about, so that she came to be defined as a sincere person with whom it was pleasant to associate. When she got to know the prisoners reasonably well, she asked if she could make notes on what they told her, and most agreed. With the few who refused, she took no notes in their presence but wrote them up from memory at the end of each day.

Line staff members in the prison were just as worried about having inappropriate job behavior reported to the prison administrators as the prisoners, so Giallombardo was careful not to be seen with prison administrators until she had spent a great deal of time interviewing correctional officers. Her demeanor in dealing with the officers was basically the same as in handling prisoners; that is to say, she tried to be uniformly pleasant and neutral about all subjects. She was courteous but brief in talking with officers unless they were out of the sight of prisoners. She found that the officer's lounge—out of bounds to prisoners—was a good place to engage officers in extended interviews.

At about the same time that Giallombardo was doing her study in an eastern penitentiary, Ward and Kassebaum[3] were conducting a parallel study in a California institution for women. Their study was introduced to the prison community by notices placed in both staff and inmate newpapers. They chose to present their research as an attempt to understand the experience of imprisonment for women, and emphasized that they were not focusing on any particular problem in the institution, nor were they interested in passing judgment on the behavior of either staff or prisoners. They admitted that any benefits accruing from their study would be for imprisoned women in general rather than the women currently incarcerated in the institution they studied. Their concern about establishing their identity as separate from the administration was so great that they decided that the interviewing room had to be as bare of any furnishings as possible in order to make sure that the furnishings did not indicate a high degree of permanance. If the furnishings did suggest permanance, then the prisoners would be more likely to see the interviewers as part of the permanent staff of the institution, and therefore unlikely to be in a position to extend full confidentiality to interviewees. Ward and Kassebaum began by recording notes by hand and then graduated to tape recordings in a second, more detailed interview. They employed both male and female interviewers, and found that equally valid results were obtained regardless of the interviewer's gender. For example, approximately the same proportion of the inmates interviewed admitted to engaging in homosexuality when the interviewers were female as did when the interviewers were male.

In a more recent application of the interview technique, Toch[4] and his staff members completed 381 interviews with suicidal prisoners in New York State. These interviews were all tape recorded and then transcribed so that the unstructured material could be analyzed using content analysis. The content analysis was accomplished by categorizing material into primary themes expressed by the prisoners and then into secondary or supporting themes. The themes were then organized into a typology of factors leading to personal breakdowns in prison settings. Toch's work exemplifies the best use that can possibly be made of interviews. By conducting unstructured interviews, Toch was able to record data that were organized in the minds of the inmates rather than forced into categories that were established by the researchers before the study began. The interviews also produced detailed vignettes that accurately portray the complexity of human relations in a prison and thus give us a feeling for the reality of prison victimization. Finally, his use of content analysis links the qualitative material developed in the unstructured interviews (which has a quasiclinical character) to a quantitative analysis of patterns of factors leading to self-destructive acts.

All of the interview studies that I have discussed so far utilized "single shot" cross-sectional research designs. That is to say, they were completed in one continuous process, and they therefore give us only a single picture of prison conditions at one point in time. It is also advisable to learn something about how prisoners change during their prison careers, and the most valid way to do this is to conduct a panel study in which prisoners are interviewed and later reinterviewed. Changes can then be calculated between the original interview and the later interview—changes that are presumably occurring due to the effects of imprisonment. Because cross-sectional studies are unable to follow individual prisoners over a period of time, they can only imply developmental changes by comparing prisoners who have been incarcerated for different periods of time.

Two recent examples of panel studies conducted in prisons are Faine and Bohlander's investigation in a Kentucky correctional facility and Alpert's comparative research on legal aid to prisoners in Washington and Texas. Faine and Bohlander interviewed all of the men admitted to the institution during a five-month period, and then interviewed them twice more—in the fifth week and after approximately nine months of institutional confinement. As a result, they were able to show that changes in the attitudes held by these prisoners over the nine-month period of imprisonment were related both to the background characteristics of the prisoners and to the conditions existing in the prison.[5]

Alpert was concerned with a different problem. He wanted to evaluate the effects of participation in legal services programs in prisons in Washington and Texas, so he interviewed samples of prisoners in these two states shortly after they had been incarcerated and then reinterviewed them six months later. Some prisoners had used legal services during this period and others had not, which allowed him to find out what background characteristics were associated with the use of legal services. He was also able to ascertain the degree to which the prisoners were satisfied with the services offered and to ask them in what way they had been helped by the provision of legal services. He then examined the effects of participation in the legal services program on two other kinds of variables: attitudes toward a variety of topics and institutional infactions. This methodological strategy enabled Alpert to conclude convincingly that the prisoners participating in legal aid programs were generally satisfied with the results of their participation, and that there were positive effects of the participation on these prisoners that went beyond the direct effects of the legal consultation provided. Prisoners participating in legal services programs showed decreased institutional misbehavior and relative attitudinal improvement when compared with prisoners who had not participated in a legal aid program.[6]

QUESTIONNAIRES

Questionnaires differ from interviews in that all of the questions are precisely formulated ahead of time and presented to the respondents in written form. Questions can be open-ended or closed. If they are open, then respondents write in the answers in their own words. Closed-ended questions have a fixed number of preprinted answers from which the respondents generally pick the most appropriate answer for each question. Questionnaires are much cheaper than interviews to administer because they can be given to groups of respondents rather than to individuals, and they also make it easier to convince respondents that their anonymity is being protected. Closed-ended questionnaires are generally precoded so that they can be directly punched onto computer cards and subjected to data processing. Questionnaires are often used when studying a representative sample of inmates and/or staff members at a correctional institution with the intent of generalizing from the data obtained to the entire population of the institution. Unfortunately, many prisoners are functionally illiterate, so any attempt at the mass administration of questionnaires must build in a mechanism for identifying those prisoners who are incapable of filling out the questionnaire so that they can have the questions read to them in a personal interview.

Sampling prisoners for questionnaire studies is not as easy as it may seem. For example, Jensen and Jones[7] administered questionnaires to female felons and misdemeanants in a prison for women in North Carolina in their study of prisonization. The prisoners were given the questionnaire in groups of two to 25, and those who seemed to have difficulty in understanding the questionnaire were either interviewed individually or allowed to indicate their responses on separate cards when the items were read to them. The institution made private rooms available for the administration of the questionnaires and there were no correctional officers present. The questionnaire administration sites were large enough so that the prisoners did not have to sit too close together and they were guaranteed complete anonymity. Despite a nominal payment for cooperating in the study, not all prisoners choose to participate. The final proportion of women completing questionnaires was 82% of the women who were present in the institution at the time of study.

An example of the application of questionnaire surveys to prison officers is Sandhu's study of prisoner officers in the state of Punjab, India.[8] Sandhu selected every third officer in all the prisons in the state of Punjab, obtaining completed questionnaires form 158 officers. Of these men, 38 were functionally illiterate and 47 more had completed only five or six years of elementary schooling. These individuals had to be aided in filling out the questionnaire by a research assistant. Although most American prisons require officers to have a high school diploma or a GED certificate, a surprisingly large proportion of officers in the less-professionalized American prison systems have as much trouble understanding printed questionnaires as the Indian officers studied by Sandhu. Therefore, it is wise to plan ahead and schedule a research assistant to be present to help in the administration of questionnaires to functional illiterates anytime that a study of correctional officers is planned.

Jacobs[9] interviewed Illinois prison officers who were being trained at the Illinois Correctional Academy instead of taking a sample of officers currently employed in correctional institutions. By doing this, he was able to get a statewide sample without having to visit all of the individual correctional institutions in the state. Some of the officers at the Academy were newly hired and others were being rotated through the Academy as part of their in-service training, so Jacobs was able to obtain data on both neophyte and experienced officers at the same time. Questionnaires were completed by 929 prisoner officers between July of one year and October of the following year, and Jacobs checked to see if this lengthy period of time showed any changes of attitudes between those officers that were interviewed early in the study and those that were interviewed nearly a year later. Again, anonymity was guaranteed to the officers so that they could state their opinions on correctional topics without fear that these opinions would be used against them later.

Three specific questionnaire devices are often used in prison studies: sociometric questions, attitude scales and prison role scales. Sociometric questions have been used by prison researchers such as Curcione,[10] Schrag[11] and Hautaluoma and Scott.[12] Sociometric scales are used as a way of plotting prisoner social relations so as to create a picture of prisoner social structure. In sociometric questionnaires, prisoners are asked about which people they would like to be friends with, or perhaps asked more indirect questions such as the names of people they would like to work with on a project or even to live with in a multiperson cell. The responses from all of the prisoners are then combined to show not only which prisoners are most popular, but which prisoners cluster together to form groups and the structure of relations between these groups. Sociometric analysis also identifies social isolates who are not affiliated with any prisoner groups. Sociometric research has established that friendship choices in prison are influenced by the criminal history of the prisoners. Each person tends to be close friends with those who have committed similar types of crimes, although there are also effects associated with propinquity (such as friendships between prisoners who cell together) and race/ethnicity. Sociometry is relevant to the study of victimization in prisons because some groups of prisoners are much more likely to be victimized than others, and social isolates are invariably more likely to be victimized than the members of even low-status groups within the prison.

Psychological attitude scaling is a way of measuring social-psychological variables such as attitudes toward the law, alienation and anomie. An example of the use of psychological attitude scaling is Guenther's unpublished doctoral dissertation, in which he used an attitude scale to measure powerlessness, which he considered to be an index of general alienation.[13] Thomas and Poole[14] also used an attitude scale to measure powerlessness and additional scales to measure the extent of inmate code adoption, attitudes toward the legal system, the extent of criminal identification, and attitudes toward the prison. Attitude scales consist of a number of attitude statements to which prisoners respond, usually with a choice of responses among strongly agree, agree, uncertain, disagree, and strongly disagree. A number of these items form a scale to measure each variable—such as powerlessness—and the items are numerically scored and summed to produce each individual's score on that scale. By comparing the scores of different inmates, one can gain a general idea of how inmates compare with their fellow inmates on that dimension. An example of an attitude scale item from the powerlessness scale used by Thomas and Poole is, "People like me have little chance of getting what we want when our wants come into conflict with the interests of groups that have a lot of power." When inmates are assigned values on a number of different attitude scales, their scores on these scales can be intercorrelated so that researchers can understand how "having" certain attitudes leads to other attitudes that are in turn presumably linked to recidivism and other measures of antisocial behavior. In their study, Thomas and Poole offered evidence to show that feelings of powerlessness were related to prisonization, which in turn was associated with increased opposition to the legal system, opposition to the administration of the prison and an increased level of criminal identification.

The idea of attitude scaling can also be adapted to the measurement of prisoner-role occupation. Prisoners usually come to occupy one or more social roles. They do not act entirely as isolated individuals. An example of the social role in prison is the "Square John," and prisoners adopting this role retain their allegiance to the legal system and law-abiding behavior while they are in the prison. They rarely engage in illegal activites in prison, and they are generally rehabilitated when they are released. When attitude scale items are used to assign inmates to prisoner social-role categories, a number of items are created for each known social role so that these items identify the relevant characteristics of that role. Inmates completing the questionnaire are assigned scores for each social role, and if one score predominates, they are considered to be occupying that social role at present. As an example of this form of analysis, Garabedian[15] included 12 attitude scale items in a questionnaire that he administered in a maximum security prison. These items were organized into four sets of three items each—each set corresponding to one of four prisoner roles. The roles used by Garabedian were the "Square John," "Right Guy," "Politician" and "Outlaw." An example of one of these items is, "The biggest criminals are protected by society and rarely get to prison." On analyzing the results of the questionnaires, Garabedian was able to classify two-thirds of his respondents as incumbents of one of the four social roles. The other prisoners were mixed types, with high scores on more than one role or low scores on all roles.

Although there is no doubt that prisoners occupy distinct social roles, there is always the danger that a study such as the one carried out by Garabedian will artificially force inmates into role constructs that are not consistent with the way the prisoners see their own role participation. Following this line of analysis, Hansel[16] argues that many of the results of role-scale analyses are no more than statistical artifacts of the analytic procedures used. He comments that inmate role scales are based on the perceptions of the researchers rather than perceptions of the prisoners themselves and that it is dangerous to rely on attitudes rather than the prisoners' reports of their own behavior. A related problem is that the general role scales cannot be sufficiently specific to delineate roles accurately in a given correctional institution. Even if a set of role scales are valid in one prison, that does not mean that they will be valid in a different correctional institution.

PARTICIPANT OBSERVATION

The only truly participating scientific observer in a correctional institution was Hans Reimer, who spent three months in a state penitentiary and two weeks in a county jail without any of the correctional officials realizing that he was more than the average prisoner.[17] More recent participant observers have actually been nonparticipant observers in that both prisoners and staff realized that they were researchers rather than prisoners, so they could not fully participate in the prisoner subculture. A prison is really too dangerous for "true" participant observation, as the typically white middle-class researchers have precisely the combination of characteristics that attract aggressors to their victims in prison settings. Reimer made a fundamental mistake when he did his participant observation study in the 1930s in that he fell inadvertently into a friendship with a young man known to submit to homosexual advances. This lowered Reimer's status and led to the refusal of older and stronger inmates to become friends with him. A mistake such as this in most modern correctional institutions would have resulted in Reimer's being gang raped.

Readers may wonder how researchers who are openly identified as such can ever expect prisoners to be honest when around them. We have already discussed Giallombardo's study of a women's penitentiary,[18] in which she found that the prisoners gradually came to include her in their discussions as a trusted confidant. Polsky experienced similar treatment when he carried out an extensive participant observation study in one of the cottages of a home for delinquent boys.[19] Like Giallombardo, Polsky underwent considerable initial testing, during which the boys responded to his presence by either whispering or leaving the room altogether when discussing private affairs. They tried to get him involved in criminal activity, which he resisted, but he also refrained from reporting the criminal activity to institutional staff members. Had a really serious criminal act been planned, Polsky would have had to report it to the prison administration, thus ruining his rapport with the youngsters and probably ruining his study at the same time. As it happened, no such serious criminal act occurred, and so he was able to avoid this eventuality.

During the testing, one boy went so far as to attack Polsky physically in a kind of boxing match. Being six and one-half feet tall, Polsky was more than a match for most of the delinquents and he easily defeated his attacker. However, two other boys came up to attack Polsky from behind while he was engaged with the first aggressor, and one of them tried to cut Polsky's arm with a knife. In another incident, one of the delinquents pulled Polsky down by his legs, and Polsky was forced to throw the boy on the ground and place his knee on the boy's stomach until the boy gave up. It is apparent from these examples that Polsky's research might not have worked out quite so well had he been a foot shorter and unskilled in self-defense. In any case, the physical attacks soon ceased, and Polsky eventually became friendly with most of the boys.

Throughout the period of severe testing, Polsky was careful never to go so far as to be a threat to the indigenous leadership or to interfere in their exploitation of the weaker prisoners. One may believe that this was not ethical or humane on his part, but we must realize that we can never obtain accurate information on prisoner victimization unless we are willing to stand aside and observe it as it occurs. The prisoners initially defined Polsky as a threatening stranger, and than gradually came to accept him as a professional outsider who was sympathetic to their gripes and who could be trusted not to report their illegal actions to the institution's administrators. They never were able to understand what it meant to be a professional psychologist or participant observer. It was just that his everyday behavior was so consistently nonthreatening that he was eventually accepted by them. Polsky felt that the seductiveness of the boys was so great that he would have had difficulty in refraining from participating in illegal activities had he not had his feet squarely planted in the law-abiding society to which he returned on a regular basis. The longer he stayed in an institution, the more he found himself to be assimilating the values and behavior of the delinquents. From his comments about this process, we can infer the strength with which the prisoner subculture molds the behavior and attitudes of "fish" and "long-termers" alike.

Three recent participant observation studies offer additional insights into the process. The first of these was written by Jacobs as a result of his participant observation in Stateville Penitentiary in Illinois. He points out that the appearance of a participant observer within a prison is a suspicious occurrence from the viewpoint of the prisoners. In his case, he was known to be associated with a famous public figure who was strongly in favor of prison reform, and this enabled him to be more easily accepted by the prisoners. When interviewing prisoners informally, Jacobs was careful to tell them that they did not have to answer all of his questions and if they didn't want to talk about something, they should simply tell him and he would gladly switch to another topic. This was his way of reducing the threat that he posed to the inmates, simultaneously gauging the degree to which they accepted him. Another advantage of this strategy is that the researcher is less likely to obtain deliberately fabricated responses. Researchers who demand answers to every question they ask often are dealt with by being given responses that are deliberate misrepresentations. This is done so that the prisoners do not have to confront directly the fact that they don't wish to deal with sensitive topics. Prisoners at Stateville quickly came to identify Jacobs with prison reform, asking him to do favors for them. He decided that it was appropriate to offer legal advice to prisoners, to contact families and lawyers for them, and to help them make plans about how to negotiate with the Stateville administration. However, these humane acts always stopped short of any illegal activity, which he steadfastly refused to engage in. Prisoners at Stateville came to understand that engaging in illegal activity would compromise the role of the researcher and endanger the entire project, and once they had included that as part of the researcher's role, requests for participation in illegal activities greatly declined.[20]

Jacobs wanted to create the appearance of being a student, so he carried a University of Chicago clipboard, and dressed more casually than staff members (with a beard!) during his period of field research. Although his professional qualifications include law and sociology, he did not want prisoners to identify him as a sociologist since the term sociologist is often used to refer to a clinical bureaucrat who writes up diagnostic classifications and parole evaluations for prisoners, which engenders much hostility. The political situation at Stateville was such that had Jacobs assumed a more balanced stance toward the requests of prisoners, he almost certainly would not have received so much cooperation from them. When prisoners are antithetically opposed to the prison administration, anyone who attempts to be strictly neutral will be perceived as being on the side of the administration and therefore an enemy to all prisoners. At the same time, Jacobs had to be careful to avoid taking the prisoners' side too vigorously lest he become persona non grata to the prison administration, and he also had to be careful not to take sides in the battles that were occurring among different factions in the prisoner subculture.

One of the most lucid and incisive discussions of participant observation in prisons is the one written by Carroll in his book, *Hacks, Blacks, and Cons.*[21] Carroll spent 15 months as a participant observer in a small state prison in eastern United States. From the beginning of his field work, he avoided more than superficial conversations with prison officers when he was being observed by prisoners in order to maintain his identity as separate from that of prison staff. His interviews with the officers were all conducted outside of the walls and included a series of lengthy in-depth unstructured interviews after the field work in the prison proper had been completed.

As a white man, Carroll began his field work by making contacts with white prisoners, subsequently asking them to introduce him to black prisoners. He matched his dress to that of the prisoners (who were not required to wear uniforms) and was sometimes mistaken for a prisoner by both prisoners and staff members who were unaware of the existence of his research project. In addition to dressing like the prisoners, he participated in as many institutional activities as possible and he used prisoner argot when talking with them. He conducted group discussions, informal conversational interviews, and formal, although still unstructured, interviews with both prisoners and staff members. His group discussions evolved as he circulated through the prison, joining first one and then another group of prisoners. His conversational interviews occurred in the same way, except that then Carroll was involved with only a single inmate and took a more active role in probing for information on the topics of interest. There was no scheduling of the conversational interviews and they occurred in natural prison settings. The formal interviews with prisoners were conducted in the prison chaplain's office, which provided the same guarantee of anonymity that prison staff members received when they were interviewed by Carroll outside of the prison walls. However, none of these interviews could be seriously pursued until Carroll had first mapped the available settings in the prison and the friendship groups into which the prisoners were organized. It is desirable to do this before getting into interviews so that one does not interview the wrong people first, thus alienating other members of the prisoner population.

When Carroll was not busy interviewing prisoners, he was examining the prison's official records—including the central files on the prisoners, disciplinary records and court transcripts. He used these data as a foil for his field observations. The material from the field observations was recorded outside of the prison rather than during the interviews and informal contacts with the prisoners. He found that he could only spend three to five hours per day within the walls if he were to have enough time to write detailed field notes on the day's observations. Spending more time in the prison resulted in his forgetting too much of what he had seen. He then sorted these field notes into three files: a chronological file by the date of the observation, a concrete file that organized material by places, activities and individuals, and an analytic file that sorted notes according to theoretical concepts such as social change and black solidarity. The use of these files enabled him to construct tentative hypotheses as he went along and then to test these hypotheses in his continuing interviews with the prisoners and staff members.

A quite different sort of participant observation study was carried out by Crouch in a southern agricultural prison. His fellow prison officers were unaware that he was scientist, but the State Department of Corrections had sanctioned his study. He followed routine job application procedures, was hired, spent three weeks as an officer in the cell blocks and then was transferred to other parts of the prison. As the study continued, he allowed it to be known that he was a professor who was studying the prison, evidently experiencing little difficulty because of this. During the time that his research role was announced, he was playing the role of a "summer hire," which is an officer who has been hired to fill in for staff members who are on vacation for the summer. Crouch carried a small notebook with him on the job and took notes surreptitiously on the basis of his informal conversations with officers and inmates. In addition, he recorded all of his notes and general impressions on tape at the end of each shift. The transcriptions of his tapes became the notes from which he summarized his findings in the study. When he had written up his findings, he submitted initial drafts of his research report to an administrator and three officers at the prison in order to make sure that he had not misinterpreted anything that he had seen.[22]

OFFICIAL RECORDS

I have already mentioned that Carroll used official records to supplement the data that he had collected in the field. Other researchers have used official records as their only source of information on prison behavior. There is an obvious disadvantage in doing this since official records reflect the biases of the staff members who created the records and there is no way to be sure of those biases when a researcher reads the records at a later point in time. In addition, the records contain only those pieces of information that were relevant to the staff members at the time that the records were made, and they exclude information that is crucial to the goals of the researcher. There is always the possibility that official records tell us more about the operation of the prison administration than they do about the behavior of the prisoners. Nevertheless, official records can tell us things that we want to know about prison events if they are carefully used. For example, Jaman et al. used frequency distribution matching to produce two equivalent groups of prisoners drawn from the central files at San Quentin. The two groups differed in that members of one group had received citations for violence or potential violence during 1960 while those in the other group had not. The researchers then compared the groups to see which recorded variables successfully differentiated between the violent and nonviolent inmates.[23]

Adelson et al. wanted to know why 91 prisoners had died unexpectedly in penal institutions in Cuyahoga County Ohio between 1956 and 1967. In historical research of this kind, official records are the only complete source of data. The researchers had access to official medical records on each of the 91 deaths—which records included autopsies and associated chemical studies as well as situational details. They did not confirm any homicides among the 91 deaths, although the majority of the deaths were not from natural causes. The most commonly found nonnatural cause of death was suicide, followed by alcohol abuse. Almost all of the suicides were accomplished by hanging in the cells.[24] Medical records were also put to good use by Jones in his study of the health risks of imprisonment in the Tennessee State Penitentiary. In this study, the state's own statistics produced a severe indictment of prison conditions, for the homicide rate suffered by prisoners was many times greater than the homicide rate for Tennessee citizens as a whole, and homicide and homosexual rape rates were particularly high for prisoners under age 25.[25]

A study that illustrates the dangers of treating official data as if they are accurate representations of what occurs in prisons is the investigation of assaults in 44 North Carolina road camps by Beshears. His measure of assaults was the number of disciplinary convictions for assault in the official records of the road camps. Using this measure, he was unable to find a relationship between population density in the road camps and the rate of prison assaults.[26] It could easily be that the lack of a statistically significant correlation between population density and the assault rates for the 44 institutions was a result of inconsistencies in recording and enforcement policies used in different institutions. Some institutions might have recorded all of the assaults that staff members were aware of while others only recorded the most serious assaults, thus masking the true differences between the institutions and confounding the analytic relationship between population density and the assault rate. Investigators of prison conditions must be careful not to be seduced by the concreteness of the data in official files. It is all too easy to accept these data as complete without second thought and then to build complicated statistical analyses based upon the data and leading to conclusions that are far removed from the empirical reality of prison life.

STRATEGIES THAT ARE LESS COMMONLY USED IN THE STUDY OF PRISON CONDITIONS

I have now completed a brief outline of the most commonly used prison research strategies. The remainder of the Appendix is devoted to supplementary techniques that have occasionally been used to shed light on prison matters.

Linguistics. Linguistics is the study of the nature, structure and systematic changes over time of human language. It has obvious application in prison studies in that prisons are characterized by a specialized slang terminology. In an early linguistic study carried out at Sing Sing Prison, Hargan presented a brief dictionary of argot words and suggested the functions that are served by the use of slang terminology in the prison. In Hargan's view, prison slang serves to neutralize the feelings of inferiority and guilt suffered by the prisoners and also functions to create class solidarity among the prisoners.[27] The father of prison studies, Donald Clemmer, continued Hargan's ideas by including a 1200 word dictionary of prison argot in his book, *The Prison Community.*[28] In his dictionary, we learn that "kid" is a young male prostitute, a "politician" is a prisoner who has a good job in the prison and has acquired special privileges for himself, and a "wolf" is an active pederast. In his analysis of these slang words and terms, Clemmer found more words relating to homosexual behavior than to heterosexual behavior, which indicates that a linguistic analysis can tell us something about the cultural emphases that are found behind the walls.

There is one linguistic analysis that has direct application to prison victimization: that is an investigation carried out by Kantrowitz on the differences in terminology used by blacks and whites in a large Illinois maximum security prison.[29] He found a number of terms used to refer to types of people either by blacks or by whites but not by both racial groups. There were 106 such names that were racially segregated, as compared with only eight terms that were used by both blacks and whites. This terminological segregation indicates how strongly the black and white groups were alienated from each other in their evaluation of their fellow prisoners. Terms used for nonracially related activities showed a more general distribution between the races. An example of this is a set of terms referring to prisoners who cheat or extort from other prisoners, of which 83% were used by both races, 17% were used only by blacks, and none was used only by whites.

Psychological Testing. Many of the psychological tests that have been developed in the past few decades for application to general population groups have also been used in prison settings. The most popular of these is the Minnesota Multiphasic Personality Inventory. These tests are commonly administered in an attempt to show differences between types of offenders, or between offenders in general and nonoffending population groups. When Hannum and Warman administered the MMPI to prisoners at the Iowa Women's Reformatory, they did not have to create their own control group because they were able to use the norming data that are provided as part of the test interpretation package.[30] These norming data can be used as a built-in comparison group that permits the rapid execution of psychological studies of prisoners without a great deal of methodological complexity.

An extension of this simple methodology is to compare test scores on different psychological tests that have been administered to prisoners in a battery. Stefanowicz and Hannum's investigation of ethical risk-taking as measured by a 16-item scale correlated risk-taking scores with a sociopathy scale and also with scores on four of the scales that are part of th MMPI.[31] Finally, psychological test scores can be used to estimate the effects of imprisonment over time. The effects of long-term imprisonment on the personality structures of prisoners were investigated by Banister et al. by administering a battery of nearly a dozen psychological tests to a sample of British prisoners.[32] The selection of the sample was constructed so as to vary systematically the amount of time that the men had spent in prison. The effects of imprisonment were then estimated by comparing the psychological test scores of a group of relatively new prisoners with a group of "long-termers." This kind of inference is always more dangerous than the direct measurement of changes over time in a panel study, but it is worth some consideration.

Artificial Experiments. Relatively few artificial experiments have been carried out in prison settings, and even fewer have attempted to replicate prison conditions in nonprison settings. Zimbardo's famous pseudoprison experiment in the basement of a Stanford University building is an outstanding example of the latter form of artificial prison experiment. Zimbardo constructed an artificial prison setting, tested college students in order to be sure that they were psychologically normal, and then randomly assigned them to be either guards or prisoners in a simulated prison experience of limited length. The experiment was extensively monitored, and it was found that these normal college students rapidly adopted the traditional roles of guards and prisoners, showing aggressive and submissive behavior, respectively. Emotional crises were noted among many of the pseudoprisoners, and sadism was noted among some of the pseudoguards. Enough psychological disturbances arose during the experiment that it had to be called off before it was scheduled to be completed.[33] The impact of the Zimbardo study is that if such negative results can be produced in an artificial prison setting with psychologically healthy volunteers who know that they are merely participating in an artificial experiment, then how can we expect a lower degree of negative effects from involvement in the affairs of a real prison? The experiment also suggests that many of the negative effects associated with prisons are due more to the social roles that are structured into the prison setting than they are to the personalities or background characteristics of the actors in that setting.

The series of studies of body buffer zones that began with the work of Kinzel exemplifies the value of artificial experiments conducted within prison walls. Kinzel took his subjects one by one into a bare room and had them stand in the center of the room, at which point Kinzel approached them from different directions and instructed them to tell him when he came too close for them to be comfortable. Using the measurements thus obtained, he calculated the size of the body buffer zones for these prisoners, and when he compared the body buffer zones for violent and nonviolent prisoners, he was able to show larger zones for the violent prisoners.[34] Paulus et al. used a different technique for testing body buffer zone perceptions. They asked prisoners to place miniature human figures in a mock-up of a room on a table. They were told that they should place the figures in the enclosure until they appeared crowded, and the number of figures placed in the artificial enclosure was then used as a measure of the subjective perception of overcrowding. Information gathered as to the housing histories of the prisoners allowed Paulus et al. to test for the possibility of a relationship between the experience of overcrowding and the experimental tolerance of crowding in the described situation.[35]

STUDIES AND ACCOUNTS BY ACTORS IN THE PRISON SETTING

Many insights can be gathered into the rigors of prison life by reading publications written by prisoners, prisoner administrators, treatment and line staff members, and investigative reporters.

Comments by Administrators. There are prison administrators who have gained specialized social science training either during or after their administrative experiences, and these officals have much to say about prison victimization. One of the early examples of this is McCleary's discussion of the impact of liberal reform on the authoritarian structure of the traditional prison.[36] Life in the Arkansas prison system was given a detailed treatment in Murton's book, *The Dilemma of Prison Reform.*[37] In a less publicized book, Fox does the same for the Michigan State Penitentiary at Jackson.[38] Major works such as these are supplemented by the publications of the American Correctional Association (in particular *Corrections Today,* previously known as *The American Journal of Corrections*) and the annual volume of *Proceedings* derived from the National Congress of Corrections. These publications almost totally exclude social science studies and pieces written by prisoners, focusing instead on the comments of administrators about the management problems that they are having and ways of solving them.

Some prison administrators are very knowledgeable about what goes on within the walls. Unfortunately, other administrators are content to sit in their offices—perhaps even fearful to get too close to the daily workings of the institution. It follows from this that some administrative commentaries are very insightful while others bear no relationship to the realities of prison life. For this reason, the main value in studying the writings of correctional administrators is not to understand what occurs within the prison but rather to understand how prison administrators view their task so that we can better see how administrative decisions and postures impact victimization phenomena.

Other Staff Writers About Prisons. Clemmer was a staff sociologist at the Menard branch of the Illinois State Penitentiary when he began writing his book, *The Prison Community.* His administrative position may have had something to do with the scant attention he gave to prison victimization, but it did not limit his insightfulness on other topics. Other publications by prison staff members include those by Fisher,[39] Coutts[40] and Bartollas.[41] Fisher worked for one year as a research associate at a California Institution for delinquent boys and remained at the institution after the research had been completed. Coutts had been a matron at the Oakalla Prison Farm for Women in British Columbia for three years before she decided to write a graduate thesis on the institution. "Runaways at Training Institution, Central Ohio" was the doctoral dissertation completed by Bartollas and led to the publication of the most significant book on juvenile prison victimization in the literature, *Juvenile Victimization: The Institutional Paradox.*[42] With his co-researchers, Bartollas provided the reader with an in-depth understanding of how staff members viewed their world and how their attitude and behavior facilitated the victimization of boys who were in their charge.

Accounts by Prisoners. The great number of accounts written by prisoners includes both memoirs and semifictionalized novels. Perhaps the most famous of these is Jackson's book, *Soledad Brother: The Prison Letters of George Jackson.*[43] Two other outstanding pieces of literature are Braly's *False Starts: A Memoir of San Quentin and Other Prisons*[44] and Elli's novel, *The Riot.*[45] Books such as these make us aware of nuances in the lives of prisoners that are rarely exposed in social science studies. Anyone reading these books will gain the ability to understand prison life from the position of the prisoner rather than from the viewpoint of an administrator or social scientist. The high proportion of these accounts that include examples of the victimization of prisoners by other prisoners and by staff members lends additional supporting evidence to data on prison victimization that have been obtained from scientific sources.

There is one volume in which an inmate account of prison life is uniquely coupled with a parallel account offered by a prison caseworker. In *The Time Game: Two Views of a Prison*, by Manocchio and Dunn, the events that are described are seen from diametrically opposing positions. There is almost no mutual understanding between the two individuals. The idealistic comments of Manocchio, the caseworker, seem strangely out of place in the drab hostile world of the prison. The cultural gap between the governors and the scientists on one hand and the governed on the other hand is revealed as almost unbridgeable.[46] What are we to think of scientific research that presents us with a view of the prison that is unidimensional? In the fractionated and polarized world of the prison, the application of approaches that assume a consensual theory of social reality is bound to be very limited. Conflict is endemic.

Investigative Reports. The category of investigative reports includes field investigations and interviews by newspaper reporters, professional writers and lawyers. Many of these reports are sensationalistic, which has tended to give them a bad name, but there are also a great many investigative reports that are as objective as scientific studies of prison life. The publications of the John Howard Association are always outstandingly objective, although they are written from a liberal management viewpoint. For example, the Association's *Survey Report: Illinois Youth Centers at St. Charles and Geneva* recounts interviews on the brutalization of delinquents by staff members and victimization among delinquents at St. Charles and compares these data with both legal standards and the administrative regulations of the Illinois Department of Corrections.[47] Because this is a technical correctional report, very few people are aware of it. Two examples of reports on prison life that have gained wide notoriety are *Weeping in the Playtime of Others* by Wooden[48] and Mitford's volume, *Kind and Usual Punishment.*[49]

An investigative report that shocked the nation and drastically changed our perceptions of prison life was the article, "Sexual Assaults in the Philadelphia Prison System and Sheriffs' Vans," by Davis.[50] Davis was the Chief Assistant District Attorney of Philadelphia at the time that his investigation was carried out, and he was responsible for the interviewing of 3,304 prisoners and 561 custodial employees of the Philadelphia Prison System. Great care was taken to substantiate claims of prison victimization that were made by the respondents, including polygraph examinations. If prisoners and staff members failed polygraph tests or if they refused to take them, their testimony was excluded from the study. Davis also used other avenues of investigation that included examination of offical records and reports and making personal inspections of the prison facilities and the sheriffs' vans. Because of his attention to detail, his multidimensional approach and the care he took to substantiate every report given, the high rate of homosexual assaults that he revealed in his conclusions cannot be questioned.

MULTIPLE COMPARISONS BETWEEN INSTITUTIONS

Almost all of the studies that I have been discussing in this appendix were conducted in single institutions. At the institutional level of analysis, these are no more than case studies, and although they allow us to examine hypotheses about the relationships between prisoners as individuals, groups of prisoners, staff members, and administrators within the institution, they do not permit controlled comparisons between institutions. This means that all of the characteristics of institutions as institutions are not available to be studied as possible causes of prison victimization. In order to understand the impact of characteristics of institutions on prison victimization, we need to conduct simultaneous studies of a number of institutions. We would be better off with a smaller number of studies of multiple institutions under controlled conditions than with a larger number of case studies of institutions, each institution being studied under different conditions and with a different analytic framework. Some of the finest multiple institutional comparisons that have been published in the last several decades are those by Glaser,[51] Propper,[52] Nelson,[53] Giallombardo,[54] Slosar,[55] Zald[56] and Berk.[57] These investigators usually limited themselves to the simultaneous comparison of two or three institutions, with Propper's research on seven American programs for juvenile delinquents being the most extensive project. Aside from the number of institutions studied, these investigations do not use research strategies that are any different from case studies of single institutions; they just apply them more broadly. Berk's finding that the attitudes held by prisoners were more positive in treatment-oriented institutions than in custody-oriented institutions is an example of the kind of generalization that can be made from multiple institution comparisons.

The easiest way to conduct a multi-institutional comparison is to rely on the administration of questionnaires rather than time-consuming interviews and participant observation. In a number of cases, this has been accomplished by simply sending questionnaires to institutional administrators—or even to the administrators of state correctional systems rather than individual institutions—and then to accept their reports as factual and analyze them without making on-site visits to any of the institutions sampled. The advantages of this technique are low cost and the ease with which data can be obtained from a representative national sample of institutions. Weighed against these advantages are the disadvantages of compounding the biases introduced in the use of official data with biases that are added when we accept the personal opinions of prison adminstrators. Mailed questionnaires were used in Sellin's studies of homicides and assaults in American prisons,[58] Baker's investigation of self-government in correctional institutions,[59] research on the relationship between population density and prisoner misconduct rates in the Federal Prison System by Nacci et al.,[60] and the recent national study of prison homicides by Sylvester et al.[61]

When Sellin attempted to amass national data on homicides and assaults in correctional institutions for 1964, he decided to send a questionnaire to the leading administrators in each of the state prison systems and the federal prison system asking about these events. These administrators then presumably summarized data in the official records of the institutions under their control and returned them to Sellin. The results were practically worthless, for some administrators reported data on only aggregated assaults, others reported data on all officially known assaults, and others included only cases of assaults that had been committed by prisoners who were serving sentences for murder.[62] The aggregation of these confused statistics was hardly inspiring, and yet it was the only national body of data on the subject, and Sellin was sufficiently satisfied with his 1964 study that he repeated the study using the same methodology for prison homicides and assaults occurring in 1965.[63]

The national study of prison homicides by Sylvester et al. also used a nationally distributed questionnaire, but they followed it up with a series of on-site visits by field staff members to each prison in which a homicide had occurred during 1973. The idea of using questionnaires to rule out prisons in which no homicides occurred during 1973 and then having on-site visits to only the remaining institutions was an efficient and intelligent use of research funds. Homicides are less likely to be distorted in questionnaire reports by administrators than assaults or other lesser crimes, and the authors also sent questionnaires to district attorneys and coroners in prison locations as a check on the information provided by the prison administrators. The only weak point in the study is that the on-site visits did not consider the question of additional homicides that might have occurred in the institutions investigated. Had they done so and found additional homicides that had been covered up or misinterpreted by prison administrators, then we would have a better estimate of the level of underreporting in the prisons claiming that no homicides had occurred during 1973. A final advantage of the on-site visits is that they were able to provide a wealth of descriptive data that would have been possible to obtain by mailed questionnaires alone. Using this research strategy, Sylvester et al. were able to go beyond categorizing homicides into a typology and to actually calculate a prevalance rate for prison homicides that was applicable to all state and federal prisons in the United States.[64]

CONCLUSION

I have attempted here to show how social scientists obtain information on prison life and prison victimization. In addition to briefly describing the methods used, I have given examples of the application of each technique and suggested some of its major advantages and disadvantages. It has been shown that valuable information on prison victimization can be obtained from the writings of administrators, literary and legal investigators, staff members and prisoners themselves. The final section of the Appendix addressed the desirability of utilizing multiple institutions in studies rather than relying on case studies of single institutions if we want to understand how structural aspects of institutional life impact prison victimization.

The array of methodological strategies that have been used in prison studies is as impressive as it is extensive. The use of reports from differing perspectives and of data gained through various methodological techniques gives us reason to accord a high degree of reliability and validity to the findings about prison victimization that have been presented in the preceding chapters. Individual investigators can be mistaken. Writers can be misleading when they present views of prison life that are distorted because of their placement as actors in the prison drama. However, when the picture that emerges from all of these diverse sources, with very few exceptions, is consistent, we have the strongest possible case made for the truthfulness of the composite description of prison victimization that is synthesized from all of these investigations.

NOTES

1. Donald Newman, Research interviewing in prison, *Journal of Criminal Law, Criminology and Police Science* 49 (1958):127–132.
2. Rose Giallombardo, Interviewing in the prison community, *Journal of Criminal Law, Criminology of Police Science* 57 (1966):318–324.
3. David A. Ward and Gene G. Kassebaum, *Women's Prison: Sex and Social Structure* (Chicago: Aldine, 1965).
4. Hans Toch, *Men in Crisis* (Chicago: Aldine, 1975).
5. John R. Faine and Edward Bohlander, Jr., The genesis of disorder: Opression, confinement, and prisoner politicization, in C. Ronald Huff (Ed.), *Contemporary Corrections: Social Control and Conflict* (Beverly Hills: Sage, 1977), pp. 54–77.
6. Geoffrey Alpert, *Legal Rights of Prisoners* (Lexington, MA: D.C. Heath, 1978).
7. Gary F. Jensen and Dorothy Jones, Perspectives on inmate culture: A study of women in prison, *Social Forces* 54 (1976): 590–603.
8. Harjit S. Sandhu, Perceptions of prison guards: A cross national study in India and Canada, *International Review of Modern Sociology* 2 (1972):26–32.
9. James Jacobs, What prison guards think: A profile of the Illinois force, *Crime and Delinquency* 24 (1978):185–196.
10. N.R. Curcione, Social relations among inmate addicts, *Journal of Research in Crime and Delinquency* 12 (1975):61–74.
11. Clarence Schrag, Leadership among prison inmates, *American Sociological Review* 19 (1954):37–42.
12. J.E. Hautaluoma and W.A. Scott, Values and sociometric choices of incarcerated juveniles, *Journal of Social Psychology* 91 (1973):229–237.
13. Anthony Guenther, "Alienation, Inmate Roles, and Release Ideology in a Penitentiary Setting," Ph.D. dissertation, Purdue University, 1972.
14. Charles W. Thomas and Eric C. Poole, The consequences of incompatable goal structures in correctional settings, *International Journal of Criminology and Penology* 3 (1975):27–42.
15. Peter Garabedian, Social roles in a correctional community, *Journal of Criminal Law, Criminology and Police Science* 55 (1964):338–347.
16. Mark V. Hansel, "The Measurement and Dimensionality of Inmate Social Roles in a Custodially Oriented Prison: An Ethnographic–Psychometric Study," Ph.D. dissertation, University of Iowa, 1974.
17. Hans Reimer, Socialization in the prison community, *Proceedings of the American Prison Association* (Washington DC: American Prison Association, 1937), pp. 151–155.
18. Giallombardo (1966).
19. Howard Polsky, *Cottage Six* (New York: Wiley, 1962).

20. James V. Jacobs, Participant observation in prison, *Urban Life and Culture* 3 (1974):221–240.
21. Leo Carroll, *Hacks, Blacks, and Cons* (Lexington, MA: D.C. Heath, 1974).
22. Ben M. Crouch, "The Book Versus the Boot: Two Styles of Guarding in a Southern Prison," paper presented at the annual meeting of the Society for the Study of Social Problems, 1978.
23. D. Jaman, P. Coburn, J. Goddard and P. Mueller, *Characteristics of Violent Prisoners: San Quentin—1960* (Sacramento: California Department of Corrections, 1966).
24. Harold Adelson, R. Huntington and D. Reay, A prisoner is dead: A survey of 91 sudden and unexpected deaths which occurred while decedent was in either police custody or penal detention, *Police* 13 (1968):49–58.
25. D. Jones, *The Health Risks of Imprisonment* (Lexington, MA: D.C. Heath, 1976).
26. Earl D. Beshears, "Assaults in Prison: A Study of the Relationship Between Living Space and Assaultive Behavior," paper presented at the annual meeting of the Academy of Criminal Justice Sciences, 1978.
27. James Hargan, The psychology of prison language, *Journal of Abnormal and Social Psychology* 30 (1935):359–365.
28. Donald Clemmer, *The Prison Community* (New York: Holt, Rinehart and Winston, 1940).
29. N. Kantrowitz, The vocabulary of race relations in a prison, *American Dialect Society Publications* 51 (1969):23–34.
30. T. Hanmum and R. Warman, The MMPI characteristics of incarcerated females, *Journal of Research in Crime and Delinquency* 1 (1964):119–126.
31. J. Stefanowicz and T. Hannum, Ethical risk-taking and sociopathy in incarcerated females, *Correctional Psychologist* 4 (1971):138–152.
32. P. Banister, F. Smith, K. Heskin, and N. Bolton, Psychological correlates of long-term imprisonment, *British Journal of Criminology* 13 (1973):312–323.
33. Philip G. Zimbardo, Pathology of imprisonment, *Society* 9(6) (1972):4–8.
34. A.F. Kinzel, Body buffer zone in violent prisoners, *American Journal of Psychiatry* 127 (1970):59–64.
35. P. Paulus, V. Cox, G. McCain and J. Chandler, Some effects of crowding in a prison environment, *Journal of Applied Social Psychology* 5 (1975):86–91.
36. Richard H. McCleary, *Policy Change in Prison Management* (Ann Arbor: Governmental Research Bureau, Michigan State University, 1957).
37. Thomas Murton, *The Dilemma of Prison Reform* (New York: Holt, Rinehart and Winston, 1976).
38. Vernon Fox, *Violence Behind Bars* (New York: Vantage Press, 1956).
39. Sethard Fisher, Social organization in a correctional residence, *Pacific Sociological Review* 4 (1961):87–93; Informal organization in a correctional setting, *Social Problems* 13 (1965):214–222.
40. Dorothy Coutts, "An Examination of the Social Structure of the Women's Unit, Oakalla Prison Farm," Master's thesis, University of British Columbia, 1961.
41. Clemens Bartollas, "Runaways at Training Institution, Central Ohio," Ph.D. dissertation, Ohio State University, 1973.
42. Clemens Bartollas, Stuart J. Miller and Simon Dinitz, *Juvenile Victimization: The Institutional Paradox* (New York: Halsted Press, 1976).
43. George Jackson, *Soledad Brother: The Prison Letters of George Jackson* (New York: Bantam, 1970).

44. Malcom Braly, *False Starts: A Memoir of San Quentin and Other Prisons* (New York: Penguin, 1976).
45. Frank Elli, *The Riot* (New York: Avon, 1966).
46. Anthony J. Manocchio and Jimmy Dunn, *The Time Game: Two Views of a Prison* (New York: Dell, 1970).
47. *John Howard Association, Survey Report: Illinois Youth Centers at St. Charles and Geneva* (Chicago: John Howard Association, 1974).
48. Kenneth Wooden, *Weeping in the Playtime of Others* (New York: McGraw-Hill, 1976).
49. Jessica Mitford, *Kind and Usual Punishment* (New York: Random House, 1971).
50. Alan J. Davis, Sexual assaults in the Philadelphia prison system and sheriffs' vans, *TransAction* 6 (December, 1968):8–16.
51. Daniel Glaser, *The Effectiveness of a Prison and Parole System* (Indianapolis: Bobbs Merrill, 1964).
52. Alice M.L. Propper, "Importation and Deprivation Perspectives on Homosexuality in Correctional Institutions: An Empirical Test of Their Relative Efficacy," Ph.D. dissertation, University of Michigan, 1976.
53. Catherine I. Nelson, "A Study of Homosexuality Among Women Inmates at Two State Prisons," Ph.D. dissertation, Temple University, 1974.
54. Rose Giallombardo, *The Social World of Imprisoned Girls* (New York: Wiley, 1974).
55. John A. Slosar, *Prisonization, Friendship and Leadership* (Lexington, MA: D.C. Heath, 1978).
56. Mayer W. Zald, Organizational control structure in five correctional institutions, *American Journal of Sociology* 68 (1972):335–345.
57. Bernard B. Berk, Organizational goals and inmate organization, *American Journal of Sociology* 71 (1966):522–534.
58. Thorsten Sellin, Homicides and assaults in American prisons, 1964, *Acta Criminologica Medicalis Legalis Japonica* 31 (1965):139–143; Prison homicides, in Thorsten Sellin (Ed.), *Capital Punishment* (New York: Harper and Row, 1967), pp. 154–160.
59. J. E. Baker, *The Right to Participate: Inmate Involvement in Prison Administration* (Metuchen, NJ: Scarecrow Press, 1974).
60. Peter L. Nacci, Hugh E. Teitelbeum and Jerry Prather, Population density and inmate misconduct rates in the federal prison system, *Federal Probation* 41 (June 1977):26–31.
61. Sawyer F. Sylvester, John H. Reed and David O. Nelson, *Prison Homicide* (New York: Halsted Press, 1977).
62. Sellin (1965).
63. Sellin (1967).
64. Sylvester et al. (1977).

Selected Bibliography

Adair, A., M. Anderson and J. Savage, Jr., Impact of incarceration on the black inmate, *Journal of Afro-American Issues* 3 (1974): 167–177.

Adelson, L., R. Huntington III and D. Reay, A prisoner is dead, *Police* 13 (1968): 49–58.

Akman, D., Homicides and assaults in Canadian penitentiaries, *Canadian Journal of Corrections* 8 (1966): 284–299.

Albany Law Review Staff, Sexual assaults and forced homosexual relationships in prison: Cruel and unusual punishment, *Albany Law Review* 36 (1972): 428–438.

Alexander, S., The captive patient: the treatment of health problems in American prisons, *Correctional Law Article Reprints* (Washington, DC: American Bar Association, 1972).

Allen, G., On the women's side of the pen, *The Humanist* 38 (September–October 1978): 28–31.

Allen, T., Psychiatric observations on an adolescent inmate social system and culture, *Psychiatry* 32 (1969): 292–302.

American Correctional Association, *Causes, Preventive Measures, and Methods of Controlling Riots and Disturbances in Correctional Institutions* (Washington, DC: American Correctional Association, 1970).

Anderson, A., "Power in Prison: House Parents and Residents in a Correctional Institution for Delinquent Girls," Ph.D. dissertation, University of Maine, 1975.

Astrachan, A., Orleans parish prison *Corrections Magazine* 2 (September–October 1975): 25–32.

Astrachan, A., Profile/Louisiania, *Corrections Magazine* 2 (September–October 1975): 9–14.

Atkins, B. and H. Glick, *Prisons, Protest and Politics* (Englewood Cliffs NJ: Prentice-Hall, 1972).

Austin, W., "An Ethological Analysis of Prisoner Social Structure," Ph.D. dissertation, University of Georgia, 1972.

Austin, W. and F. Bates, Ethological indicators of dominance and territory in a human captive population, *Social Forces* 58 (1974): 447–455.

Austin, W. and C. Unkovic, Prison suicide, *Criminal Justice Review* 2 (1977): 103–106.

Bartollas, C., S. Miller and S. Dinitz, The exploitation matrix in a juvenile institution, *International Journal of Criminology and Penology* 4 (1976): 257–270.

Bartollas, C., S. Miller and S. Dinitz, *Juvenile Victimization, The Institutional Paradox* (New York: Wiley, 1976).

Bartollas, C., S. Miller and S. Dinitz, "Emotional Disturbance and Victimization in an End-of-the-Line Juvenile Institution," unpublished paper, The Ohio State University, 1975.

Bartollas, C., S. Miller and S. Dinitz, The inmate code in juvenile institution: Guidelines for the strong, *Southern Journal of Criminal Justice* 1 (1975): 33–52.

Bartollas, C., S. Miller and S. Dinitz, Staff exploitation of inmates: The paradox of institutional control, in E. Viano and I. Drapkin (Eds.), *Exploiters and Exploited: The Dynamics of Victimization* (Lexington, MA: D.C. Heath, 1975), pp. 157–168.

Bartollas, C., S. Miller and S. Dinitz, Becoming a scapegoat: Study of a deviant career, *Sociological Symposium* 11 (Spring 1974): 84–97.

Bartollas, C., S. Miller and S. Dinitz, The 'booty bandit': A social role in a juvenile institution, *Journal of Homosexuality* 1 (1974): 203–212.

Baunach, P. and T. Murton, Women in prison: An awakening minority, *Crime and Corrections* 1 (Fall 1973): 4–12.

Beshears, E., "Assaults in Prison: A Study of the Relationship Between Living Space and Assaultive Behavior," paper presented at the annual meeting of the Academy of Criminal Justice Sciences, 1978.

Bidna, H., Effects of increased security on prison violence, *Journal of Criminal Justice* 3 (1975): 33–46.

Bloch, H., Social pressures of confinement towards sexual deviation, *Journal of Social Therapy* 1 (1975): 112–125.

Boettner, J., "Prisoner's Right of Access to the Courts: The Impact of the Federal Judiciary on the Texas Department of Corrections," Ph.D. dissertation, University of Texas, Austin, 1976.

Bowker, L., Victimization in correctional institutions: An interdisciplinary analysis, in John A. Conley(Ed.), *Theory and Research in Criminal Justice: Current Perspectives* (Cincinnati: Anderson, 1979), pp. 109–124.

Bowker, L., Prisoner violence: A permanent epidemic? *Proceedings of the*

American Correctional Association (Washington, DC: American Correctional Association, 1977), pp. 209–216.

Bowker, L., *Prisoner Subcultures* (Lexington, MA: D.C. Heath, 1977).

Bowker, L., Volunteers in correctional settings: Benefits, problems, and solutions, *Proceedings of the American Correctional Association* (Washington, DC: American Correctional Association, 1973), pp. 298–303.

Boyd, J., "Race of Inmate, Race of Officer, and Disciplinary Proceedings at a Federal Correctional Institution" (Tallahassee: *FCI Research Reports* 8, 1976)

Brierley, J., Legal controversy as it relates to correctional institutions—A prison administrator's view, *Villanova Law Review* 16 (1971): 1070–1076.

Brown, B. and J. Spevacek, Disciplinary offenses and offenders at two differing correctional institutions, *Correctional Psychiatry and Journal of Social Therapy* 17 (1971): 48–56.

Buffum, P., Homicides in Pennsylvania prisons, 1964–1973: A preliminary research note, in *Report of the Governor's Study Commission on Capital Punishment* (Harrisburg: Commonwealth of Pennsylvania, 1973), pp. 111–114.

Buffum, P., *Homosexuality in Prisons* (Washington, DC: U.S. Government Printing Office, 1972).

Buffum, P., Prison killings and death penalty legislation, *Prison Journal* 53 (1968): 49–57.

Bullard, C., "A Sociological Study of Prison Officers in New South Wales: A Stressful Occupation," Ph.D. dissertation, University of New South Wales, Australia, 1977.

Burns, H., The black prisoner as victim, in M. Hermann and M. Haft(Eds.), *Prisoners' Rights Sourcebook* (New York: Clark Boardman, 1973), pp. 25–31.

Burns, H., Jr., Prison Reform—'To minimize the damage,' *Discovery* 8 (May 1977): 9–15.

Burns, H., Jr., A miniature totalitarian state: Maximum security prison, *Canadian Journal of Criminology and Corrections* 11 (1969): 153–164.

Caffrey, T., "Assaultive and Troublesome Behavior Among Adolescent Homosexual Prison Inmates,", Ph.D. dissertation, City University of New York, 1974.

California Board of Corrections, *Report to Governor Regan on Violence in California Prisons* (Sacramento: California Board of Corrections, 1971).

California Department of Corrections Research Division, *Brief Analysis of Characteristics of Male Felon Inmates Designated as Aggressors in Stabbing Incidents* (Sacramento: California Department of Corrections, 1974).

Carleton, M. *Politics and Punishment* (Baton Rouge: Louisiana State University Press, 1971).

Carroll, L., Humanitarian reform and biracial sexual assault in a maximum security prison, *Urban Life* 5 (1977): 417–437.

Carroll, L., "Race and Three Forms of Prisoner Power: Confrontation, Censoriousness, and the Corruption of Authority," paper presented at the annual meeting of the American Society of Criminology, 1976.

Carroll, L., Race and sexual assault in a prison, paper presented at the annual meeting of the Society for the Study of Social Problems, 1974.

Carroll, L., *Hacks, Blacks, and Cons* (Lexington, MA: D.C. Heath, 1974).

Carter, R., D. Glaser and L. Wilkins, *Correctional Institutions*, 2nd ed. (Philadelphia: Lippincott, 1977).

The case of Joanne Little, *Crime and Social Justice* 3 (Summer 1975): 42–45.

Castro, A., Violence in the urban prison, in V. Fox (Ed.), *Proceedings, Twentieth Annual Southern Conference on Corrections* (Tallahassee: Division of Continuing Education, Florida State University, 1975), pp. 8–21.

Chang, D. and C. Zastrow, Inmates' and security guards' perceptions of themselves and of each other: A comparative study, *International Journal of Criminology and Penology* 4 (1976): 89–98.

Chase, N., *A Child Is Being Beaten* (New York: McGraw-Hill, 1975).

Claghorn, J. and D. Beto, Self-mutilation in a prison mental hospital, *Corrective Psychiatry and Journal of Social Therapy* 13 (1967): 133–141.

Clark, N., "Behavioral Indicators of Longitudinal Inmate Change in a Maximum Security Prison," Ph.D. dissertation, Northwestern University, 1976.

Clark, R., When punishment is a crime, *Playboy* (November 1970): 100–102, 118, 200–201.

Clemmer, D., *The Prison Community* (New York: Holt, Rinehart and Winston, 1940).

Cloward, R., "Social Control and Anomie: A Study of a Prison Community," Ph.D. dissertation, Columbia University, 1959.

Cohen, A., G. Cole and R. Bailey, *Prison Violence* (Lexington, MA: D.C. Heath, 1976).

Cole L., *Our Children's Keepers: Inside America's Kid Prisons* (New York: Grossman, 1972).

Conley, J., "The Political Manupulation of a Social Problem: Penal Reform as Symbolic Justice," paper presented at the annual meeting of the Society for the Study of Social Problems, 1979.

Conley, J., "A History of the Oklahoma Penal System, 1907–1967," Ph.D. dissertation, Michigan State University, 1977.

Conrad, J., Violence in prisons, *The Annals of the American Academy of Political and Social Science* 364 (March 1966): 113–119.

Cooper, H., Self-mutilation by Peruvian prisoners, *International Journal of Offender Therapy* 15 (1971): 180–188.

Cooper, H. Penological study: Peru's island prison of El Fronton, *International Journal of Offender Therapy* 13 (1969): 183–187.

Criminal law—California court holds the defense of necessity available to prison escapees—People v. Lovercamp, 43 Cal.App. 3d 823, 118 Cal. Rptr.110 (1974), *University of Illinois Law Forum* 1975 (1975): 271–280.

Crouch, B., "The Book Versus the Boot: Two Styles of Guarding in a Southern Prison," paper presented at the annual meeting of the Society for the Study of Social Problems, 1978.

Curran, S., R. Blatchley and T. Hanlon, The relationship between body buffer zone and violence as assessed by subjective and objective techniques, *Criminal Justice and Behavior* 5 (1978): 53–62.

Davidson, R., *Chicano Prisoners, The Key to San Quentin* (New York: Holt, Rinehart and Winston, 1974).

Davis, A., Sexual assaults in the Philadelphia prison system and sheriffs' vans, *TransAction* 6 (December 1968): 8–16.

Deckert, D., Criminal law—Prisons—Necessity a defense to escape when avoiding homosexual attacks—People v. Lovercamp, 43 Cal App. 3d 823, 118 Cal Rptr.110 (1974), *Western State University Law Review* 3 (1975): 164–175.

Desroches, F., April 1971 Kingston penitentiary riot, *Canadian Journal of Criminology and Corrections* 16 (1974): 317–331.

Desroches, F., Patterns in prison riots, *Canadian Journal Criminology and Corrections* 16 (1974): 332–351.

Devereaux, G. and M. Moos, The Social Structure of Prisons, and the Organic Tensions, *Journal of Criminal Psychopathology* 4 (1942): 306–324.

Dimick, K., *Ladies in Waiting Behind Prison Walls* (Muncie, IN: Accellerated Development, 1979).

Dinitz, S., S. Miller and C. Bartollas, Inmate exploitation: A study of the juvenile victim, in E. Viano and I. Drapkin (Eds.), *Exploiters and Exploited: The Dynamics of Victimization* (Lexington, MA: D.C. Heath, 1975), pp. 135–142.

Drapkin, I., The prison inmate as victim, *Victimology* 1 (1976): 98–106.

Elli, F., *The Riot* (New York: Coward-McCann, 1966).

Ellis, D. and P. Austin, Menstruation and aggressive behavior in a correctional center for women, *The Journal of Criminal Law, Criminology and Police Science* 62 (1971): 388–395.

Ellis, D., H. Grasmick and B. Gilman, Violence in prisons: A sociological analysis, *American Journal of Sociology* 80 (1974): 16–43.

Esparza, R., Attempted and committed suicide in county jails, in B. Danto (Ed.), *Jailhouse Blues* (Orchard Lake, MI: Epic Publications, 1973), pp. 27–46.

Evans, D., "American Prisoners at Lecumberri (Black Palace in Mexico)," paper presented at the annual meeting of the Academy of Criminal Justice Sciences, 1978.

Faine, J. and E. Bohlander, Jr., Prisoner radicalization and incipient violence, in C. Huff (Ed.), *Contemporary Corrections* (Beverly Hills: Sage, 1977), pp. 54–77.

Feld, B., *Neutralizing Inmate Violence* (Cambridge, MA: Ballinger, 1977).

Ferracuti, F., S. Dinitz and A. Piperno, *Mental Deterioration in Prison* (Columbus: Ohio State University, School of Public Administration, 1978).

Fisher, S., Informal organization in a correctional setting, *Social Problems* 13 (1965): 214–222.

Fisher, S., Social organization in a correctional residence, *Pacific Sociological Review* 4 (1961): 87–93.

Fishman, J., *Sex in Prison* (National Library Press, 1934, no location given).

Fitzpatrick, J. and S. Kruger, Control of violence in a maximum security prison or the taming of the few, *Proceedings of the American Correctional Association.* (Washington, DC: American Correctional Association, 1972), pp. 232–240.

Ford, C., Homosexual practices of institutionalized females, *Journal of Abnormal and Social Psychology* 23 (1929): 442–448.

Fox, V., Analysis of prison disciplinary problems, *Journal of Criminal Law and Criminology* 49 (1958): 321–326.

Fox, V., *Violence Behind Bars* (Westport: Greenwood Press, 1973, originally published in 1956).

Fuller, D., T. Orsagh and D. Raber, "Violence and Victimization Within the North Carolina Prison System," paper presented at the annual meeting of the Academy of Criminal Justice Sciences, 1977.

Gardner, M., The defense of necessity and the right to escape from prison—A step toward incarceration free from sexual assault, *Southern California Law Review* 49 (1975): 110–152.

Garson, G., The disruption of prison administration: An investigation of alternative theories of the relationship among administrators, reformers, and involuntary service clients, *Law and Society Review* 6 (1972):531–561.

Garson, G., Force vs. restraint in prison riots, *Crime and Delinquency* 18 (1972): 411–421.

Giallombardo, R., *The Social World of Imprisoned Girls* (New York: Wiley, 1974).

Giallombardo, R., *Society of Women* (New York: Wiley, 1966).

Gibbs, J. "Stress and Self-Injury in Jail," Ph.D. dissertation, State University of New York at Albany, 1978.

216

Gilman, D., Did the highest court in Massachusetts give inmates the *right* to use force against guards? *Corrections Magazine* 2 (1976): 13–16.

Gilman, D., Courts and corrections, *Corrections Magazine* 2 (1976): 51–53.

Gochras, H., The sexually oppressed, *Social Work* 17 (1972): 16–23.

Goffman, E., *Asylums* (Garden City, NY: Doubleday, 1961).

Goldfarb, R., *Jails: The Ultimate Ghetto of the Criminal Justice System* (Garden City, NY: Doubleday, 1976).

Goshen, C., Transcultural studies: A state prison population of youthful offenders, *Adolescence* 4 (1969): 401–430.

Grasewicz, L., "A Study of Inmate Assaults in Major Institutions," (Richmond: Bureau of Research, Reporting and Evaluation, Virginia Department of Corrections, 1977.

Grosz, H., H. Stern and E. Feldman, A study of delinquent girls who participated in and who abstained from participating in a riot, *American Journal of Psychiatry* 125 (1969): 1370–1379.

Guenther, A., Prison rackets, in N. Johnson and L. Savitz (Eds.), *Justice and Corrections* (New York: Wiley, 1978), pp. 531–540.

Guenther, A., Compensations in a total institution: The forms and functions of contraband, *Crime and Delinquency* 21 (1975): 243–254.

Guenther, A., "Violence in Correctional Institutions: A Study of Assaults," unpublished paper, College of William and Mary, 1974.

Guenther, A. and M. Guenther, Screws versus thugs, *Society* 11 (July–August 1974): 42–50.

Gunn, J., *Epileptics in Prison* (New York: Academic Press, 1977).

Gunn, J., G. Robertson, S. Dell and C. Way, *Psychiatric Aspects of Imprisonment* (New York: Academic Press, 1978).

Hallman, L. and V. Johnson., Glick-section 1983 damages for brutality, *New England Journal on Prison Law* 1 (1974): 125–137.

Haney, C., C. Banks and P. Zimbardo, Interpersonal dynamics in a simulated prison, in R. Leger and J. Stratton (Eds.), *The Sociology of Corrections* (New York: Wiley, 1977), pp. 65–92.

Hanks, L., Jr., Preliminary study of problems of discipline in prisons, *Journal of Criminal Law and Criminology* 30 (1940): 879–887.

Hartman, C., The key jingler, *Community Mental Health Journal* 5 (1969): 199–205.

Hartung, F. and M. Floch, A social-psychological analysis of prison riots: An hypothesis, *Journal of Criminal Law, Criminology and Police Science* 47 (1956): 51–57.

Heffernan, E., *Making It in Prison: The Square, the Cool, and the Life* (New York: Wiley, 1972).

Heise, R., *Prison Games* (Fort Worth, TX: privately published, 1976).

Held, B., D. Levine and V. Swartz, Interpersonal aspects of dangerousness, *Criminal Justice and Behavior* 6 (1979): 49–58.

Helgemoe, R., "A Preliminary Inquiry into the Prediction of Self-Injury Among Prison Inmates Based on Stressful Incidents," paper presented at the annual meeting of the Academy of Criminal Justice Sciences, 1979.

Hildreth, A., L. Derogatis and K. McCusker, Body buffer zone and violence: A reassessment and confirmation, *American Journal of Psychiatry* 127 (1971): 1641–1645.

Hirschkop, P. and M. Millermann, The unconstitutionality of prison life, *Virginia Law Review* 55 (1969): 795–839.

Howard League for Penal Reform, Prison officers in the news, *Newsletter* 23 (Summer 1978): 1–2.

Huffman, A., Problems precipitated by homosexual approaches on youthful first offenders, *Journal of Social Therapy* 7 (1961): 216–222.

Huffman, A., Sex deviation in a prison community, *Journal of Social Therapy* 6 (1960): 170–181.

Ibrahim, A., Deviant sexual behavior in men's prisons, *Crime and Delinquency* 20 (1974): 38–44.

Illinois Legislative Investigating Commission, *The Joliet Correctional Center Riot of April 22, 1975* (Chicago: Illinois Legislative Investigating Commission, 1975).

Irwin, J., The big house: The great American prison, in C. Huff (Ed.), *Contemporary Corrections* (Beverly Hills: Sage, 1977), pp. 14-39.

Irwin, J., *The Felon* (Englewood Cliffs, NJ: Prentice-Hall, 1970).

Jackson, G., *Soledad Brother: The Prison Letters of George Jackson* (New York: Bantam, 1970).

Jacobs, J., What prison guards think: A profile of the Illinois force, *Crime and Delinquency* 24 (1978): 185–196.

Jacobs, J., *Stateville* (Chicago: University of Chicago Press, 1977).

Jacobs, J., Stratification and conflict among prison inmates, *Journal of Criminal Law and Criminology* 66 (1976): 476–482.

Jacobs, J., Street gangs behind bars, *Social Problems* 21 (1974): 395–411.

Jacobs, J. and L. Kraft, Integrating the keepers: A comparison of black and white prison guards in Illinois, *Social Problems* 25 (1978): 307–317.

Jacobs, J. and H. Retsky, Prison guard, *Urban Life* 4 (1975): 5–27.

Jaman, D., *Behavior During the First Year in Prison, Report Three— Background Characteristics as Predictors of Behavior and Misbehavior* (Sacramento: Research Division, California Department of Corrections, 1972).

Jaman, D., P. Coburn, J. Goddard and P. Mueller, *Characteristics of Violent Prisoners (San Quentin—1960)* (Sacramento: Division of Research, California Department of Corrections, 1966).

James, H., Children in trouble: A national scandal, *Proceedings*. Fifth Annual Interagency Workship of the Institute of Contemporary Corrections and the Behavioral Sciences (Huntsville, TX: Sam Houston State University, 1970), pp. 285–307.

John Howard Association, *Illinois Youth Centers at St. Charles and Geneva* (Chicago: John Howard Association, 1974).

John Howard Association, *Report on the Indiana State Reformatory, Pendleton* (Chicago: John Howard Association, 1970).

Johnson, E., The homosexual in prison, in J. Susman (Ed.), *Crime and Justice, 1971–1972* (New York: AMS Press, 1974), pp. 99–111.

Johnson, E.H., *Correlates of Felon Self-Mutilations* (Carbondale, IL: Center for the Study of Crime, Delinquency and Corrections of Southern Illinois University, 1969).

Johnson, E.H. and B. Britt, *Self-Mutilation in Prisons: Interaction of Stress and Social Structures* (Carbondale IL: Southern Illinois University, Center for the Study of Crime, Delinquency and Corrections, 1967).

Johnson, R., "Youth in Crisis: Patterns of Self-Destructive Conduct Among Adolescent Prisoners," paper presented at the annual meeting of the Academy of Criminal Justice Sciences, 1978.

Johnson, R., *Culture and Crisis in Confinement* (Lexington, MA: D.C. Heath, 1976).

Jones, D., *The Health Risks of Imprisonment* (Lexington, MA: D.C. Heath, 1976).

Jones, F., A betting shop in prison, *Prison Service Journal* 5 (No. 19) (1966):37–40.

Karpman, B., *The Sexual Offender and His Offenses* (New York: Julian Press, 1954).

Kassebaum, G., Sex in prison, violence, homosexuality, and intimidation are everyday occurrences, *Sexual Behavior* 2 (January 1972):39–45.

Keve, P., *Prison Life and Human Worth* (Minneapolis: University of Minnesota Press, 1974).

King, R. and K. Elliott, *Albany: Birth of a Prison—End of an Era* (London: Routledge and Kegan Paul, 1977).

Kinzel, A., Body-buffer zone in violent prisoners, *American Journal of Psychiatry* 127 (1970):59–64.

Kirkham, G., Homosexuality in prison, in J. Henslin (Ed.), *Studies in the Sociology of Sex* (New York: Appleton-Century-Crofts, 1971), pp. 325–349.

Lejins, P., *Prevention of Violence in Correctional Institutions* (Washington, DC: U.S. Government Printing Office, 1973).

Lembo, J., Research notes: The relationship of institutional disciplinary infractions in the inmate's personal contact with the outside community, *Criminologica* 7 (1969):50–54.

219

Leonard, R., "Communication in the Total Institution: An Investigation of Prisoner–Guard Interaction in a State Penitentiary," Ph.D. dissertation, Purdue University, 1976.

Lindquist, C., "Female Violators of Prison Discipline: Backgrounds and Sanctions," paper presented at the annual meeting of the American Society of Criminology, 1978.

Lockwood, D. *Prison Sexual Violence* (New York: Elsevier, 1980).

Lockwood, D., "Maintaining Manhood: Prison Violence Precipitated by Aggressive Sexual Approaches," paper presented at the annual meeting of the Academy of Criminal Justice Sciences, 1978.

Mabli, J., C. Holley, J. Patrick and J. Walls, Age and prison violence, *Criminal Justice and Behavior* 6 (1979):175–186.

McCorkle, L. and R. Korn, "Resocialization Within Walls," *Annals of the American Academy of Political and Social Science* 293 (May, 1954):88-98.

Mann, W., *Society Behind Bars: A Sociological Scrutiny of Guelph Reformatory* (Toronto: Social Science Publishers, 1967).

Mann, W. Socialization in a medium-security reformatory, *Canadian Review of Sociology and Anthropology* 1 (1964):138–155.

Martinson, R., Collective behavior at attica, *Federal Probation* 36 (September 1972):3–7.

Mattick, H., The prosaic sources of prison violence, in J. Susman (Ed.), *Crime and Justice, 1971–1972* (New York: A.M.S. Press, 1974), pp. 179–187.

Mayhew, S., Prisoner's rights: Personal security, *University of Colorado Law Review* 42 (1970):305–385.

Menninger, K., *The Crime of Punishment* (New York: Viking, 1968).

Michigan Department of Corrections Program Bureau, "Analysis of Inmate Assaults on Officers, 1972–1973," Lansing: Michigan Department of Corrections, 1974.

Miller, S., C. Bartollas, D. Jennifer, E. Redd and S. Dinitz, Games inmates play: Notes on staff victimization, in E. Viano and I. Drapkin (Eds.), *Exploiters and Exploited: The Dynamics of Victimization* (Lexington, MA: D.C. Heath, 1975), pp. 143–153.

Miller, W.A., Crime in our prisons, *FBI Law Enforcement Bulletin* 46 (October 1977):5–9.

Miller, W.B., *Handbook of Correctional Psychiatry*, Vol. 1 (Washington, DC: U.S. Government Printing Office, 1968).

Mitford, J., *Kind and Usual Punishment* (New York: Random House, 1971).

Moore, J., *Homeboys: Gangs, Drugs, and Prison in the Barrios of Los Angeles* (Philadelphia: Temple University Press, 1978).

Morello, M., "A Study of the Adjustive Behavior of Prison Inmates to Incarceration," Ed.D. dissertation, Temple University, 1958.

Morris, T. and P. Morris, *Pentonville: A Sociological Study of an English Prison* (London: Routledge and Kegan Paul, 1963).

Murton, T., *The Dilemma of Prison Reform* (New York: Holt, Rinehart and Winston, 1976).

Murton, T. and J. Hyams, *Inside Prison U.S.A.* (New York: Grove Press, 1969).

Nacci, P., Sexual assault in prisons, *American Journal of Correction* 40 (1978):30–31.

Nacci, P., H. Teitlebaum and J. Prather, Population density and inmate misconduct rates in the federal prison system, *Federal Probation* 41 (June 1977):26–31.

Nachshon, I. and M. Rotenberg, Perception of violence by institutionalized offenders, *The Journal of Criminal Law and Criminology* 68 (1977):454–457.

National Center on Child Abuse and Neglect, *Child Abuse and Neglect in Institutions: Selected Readings on Prevention, Investigation, and Correction* (Washington, DC: U.S. Government Printing Office, 1978).

Newfield, J., *Cruel and Unusual Justice* (New York: Holt, Rinehart and Winston, 1974).

Orsagh, T., D. Fuller and D. Raber, *Assaults and Assaultive Victimization Within Ten North Carolina Correctional Institutions* (Raleigh: North Carolina Department of Correction, 1977).

Otten, L., *Colloquium on the Correlates of Crime and the Determinants of Criminal Behavior* (McLean, VA: MITRE, 1978).

Paulus, P., V. Cox, G. McCain and J. Chandler, Some effects of crowding in a prison environment, *Journal of Applied Social Psychology* 5 (1975):86–91.

Pearman, R., The whip pays off, *Nation* (December 26, 1966):201–204.

Plotkin, R., Surviving justice: Prisoners' rights to be free from physical assault, *Cleveland State Law Review* 23 (1974):387–422.

Polansky, N., The prison as an autocracy, *Journal of Criminal Law and Criminology* 33 (1942):16–22.

Polsky, H., *Cottage Six* (New York: Wiley, 1962).

Powledge, F., *The Seeds of Anguish: An ACLU Study of the D.C. Jail* (Washington, DC: ACLU of the National Capital Area, 1972).

Prassel, F., Rebellion in miniature: A sociological analysis of the prison riot, *Proceedings of the Southwestern Sociological Association* 20 (1970):369–373.

The Prison Journal 34 (April 1954). Special issue on prison riots.

Quinn, L., Militant black: A correctional problem, *Correctional Psychologist* 4 (1970):40–48.

Rees, C., Arsenals behind prison walls, *Guns and Ammo* (January 1970):29–33.

Richmond, R., The homosexual in prison, *Canadian Journal of Criminology and Corrections* 12 (1970):553–555.

Rosenblatt, I., "The Effect of Punitive Measures on Attitudes of Prison Inmates Toward Authority," Ph.D. dissertation, New York University, 1961.

Ross, B., *Changing of Guard: Citizen Soldiers in Wisconsin Correctional Institutions* (Madison: League of Women Voteers of Wisconsin, 1978).

Roth, L., Territoriality and homosexuality in a male prison population, *American Journal of Orthopsychiatry* 41 (1971):510–513.

Rothbart, G., "Social Confinement in Prison Organization," Ph.D. dissertation, University of Washington, 1964.

Rubenfeld, S. and J. Stafford, An adolescent inmate social system: A psychosocial account, *Psychiatry* 26 (1973):241–256.

Rubenstein, E., "Body Buffer Zones in Female Prisoners," Ph.D. dissertation, Long Island University, 1975.

Rudoff, A., "Prison Inmates: An Involuntary Association," Ph.D. dissertation, University of California, Berkley, 1964.

Rudovsky, D., "Prison Sexual Assaults and the Law," unpublished paper, Pennsylvania Prison Society, Philadelphia, 1971.

Sacks, J., "Troublemaking in Prison, A Study of Resistant Behavior as an Administrative Problem in a Medium-Security Penal Institution," Ph.D. dissertation, Catholic University of America, 1942.

Sagarin, E. and D. MacNamara, The homosexual as a crime victim, *International Journal of Criminology and Penology* 3 (1975):13–25.

Sandhu, H., Therapy with violent psychopaths in an Indian prison community, *International Journal of Offender Therapy* 14 (1970):138–144.

Sarsfield, E., *A Policy for Prison Uprisings* (Washington, DC: Department of Corrections, 1973).

Scacco, A., *Rape in Prison* (Springfield, IL: Charles C. Thomas, 1975).

Schrag, C., The sociology of prison riots, *Proceedings of the American Correctional Association* (Washington, DC: American Correctional Association, 1960), pp. 138–145.

Sellin, T., *Slavery and the Penal System* (New York: Elsevier, 1976).

Sellin, T., Prison homicides, in T. Sellin (Ed.), *Capital Punishment* (New York: Harper and Row, 1967), pp. 154–160.

Sellin, T., Homicides and assaults in American prisons, 1964, *Acta Criminologica Medicalis Legalis Japonica* 31 (1965):139–143.

Serrill, M., Walpole, prison: After the storm, *Corrections Magazine* 2 (December 1975):49–54.

Serrill, M., Lockdown, *Corrections Magazine* 1 (September 1974):32–34.

Shaw, C., *The Jack-Roller* (Chicago: University of Chicago Press, 1930).

Sherwin, R. and A. Straus, Inmate rioters and non-rioters, a comparative analysis, *American Journal of Corrections* 37 (1975):34–35, 54–58.

Shoemaker, D. and G. Hillery, Jr., "Violence and Commitment in Custodial Settings," paper presented at the annual meeting of the American Sociological Association, 1978.

Simmons, I., "Interaction and Leadership Among Female Prisoners," Ph.D. dissertation, University of Missouri—Columbia, 1975.

Skelton, W., Prison riot. Assaulters versus defenders, *Archives of General Psychiatry* 21 (1969):359–362.

Slosar, J., Jr., *Prisonization, Friendship and Leadership* (Lexington, MA: D.C. Heath, 1978).

Sommer, R., *The End of Imprisonment* (New York: Oxford University Press, 1976).

Spencer, E., "The Social System of a Medium Security Women's Prison," Ph.D. dissertation, University of Kansas, 1977.

Spevacek, J., Characteristics of chronic disciplinary offenders in the Lorton Correctional Complex, *Research Memorandum 71–3* (Washington, DC: Department of Corrections, 1971).

Srivastava, S., *The Indian Prison Community* (Lucknow, India: Pustak Kendra, 1977).

Srivastava, S., The exercise of authority in prison (An analysis of the problems of discipline in a central prison of Uttar Pradesh), *Indian Journal Criminology* 4 (1976):50–61.

Srivastava, S., The feel of imprisonment: An evaluative study of the impact of incarceration on 400 long-term prisoners of a central jail in U.P., *Indian Journal of Criminology* 2 (1974):46–54.

Srivastava, S., Sex life in an Indian male prison, *Indian Journal of Social Work* 35 (1974):21–33.

Srivastava, S., Social profile of homosexuals in an Indian male prison, *The Eastern Anthropologist* (1973):313–322.

Srivastava, S., The quality of basic necessities in prison, *The Indian Journal of Social Work* 33 (1973):337–346.

Sykes, G., *The Society of Captives* (New York: Atheneum, 1966).

Sykes, G., Men, merchants, and toughs: A study of reactions to imprisonment, *Social Problems* 4 (1956):130–138.

Sykes, G., The corruption of authority and rehabilitation, *Social Forces* 34 (1956):257–262.

Sylvester, S., J. Reed and D. Nelson, *Prison Homicide* (New York: Spectrum 1977).

Szabo, D. and S. Katzenelson, *Offenders and Corrections* (New York: Praeger, 1978).

Task Force Investigating Allegations of Discriminatory Practices at the Joliet and Stateville Correctional Centers, *Report* (Springfield: Illinois Department of Corrections, 1978).

Thomas, J., Killed on duty: An analysis of murders of English prison service staff since 1850, *Prison Service Journal* 7 (1972):9–10.

Toch, H., Social climate and prison violence, *Federal Probation* 42 (December 1978):21–25.

Toch, H., *Living in Prison: The Ecology of Survival* (New York: Free Press, 1977).

Toch, H., *Police, Prisons, and the Problem of Violence* (Washington, DC: U.S. Government Printing Office, 1977).

Toch, H., *Men in Crisis, Human Breakdowns in Prison* (Chicago: Aldine, 1975).

Tolley, H., Politics and prison reform—Three test cases, *Intellect* 105 (1971):93–96.

Train, G., Unrest in the penitentiary, *Journal of Criminal Law, Criminology and Police Science* 44 (1953):277–295.

Trupin, J., *In Prison* (New York: New American Library, 1975).

United States Congress, Senate Committee on the Judiciary, *Juvenile Delinquency—Past Twenty—Conditions in Juvenile and Young Offender Institutions* (Washington, DC: U.S. Government Printing Office, 1971).

Veno, A. and M. Davidson, Prison violence: Some different perspectives, *International Journal of Criminology and Penology* 5 (1977):399–409.

Vinter, R., T. Newcomb and R. Kish, *Time Out, A National Study of Juvenile Correctional Programs* (Ann Arbor: The University of Michigan, 1976).

Violence statistics for 1974 and 1975, *Corrections Compendium* (February and March 1977 issues).

Walsh, J., Prisoners' rights—Jailers' duty of protection, *Louisiana Law Review* 34 (1974):685–691.

Ward, D. and G. Kassebaum, *Women's Prison, Sex and Social Structure* (Chicago: Aldine, 1965).

Ward, J., Homosexual behavior of the institutionalized delinquent, *Psychiatric Quarterly Supplement* 3 (1958):301–314.

Webb, G. and D. Morris, *Prison Guards: The Culture and Prospective of an Occupational Group* (San Marcos, TX: Coker Books, 1978).

Weinberg, S. Aspects of the prison's social structure, *The American Journal of Sociology* 47 (1942):717–726.

Weiss, C. and D. Friar, *Terror in the Prisons: Homosexual Rape, and Why Society Condones It* (Indianapolis: Bobbs-Merrill, 1974).

Wendel, M. and M. Hirleman, *Jail Space Utilization Study* (Sacramento: California Bureau of Criminal Statistics, 1974).

Wenk, E., J. Robinson and G. Smith, Can violence be predicted? *Crime and Delinquency* 18 (1972):393–402.

Wicks, R., Suicide prevention—A brief for corrections officers, *Federal Probation* 36 (September 1972):29–31.

Wilbanks, W., The report of the commission on Attica, *Federal Probation* 37 (March 1973):3–7.

Williams, V. and M. Fish, *Convicts, Codes and Contraband: The Prison Life of Men and Women* (Cambridge: Ballinger, 1974).

Wilson, R., The end of the Gatesville era, *Corrections Magazine* 4 (September 1978):26–28.

Wilson, R., Homosexual rape: Legacy of overcrowding, *Corrections Magazine* 3 (March 1977):10–11.

Wolfson, W., "The Patterns of Prison Homicide," Ph.D. dissertation, University of Pennsylvania, 1978.

Wood, B., G. Wilson, R. Jessor and J. Bogan, Troublemaking behavior in a correctional institution: Relationship to inmates' definition of their situation, *American Journal of Orthopsychiatry* 36 (1968):795–802.

Wooden, K., *Weeping in the Playtime of Others* (New York: McGraw-Hill, 1976).

Wright, E., *The Politics of Punishment* (New York: Harper and Row, 1973).

Yee, M., *The Melancholy History of Soledad Prison: In Which a Utopian Scheme Turns Bedlam* (New York: Harper's Magazine Press, 1973).

Zimbardo, P., Pathology of imprisonment, *Society* 9(6)(1972):4–8.

Index